LIVING WITH BALLADS

LIVING WITH BALLADS

By

Willa Muir

NEW YORK
OXFORD UNIVERSITY PRESS
1965

Library of Congress Catalog Card Number: 65-14597

Printed in Great Britain

Dedicated to the memory of

EDWIN MUIR

Contents

Acknowledgments

I HAVE many kind people to thank for help and encouragement in preparing this book. First and foremost, the Bollingen Foundation of New York, who made it possible for me to write it at all. Next, the Chapelbrook Foundation of Boston, who enabled me to engage as assistant a Cambridge graduate, Miss Alison Souper, now Mrs Charles Richards, who brought me from the University Library the books I could not fetch myself, and to whom I am very grateful. Mrs John Macmurray lent me an essential work: Greig's Last Leaves of Aberdeen Ballads and Ballad Airs. The School of Scottish Studies in Edinburgh University, under the direction of Mr Basil Megaw, supplied me with tape-recordings of Jeannie Robertson's Ballads, and one of its officers, Mr Hamish Henderson, allowed me to quote from a paper of his. Mr and Mrs William Montgomerie gave me an excerpt from the Bannatyne MS. besides allowing me to quote from their book 'Sandy Candy'. Mr E. V. Rieu, editor of the Penguin Classics, and Miss N. K. Sandars, who translated the Epic of Gilgamesh, graciously allowed me to lean heavily on that volume out of the Penguin series. All the others, whose books have helped to provide evidence I was glad of, I wish to thank now very heartily.

Finally I should like to thank Miss Kathleen Raine for continuous encouragement and kindness in listening to chapter after chapter.

Index of Ballads

INDEX OF BALLADS

INTRODUCTORY

I

Children's Singing Games

I WISH first to examine a simple, rudimentary form of oral poetry, the singing games played daily in our school playground, when I was a child of eleven and twelve, in a small town on the North-East Coast of Scotland. These singing games, transmitted orally from generation to generation of schoolgirls, were an inheritance from the same kind of people who made and sang the Scottish Ballads. The Ballads were made and sung by grown-ups, while our games, whoever made them up, were sung and passed on only by children, yet I feel that they were closely related to the Ballad world. As my experience of them was a living experience not drawn from books, I think some valuable insights might be gained from it.

We were both singers and audience in our singing games, and I had better make it clear what kind of audience we were. The school was an elementary Board School for working-class children, where education in the three R's was provided free. It was a drab, gabled grey stone building on the outskirts of the town, with two playgrounds, a larger one of beaten earth for the boys and a smaller one, partly concreted, for the girls and infants. The boys' playground was left open on two sides, but the girls' playground was walled round except for the gate we went out and in by, which opened on a country road. There were as many girls as boys in the school, and since our playground cramped us, we used to run out through the gate in fine weather and play on the road. The year was 1901, and there were no motor-cars; nothing came down our road except an occasional farm-cart or tradesman's van. Out there we had an open horizon looking over fields; we could and did turn our backs on the school, especially in our singing games.

Inside the school our education was wholly utilitarian. What we read and wrote mattered little, but failures in memory, in accuracy, especially in spelling and arithmetic, or misdemeanours like whispering in class, were punished by blows on the palm of the hand from a hard leather tawse. All the boys and girls were due to leave school at the age of fourteen. Their parents were labourers, washerwomen, mill-workers or small tradesmen.

I went to that school at the age of nine and left it three years later because I won a bursary to the Academy, a fee-paying school where the middle classes of the town sent their children. In the new playground of the Academy I found no singing games; I was lucky to have learned them when I did. Only the working-class girls in our town kept that tradition alive, and only in the school playtime. Their mothers may have learned these songs as children, but they did not sing them at home. The girls sang them no longer when they went out to work. These singing games were not made for solitary performers; they needed to be set going by a social group. Our group of schoolgirls, eleven-, twelve-, and thirteen-year-olds, answered that need, as the singing games answered ours.

We eleven-year-olds were proud to be included in the singing games. Admission to them was a promotion, a step towards being grown-up, which for us meant chiefly being mated and married. The rhythms of puberty, already stirring in us, directed our attention to the future bliss of choosing and being chosen by a sweetheart, but until invited to join the ring of senior girls we had to make do with solitary attempts to divine that future by skipping-rope, a frenzy of skipping which was merely self-made magic, not to be compared with the communal choosing practised in the singing games. These games left us all satisfied and happy. While they went on we became progressively happier, so that there was a notable freedom from squabbling. None of us was willing to have a game held up for one moment by a quarrel over precedence or choice. We felt that the rhythm, the beat of the singing and dancing must go on to our common, harmonious satisfaction. Among our rough-tongued and noisy girls that was remarkable.

The elder girls pushed us into place and left us to learn the words and actions. Round and round we went in a circle with joined hands, moving clockwise, till a protagonist was chosen from among the seniors and set in the middle of the ring. Then the game was under way. Here is one of them, a typical specimen.

The girl in the middle sings to the dancing circle:

'Father, Mother, may I go?
May I go? May I go?
Father, Mother, may I go,
On a cold, cold frosty morning?

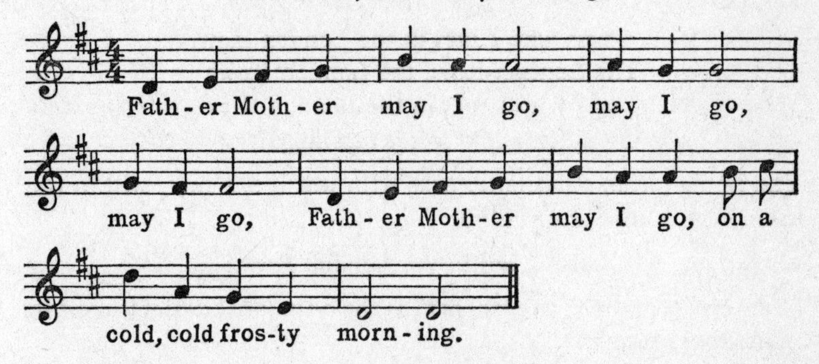

The answer comes from the circle, still dancing round:

'Yes, my darling, you may go,
You may go, you may go.
Yes, my darling, you may go,
On a cold, cold frosty morning.'

At once, we have, all of us, set a good distance between our ordinary world and that of the song, for we are singing the words as I have written them, with Scottish vowels certainly, but in what we take to be English. Had we sung them in our habitual mode of speech, this is how they would have gone:

'Faither, Mither, can I ging?
On a cauld, cauld frosty moarnin'.'

Nor would any father or mother of our girls have said: 'Yes, my darling.' What they might have said would be: 'Ay, my dearie.' It does not occur to any of us to note this peculiarity; we do not think of it as an affectation. That is the traditional way to sing this song, and so we sing it like that.

On receiving this favourable answer, the heroine, collecting in one hand her brief skirt, ducks between two of the circle and dances round outside it, also clockwise, singing:

> 'I gather up my tails and away I go,
> Away I go, away I go.
> I gather up my tails and away I go,
> On a cold, cold frosty morning.'

Then she ducks back into the middle and sings:

> 'Guess who I met in the London Row,
> The London Row, the London Row?
> Guess who I met in the London Row,
> On a cold, cold frosty morning?'

The home circle obediently asks who was it she met, still in the same metre, and she replies:

> 'I met my lad in the London Row.'

Lad here, meaning 'sweetheart', is the only local dialect word in the whole game.

Now, without any naming of names, the heroine picks one of the circle to be her 'lad', and they stand together in the middle, holding hands, while she tells the circle, in the same verse-metre:

> 'He gave me a kiss and a guinea-gold ring,
> On a cold, cold frosty morning.'

The couple then kiss, swiftly so as not to lose the beat of the tune, and the first heroine joins the circle while the chosen one becomes the protagonist of the renewed game. Simple as it is, this game can and usually does go on until all the girls in the circle have had their 'turn' of choosing, being chosen and exchanging a kiss. It was a prime favourite and we never tired of it.

What really happened to us in this singing game? We had and expected no direction from adults. Our teachers never came into the playgrounds; had one of them come out to direct our games, the magic would have faded. Holding hands and dancing in a circle, or linking arms and advancing in a row, is a primitive way of establishing a communal flow of feeling, which in turn releases imaginative energies that need to take on shape. We did not compose the shape of this game, but we enacted it and our feelings flowed out into a new world well away from the alleged facts of our school curriculum, bearing no obvious relation to the routine of our working days, a world that touched the frontiers of the imaginative world. Closed away from daily life in our dancing ring as in a magic circle, we played out the drama of choosing a mate and being chosen; we entered the vague, as yet unrealized, heaven of a love-affair; underlying currents of emotion generated by the group took us into an exciting world of anticipation, of potentiality. It was a rehearsal of what might happen to us later on in real life.

The Father, the Mother and the Lad were all token figures; one could mentally fill in details, if one wished, to correspond to a private dream, but the figures were mere masks, labels, reach-me-downs. We were rehearsing a situation, not looking for this person or that to fulfil our desires. Nor were we asking any questions. We took everything in the game for granted, as if its statements were virtual fact: the given elements were accepted without explanation or comment. To us, the various actions were as good as real. One ducked outside the dancing circle and it felt exactly like leaving the home circle. One came back announcing that one had been in the London Row: why not, if the song said so? Gathering up one's 'tails' was exactly what grown-up women did and what one would eventually do oneself. And a gold ring was the normal respectable climax of a love-affair. The values of the society we were growing up in were not examined; they did not take shape enough for that: the framework of the situation was immediate and unquestioned.

It was not open-eyed curiosity, then, that set this game moving. What prompted it was an emotional need, an urge of feeling, the desire to be loved and chosen, an urge coming from well below the threshold of consciousness. The general consent and harmony of the participants implicitly recognized that this was for all of us a practice rehearsal for later life; the same surge of feeling pulsed through each one and seemed self-evident; a tension in each of us was temporarily resolved. But there was no explicit recognition of the total situation. Our game was an expression of energies, a release of tension; it was not concerned with concepts or categories. It was a stage in the process of growing up, but by itself was not sufficient to help us to self-consciousness. It was a game for children on the verge of puberty, not for grown-ups or half grown-ups.

Yet it was informed by imagination, and not only through its embodied actions. Let us look again at the refrain, which seems at first sight oddly remote from the theme. Does it not provide a clue to the emotional need? On a cold, cold frosty morning—the cold is emphasized—one needs the warmth of declared affection. These token figures, Father and Mother, may call one 'darling', yet this is a cold, *cold* frosty morning. Here we find ourselves recognizably in the world of imaginative symbol, where an icy landscape denotes lovelessness and morning means youth. In its simplest terms this symbol affirms that love is warmth and sunshine, and so it enfolds the germ of a concept, but it is not stated in conceptual form. It is merely embodied in a refrain added to the song without link or explanation—a last touch which grown-ups might call poetry—a residue of feeling left unformulated in the stanza which curls up at the end of it like the back-lash of a wave.

The lack of any explanation suggests that the image, the symbol, conveys its own meaning, that its relationship to the stanza can be taken for granted. In this realm of unconscious feelings—or shall we say imperfectly conscious feelings?—there is an immediate awareness of close links between symbol and narrative. This is a world which does not need formulated concepts to show relationship, where meaning and import are simply 'felt in the blood and felt along the heart'. The use of this refrain in our singing game goes right back to the similar use of imagery in the early songs of other countries and continents. Arthur Waley[1] puts it like this, that in early Chinese songs the image or comparison is stated 'on the same footing' as the facts narrated. On the same footing, immediately comprehensible like facts, no explanation being needed. Such symbolic images thrown up by the underworld of feeling are a common inheritance drawn upon by poets everywhere and need no explanation to people who have kept open the lines of communication from the unconscious to the conscious self.

The embodied symbol in a singing game comes sometimes at

[1] Introduction to *The Book of Songs* translated from the Chinese

the beginning of it instead of in a refrain. Here is one song which starts with a melancholy picture:

Water, water wallflower, growing up so high,
We are all maidens and we must all die.

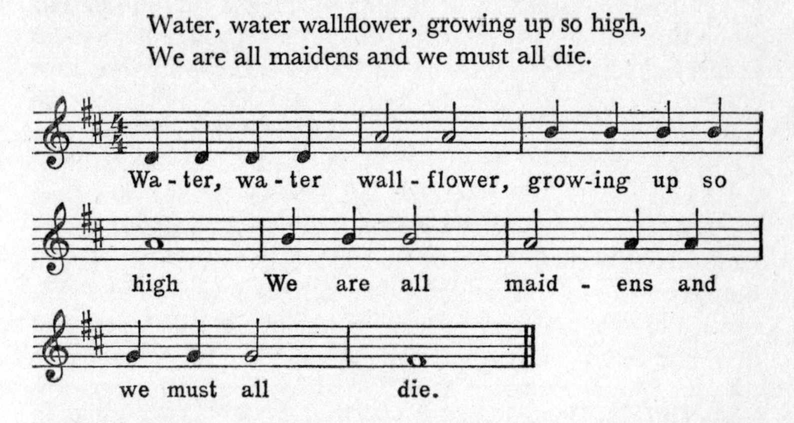

Involved in that image lies our fear of being 'wallflowers' and so old maids, felt to be a kind of death. The tune for these two lines is a slow tune with a falling cadence. But we exorcise that fear at once, with brisk reassurance:

All except (So-and-so).
She is young and she is pretty,
She is the girl of the golden city.

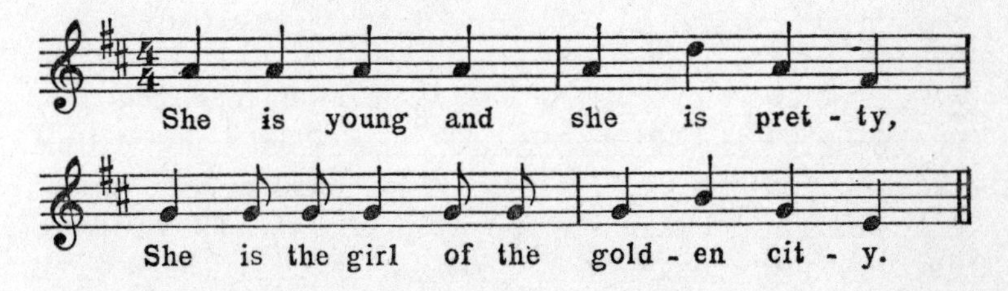

Thus excepted from the common fear, the protagonist goes on merrily to the usual love adventure. No further reference to wall-flowers is needed: we shall all have our 'turn' at being reassured: the symbol is therefore not repeated.

But did we recognize the import of these symbols as we sang? Not consciously, any more than we recognized the import of symbols in dreams. As in dreams, we accepted them without surprise; yet our feelings about them, which must have existed, did not get very far, if at all, across the threshold of consciousness. The impulses that moved us to dance and sing, that threw up the verses of our games one after another, sank again into the underworld of feeling when the games ended, leaving nothing that could be formulated except a memory of the verbal and dancing patterns and the shapes defined by the tunes. The foundations were being laid for a bridge between unconscious feelings and conscious personalities; there was not yet much traffic to cross the bridge and the territory beyond it was largely unexplored, but the lines of communication were being kept open.

Yet although we neither queried nor analysed our feelings, we were aware of a profound satisfaction that made us play the games again and again, day after day. What we understood in this underworld of fluid feelings that merged easily into each other was just enough to make rational explanation superfluous, enough, anyhow, to keep us pleased and happy.

Most of our singing games were concerned with sweethearting, but there were other cross-currents and swirls of feeling that found expression, especially those arising between mothers and daughters. In the mother-and-daughter games we did not seclude ourselves in a dancing ring; we linked arms in two lines that faced each other, advancing and retreating with a processional dancing step, a formation that could be called the classical embodiment of two opposing forces. Being thus symbolically split, we needed no further symbol. These were teasing games, faintly sadistic like all teasing; the daughters kept the mothers on tenterhooks and tried to outwit them. The refrains had some emotional force, being chanted in a sardonic, flouting manner, but they were mostly jeering nonsense syllables that filled up gaps in a tune. The mothers asked the questions, advancing across the road while the daughters retreated; then in turn the daughters advanced upon their retreating mothers and answered the questions, sometimes improvising the answers.

Here is the pattern of one of these games. Some strangers have arrived as visitors, unknown men from outside, and the mothers consult the daughters about where they are to sleep. The daughters answer:

Put them in the boys' bed, mother, mother.
Put them in the boys' bed, La la la
La la la.

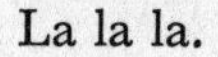

The mothers ask:

Where will the boys sleep, daughter, daughter,
Where will the boys sleep? La la la
La la la.

The girls suggest:

Sleep in the wash-tub, mother, mother.

The mothers naturally ask:

Where shall we wash the clothes, daughter, daughter?

Up to this point the questions and answers are traditional, but now the fun of improvising begins. While pirouetting backwards under the mothers' questioning, the daughters are thinking out what they can say; the loudest, quickest, most confident voice leads the answering chorus.
For instance:

Wash them in the porridge pot, mother, mother.

Or perhaps:

Wash them in the broth-pot, mother, mother,

which opens up a vista of alternative expedients for making the porridge or cooking the dinner, making porridge in a pillowslip or cooking stew in a boiler, and so on, until, as I remember, by way of the kitchen sink and the water butt, the daughters recommend throwing all the clothes and all the dishes and all the boys into the midden, and with hoots of laughter the game breaks up.

In this game we are not tranced into quietude, closed in a magic circle: we incline to be boisterous. The opposition between mothers and daughters comes farther into our consciousness than the dream-prospect of a sweetheart, because we have already experienced it in daily routine. And we shift the emphasis about which bed one is to sleep in, probably the original emphasis in the game and the underlying reason for it, into a farcical disruption of kitchen chores to annoy the mothers. This we do because we enjoy discomfiting them. Somewhere in the past history of this game the senior girls, who always choose to be the daughters rather than the mothers, have changed its whole mood.

This was my guess, and I confirmed it when I found a simpler version of the same game recorded in Antrim and Tipperary in Ireland.[1] The Irish game runs like this:

> Mother will you buy me a milking-can,
> With my one, two and three?

The mothers ask:

> Where will the money come from?

The daughters say:

> Sell our father's feather-bed.

The next question, coming close to the real preoccupation behind the game, asks:

> Then where shall the father lie?

To which the answer comes:

> In the girls' bed.

And where shall the girls lie?

> In the boys' bed.

Where shall the boys lie?

> In the washing-tub.

Here the Irish game ends, just where our free improvisations begin. Our improvisations are an almost daring extra advance into self-conscious territory. We are covering up possibly naughty unconscious desires by inventing consciously naughty tricks. All our mother-and-daughter games mark a certain advance into greater self-consciousness.

[1] Leslie Daiken, *Children's Games Throughout the Year*

In Ireland there are also more complete versions of two other games we played, in the mother-and-daughter series. As we sang it, the first of these began with the daughters chanting:

Have you any bread and wine,
Bread and wine, bread and wine,
Have you any bread and wine,
Mitheerie and mithorie?

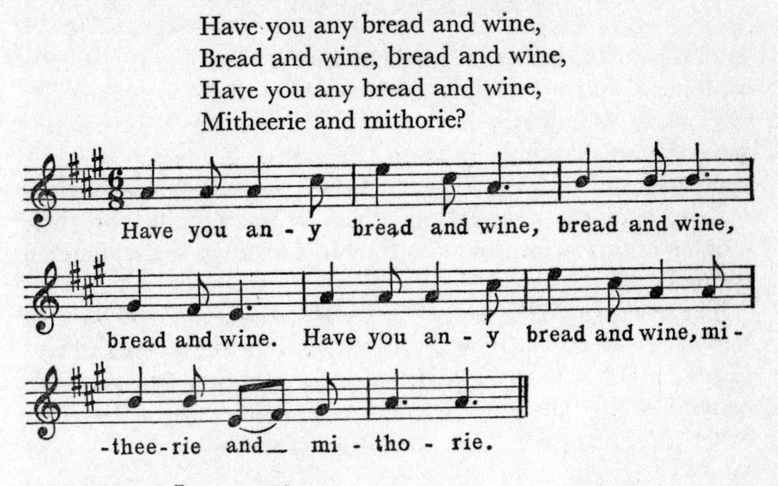

The mothers answered:

Yes, we have some bread and wine,

but refused to hand any of it over, even after much inquisition. Now in Ireland this is a combat not between mothers and daughters but between Roman soldiers and English soldiers.

Have you any bread and wine?
For we are the Romans.
Have you any bread and wine?
For we are Roman soldiers.
Yes, we have some bread and wine,
For we are English soldiers.
Then we will have one cup full.
No, you sha'n't have one cup full.
Then we will have two cups full.
No, you sha'n't have two cups full.
We will tell the Pope of you.
We don't care for the Pope or you.
We will send our cats to scratch.
We don't care for your cats or you.

We will send our dogs to bite.
We don't care for your dogs or you.
Are you ready for a fight?
Yes, we're ready for a fight.

A spirited defiance in an ancient mode, once usual before a combat. This was certainly a game played by boys, perhaps by boys and girls, whereas in our school boys and girls were segregated during playtime. That may have been the reason why our combat game had lost its ferocious directness and garbled its refrain, since the girls did not want an actual fight with their mothers. This game had clearly broken down somewhere in transmission.

The second game preserved in Ireland was found in Belfast. In our version of it, we came as near to miming as ever we did and ventured some way into the strange territory where other people's doings became our concern. A mother and a daughter stood together, while three girls advanced towards them, very slowly, singing:

We are three Jews,
New come from Spain,
To call upon
Your daughter Jane.

In the same slow tempo the mother replied:

My daughter Jane,
She is too young,
She cannot bear
Your clattering tongue.

At this point our tradition simply broke down. We had lost the words and the shape of the game, as can be seen from the fuller

Ulster version, but we had a feeling that Jane was now due to be snatched away by the intruders, a feeling which was correct enough yet, lacking words and shape, could express itself only through violence. So our 'Jews' fought for and kidnapped Jane: successive Janes were snatched or rescued: the whole rough-and-tumble became in the end a kind of pogrom, had we only known the word, against the villainous Jews. Yet in Ulster the game went on decorously. It began also on a more courtly level, boys on one side, girls on the other, taking alternate parts, like this:

Boys: We are three Lords
Come out of Spain
That we might coort
Your daughter Jane.
Girls: My daughter Jane,
She is too young,
She cannot bear
Your flattering tongue.
Boys: Then fare thee well,
Oh fare thee well,
We'll go and coort
Some other girl.
Girls: Come back, come back!
Your coat is white
And choose the fairest
To your sight.
Boys: The fairest one
That we can see
Is (So-and-so)
Come out to me.

One by one the girls are all chosen, until last of all the Leader succumbs, and to the tune of Nuts in May a general dance begins.

Because the boys and girls shared in this game, it must have conveyed a thrilling satisfaction to the girls who were chosen; it approximates more nearly to a parlour game played at a mixed party; the excitement of the sweethearting *motif* is heightened. Our game, lacking boys, was a more sinister performance. Yet I incline to think that it was also nearer the original tradition. How else did three Jews from Spain rather than three Lords come into our play? In our daily life we were not aware of Jews except as figures in the Bible. There is another version of this game, not a Scottish one, which begins: 'We are three Dukes', an easy oral transposition from 'Jews' that could easily in turn be transformed into 'Lords'. But I cannot believe that we, unaided, historically ignorant as we were, could have invented Jews from Spain. They must have been traditional. We were, too, genuinely traditional in feeling that an aura of villainy surrounded these alien figures, who might have been found in an old Ballad or a mediaeval play. In our other games we usually acted ourselves, simply, within our limited range of experience as daughters or possible sweethearts; in this game we mimed complete strangers from an unknown land speaking a 'clattering' tongue, unlike the Ulster Lords whose tongue was merely flattering.

Our style of acting and singing this game was slower and more formal than in any other. Were we unknowingly passing on from generation to generation slow struttings that originated on a mediaeval stage, so that our movements were weighted by tradition? Or were we slowed down by a greater degree of self-consciousness in miming figures so alien to us, venturing as we did on novel and dangerous territory haunted by villains? Whatever the reason, the three Jews, as we played them, stalked forward stiffly instead of dancing. They chanted slowly in time to their strutting, prolonging the last note in each line of the verse to the length of three struts forward. This measured advance was sinister. The mother also chanted her verse in the same slow, deliberate mode. The drama went suddenly into top gear, as it were, when the Jews grabbed at the daughter, headed off by the mother and by all the extras concealed near by; formality was thrown to the winds; the ensuing rough-and-tumble became shapeless. Yet the first two verses were the beginning of a story about people with whom we could not wholly identify ourselves. They marked, that is to say, a transition, however imperfect, into the world of grown-ups, the world in which the Ballads took shape.

In only one of our singing games did we revert to our local dialect. The distance between us and the feeling expressed in the game was thus lessened; it was nearer to daily life, and we sang it in a noisy, defiant manner. It was a very direct resolution of tension, a wholesome enough repudiation of romantic sentiment. Rushing round in a kind of gallop we shouted rather than sang:

O, I've lost my lad an' I care-nae,
I've lost my lad an' I care-nae,
I've lost my lad an' I ca-are-nae,
A ramshy-damshy-doo!
O, we'll get anither canary,
We'll get anither canary,
We'll get anither cana-a-ry,
A ramshy-damshy-doo!

We always sang it last of all, before running into school again, so it was never sung more than once. It was, so to speak, the satyr comedy at the end of our dramatic performances, helping to let us down to the level of daily life. Entirely by instinct we followed the right artistic pattern, as poets have probably done everywhere. In the Ballads, for instance, the last stanza or two in a story are often of this nature—a return to daily life, a slackening of tension. Our closing measure, it is true, was not a gentle, dying fall, but the daily routine to which we returned was not gentle: we had had our interlude of gentleness in our sweethearting games and the rough therapy we administered to ourselves was doubtless salutary.

It will be clear by this time that the lines of communication kept open by singing games between our unconscious and our conscious energies did not extend very far in either direction, neither into the depths of traditional feeling nor into the heights of conscious personality. But they did exist, and they did form a habit of mediating these energies into artistic expression, which with any encouragement could have been continued and developed in later life. Our most obvious defect lay in the higher reaches of personality, for we were poor in stories, a defect that was social rather than personal. Most unfledged and tentative youngsters have the chance of listening eagerly to or reading stories about grown-up experience, but there was a general dearth of story material in the lives of my schoolmates. Their mothers gossiped, but did not tell stories to their children. And, for them, stories in books did not exist. To my friends, reading was a hated school exercise, performed aloud in class, slowly, unwillingly and with apparent incomprehension. These girls did not sit enthralled with their noses in story-books, nor had their mothers and grandmothers done so. Indeed the prejudice was still perceptible which felt that a female should not waste time in reading books when she might be sewing or knitting, or, in earlier times, spinning or weaving. (The vestiges of this prejudice may still be responsible for the great space allotted to sewing and knitting in women's magazines today.) Ballads and folk-tales alike were unknown to the working classes in our town, although, as I was to discover five years later, some traditional Ballads were still being sung by ploughmen in the surrounding countryside. For lack of story-material, then, we tended to circle round and round the same story in varying guise: the acquisition of a sweetheart. Partly for the same reason, lack of scope and experience, our feelings did not reach outside the common biological urges towards puberty and motherhood. In our games we did not enter into a world of passions such as jealousy or revenge; if we had any rebellious ambitions we kept them vague and private, like the possibility of passionate love. Our most articulate defiance, a feeling of rivalry with our mothers, skirted only very delicately round one of its prime causes, the cross-pull that draws girls towards their fathers, as boys are drawn to their mothers. In general, then, our singing games were as rudimentary as we were ourselves. And yet they carried with them a certain weight of tradition.

Most of them, for instance, contain evidence that they have come from a long way off. To begin with, the traditional way of singing them was in what we took to be English. This may have been a mode of setting a distance between us and them, which seems to be a necessary process in the making of any work of art, yet there are other indications that some of these songs had come by way of England. Our very simple 'frosty morning' game brought in 'the London Row' as a glamorous place where one met one's sweetheart; it remained glamorous and unknown to us, for none of us had been in or heard of the London Row in Newcastle or Rotten Row in Hyde Park, London. Even if 'the London Row' is a deformation of 'the London Road', which I hardly believe, the reference was well outside our daily lives. The 'guinea-gold ring' also, which may have supplanted the 'gay gold ring' of the Ballads, has an English, even a Hanoverian feeling about it. 'Have you any bread and wine?' suggests a Catholic setting, certainly an earlier setting than our time, for among our Presbyterian people wine was only a name, except at the church communion service. The usual 'drink' was beer or whisky, not wine, since the lavish claret that once flowed in Edinburgh when Scotland was an ally of France had vanished from common use. The teasing concatenation of riddles about where the visiting strangers are to sleep may reach even farther out, into Northern Europe, for there was once upon a time an old and widespread custom in Northern lands—earlier on in Southern Europe too—that important male visitors shared the beds of the daughters of the house; this was an accepted rite of hospitality. And there were also our three Jews from Spain, who came down to us, as I believe, from mediaeval times.

In thus recognizing no frontiers of centuries or countries, bringing with them vestiges of other and earlier modes of living, our singing games, humble and rudimentary as they were, showed themselves to be waves, even if small waves, in the great surge of oral tradition. What was it that kept them going and made them survive? For they survived as by a miracle in a precarious enclave of their own, outside of which they had no prestige.

The boys despised them. Unlike the Ulster boys, our young males shared in no singing games and did not know any. Their playground was used chiefly for football. The sounds that rose in the air from it were the yells of aggressive solitaries punching and kicking each other into combined action. The climate of expectation in which these boys were reared permitted no dancing or singing games as an outlet for their energies. Only war-like combat, emulation, beating the other fellow or the other 'side', were regarded as proper male activities. A war dance might have been allowed, but war dances had long died out among the Lowland Scots. In their school playground our boys rehearsed only warfare: the symbols in which their energies found relief were conditioned solely by combat. Like us, they simply accepted their playground tradition, which, like ours, was uncontaminated by adult instruction. Yet their tradition was the prevailing social tradition of that time, outside school hours as well as in. Man, working-class man at least, was assumed in our town to be primarily a fighting animal, needing little other culture than the mediation of his energies by some kind of collective team spirit. Girls, not being fighters, mattered much less, and their activities had no prestige. That was perhaps why, in the Academy to which I was later promoted, the boys were still playing football while the girls had no singing games, none at all.

The culture that originally shaped our singing games, as it shaped the Ballads, must have been a wider culture, shared by both sexes, as in Ulster, not yet narrowed down, like ours, to utilitarian techniques and fighting. I call it a wider culture because it allowed room for the imagination; it kept open the lines of communication between unconscious and conscious energies; it formed a habit of imaginative expression which our girls inherited and for a year or two practised—for most of them, I fear, the too brief opening of a single door. Yet, in our day and time, it had become precarious. Our singing games were kept going because we found an emotional satisfaction in them, which came from sources deep enough to recur with vitality and persistence in each new generation of schoolgirls. They answered a human need, these simple singing games of ours, but the need was not recognized by convention outside the playground and so was not provided for in the social pattern of our time.

It was, and remains, a general human need. The energies informing the underworld of human feeling search for an objective shape in the light of day, and until they find it are unsatisfied. Mere violence, the chaotic eruption of formless energy, does not bring the peculiar satisfaction which arises from works of the imagination, whether in words or paint or music. Whenever our games broke down through a failure in transmission and lapsed into violence, they became shapeless and unsatisfactory; they turned into something else and we returned with noise and squabbling to our daytime selves. When our energies did find shape, a profound and different satisfaction was conveyed to all of us. The transmission of this immediate, imaginative satisfaction, I do believe, is what keeps an oral tradition going.

The satisfaction cannot arise, the tradition cannot survive for long, unless the unformulated energies of the underworld have found a shape to flow into which is accepted directly, without question, by all the participants. It looks as if the shape to be achieved takes a rhythmic form naturally and spontaneously. Human beings are symmetrically fashioned and each day is rounded for them by the sun; when they run or skip or hop they cannot help doing so rhythmically any more than waves on the sea can help following a rhythm. Children combining in play shape a rhythm for their games without thinking about it. Even combined naughtiness turns into rhythmic action. I remember joining in the baiting of a half-wit in our town whose name was Jimmy Rattray; we pursued him with a song which had a simple enough rhythm yet one which demanded a change in the syllables of his name, so we just changed them and yelled at his heels, keeping admirable time:

Jimmy Rat-at-airy,
Tea-pot nose,
One, two, three and
Away he goes.

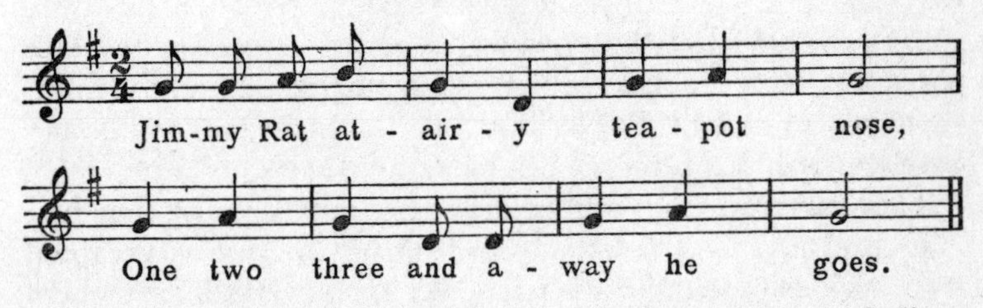

Rhythm alone, even when combined with passionate feeling, as when an angry child sobs rhythmically in his rage, does not make a work of art. But rhythm that takes on a shape fixed by a pattern of dancing feet or music or words, or, as in our games, by all three together, can make a work of art. Our singing games had this kind of shape: they were strongly rhythmical; the dance-steps, the tune, corresponded to the beat of the word-stresses, and much repetition fixed the shapes indelibly in our memories. (It is worth noting that the dancing never hampered the singing or the actions: the governing rhythm was never broken. I therefore find it easy to believe that once upon a time dance and song had a simultaneous origin.) We did not think of the shape as a shape, but we felt it, exactly as we did not think of the symbols we embodied, although we felt them. Our emotional energies did not emerge as concepts, but as primarily rhythmical and often symbolical waves of feeling, which fell into concrete shape. The embodied pattern or image governed the expression of our feelings, which were thus mediated by the whole effect of the embodiment. This set a certain distance between any feeling and the expression of it, and set a distance also between our ordinary selves and the selves absorbed in the game. In a sense, we were liberated from our ordinary selves. That was part of the satisfaction.

The closed ring-games, indeed, held us tranced in a kind of dream-world. As in a dream, everything was immediate but also in flux; no conceptual categories divided dance from song or song from drama. But it was a waking dream-world, and therefore distinctively human. We share with animals an underworld of sleeping dreams, yet, so far as we know, the human imagination alone brings its dreams into the open and shapes them in sunlight or moonlight, with paint-brush or carving-knife, with dance and song and drama, with patterned, rhythmic ritual. The frieze along a temple-front, the repeated pattern round an earthenware pot, come from the same source as our singing games, the fluid, unshaped underworld of feeling. I do not insist that our games were works of art, but they did have the makings of art.

They survived as an oral tradition not only because they had shape and gave us profound satisfaction, but because we accepted them seriously, without question. We took everything in them for granted: we queried nothing. This does not mean that we were passive little conformists. It may be that in every category we invent to describe a pair of polarized opposites there lurks a fallacy; there is certainly a fallacy in our use of the terms 'active' and 'passive'. We identify ourselves with the 'active' component and regard the 'passive' component as a blank negation: a complete misunderstanding of any reciprocal relationship. There was a strongly reciprocal relationship between us and our singing games. It was our energy that flowed into and informed them; if we accepted them without question, it was because we were concerned with energies, not concepts; because we wanted to accept them as they were; because we enjoyed the experience of releasing our nebulous feelings into an expressive shape. One could not call our attitude even a suspension of disbelief, since disbelief implies some conceptual thinking. The free flow of feeling was what mattered most to us; we did not want to impede it with conscious criticisms, even had we been capable of them. Our common need for accepted emotional expression overrode any tendencies we might have had to contrary self-assertion or quibbling. So we were not passive little conformists, such as are usually called 'good' little girls. We were far from being good little girls. In school, for instance, most of us put up a successful resistance to instruction, despite exhortation and punishment. In the playground when not playing singing games we were noisy, rough-tongued and frequently aggressive. Yet while we danced we were harmonious little girls, keeping the same time, accepting the same convention. While we danced we were outside the conscious categories of good and evil; we were neither good nor bad little girls; we were simply forming the habit of mediating our energies into artistic expression.

This attitude of acceptance characterizes, I think, all audiences who listen to oral poetry. Without it, I do not believe that oral tradition could long survive. The spoken word, or the sung word, seems to penetrate more immediately, more directly, into the underworld of feeling than the word looked at on a printed page. Most people have had the experience of being moved by a poem impressively declaimed by the human voice and of discovering later, on reading it silently, that it is a bad poem. The critical conscious self seems to live behind the eyes rather than in the midriff, where the human voice reverberates with potent effect. That may be why oral poetry needs and gets absorbed audiences who accept it without question, who are involved in a flow of feeling rather than in what is nowadays called evaluation. Once the reciprocal flow of feeling stops, there will be no more listeners and no more traditional singers. The audience for oral poetry is not passive.

Our singing games, then, provide indications of what to look for in oral poetry. They fell into simple, patterned forms that allowed room for contrary or supplementary swirls of feeling and for subsequent changes of mood within the framework of the whole. They were strongly rhythmic. They were repetitive without self-consciousness. They concentrated on the tension and release of emotion in action, not on the elaboration of characters or personalities. They depended on a reciprocal flow of feeling among the participants, either as singers or audience. In all these respects they resembled the Ballads, and, like the Ballads, they were anonymous. Like the Ballads, too, as I believe, they were a profoundly satisfying form of play.

2

Singing and Listening to Oral Poetry

'one of these wild and monotonous strains so common in Scotland, and to which the natives of that country chant their old ballads.'

Sir Walter Scott, *Heart of Midlothian*, chap. xv

THE audience for oral poetry is not passive, but that does not necessarily mean that the listeners compose the songs. It means that there is a flow of sympathy between the listeners and the singer, of which all are more or less aware; the quality of this sympathetic *rapport* may lead the Ballad-singer, almost unconsciously, to shift an emphasis here or change a phrase there to fit the mood of his audience. Oral poetry lives only while it is being performed, and with every Ballad performance the singer creates it anew, with possible variations in the tune or the stanzas. What he does not change is the pattern followed by deep currents of feeling that sweep through the song and through his listeners. This unanimity of feeling is something he takes for granted. The listeners have the same background as himself; their likes and dislikes, fears and prejudices, come from experiences similar to his own, and out of an underworld of imagination common to all he does not need to persuade or cajole or explain; he can concentrate on the story he is singing.

For this reason Ballads must flourish best in a close, small community. In a wider setting oral poetry tends to become public entertainment, and that is something else, since the audience is in a different relationship to the singer. The warmth of intimacy is needed for the right rendering of a Ballad. I first met a Ballad on a late summer evening of 1906, when a ploughman sang it to me, and I find that I ought to explain how I achieved a friendship with him that encouraged him to sing it.

My mother at that time rented for summer holidays a four-roomed cottage or 'cottar house' on a farm beside the sea, five miles from our home town. The farmer whose cottage we rented had no ploughman; he himself, two sons, a daughter and his wife did the work of the farm, all living in squalid discomfort while he put large sums of money in the bank. But the neighbouring farmer, a kindly old man whose comfortable sister kept house for him, had ploughmen. Two of them were married and lived in cottar houses; two were bachelors accommodated in the traditional 'bothy', along with the 'halflin', a boy of fifteen. There were many farm bothies at that time in Kincardine, as also in Aberdeen farther north, and in all of these, I believe, Ballads were still being sung.

The bothy ploughmen, besides getting free oatmeal and milk, were fed at noon and supper-time in the farm kitchen. Nether Warburton—the farmer was always referred to by the name of his farm—treated them well. But the bothy itself was comfortless. It had a stone floor, a meal-chest, a rough table and benches, box-beds to sleep in—mere holes in the wall—and old sacks thrown down on the floor for rugs; the whole place smelt musty and damp. Now there were six of us young people in the cottage, including visiting cousins, and we used to dance out of doors at the nearby cross-roads: it was not surprising that the bothy men formed the habit of joining in our fun at the cross-roads every fine night. They had nowhere else to go, unless they bicycled to our home town, to drift along the streets chaffing mill-girls and drop into a public-house for a drink. They preferred our company at the cross-roads, where there was room for energetic dancing and a long wooden fence to sit on. The halflin brought his melodeon with him, so that we had music. We became very friendly both with Nether Warburton and his men. Indeed, before we left at the end of the summer, Nether Warburton gave us a dance in his barn, with fresh melons and ice-cream as well as a fiddler and a piper to play for us; all the ploughmen came to it, in their tackety boots; it was a grand dance.

I was on especial terms of friendship with the senior bachelor, Harry, a man of twenty-seven whose heart's desire was to farm in Canada. His lean shoulders, like Robert Burns's, were slightly bent with premature hard labour at the plough; he was gentle with animals and shy with people. After I had tramped hay on the stacks, stooked oats and barley and hoed many turnips at the cliff-foot, he allowed me to take charge of his two cherished horses and plough up a couple of 'furs' in the potato field, a supreme mark of confidence.

One moonlit evening after this, when the others were dancing 'Petronella' and I sat on the fence listening to Harry's news from his brother-in-law in Alberta, he said unexpectedly: 'Wad ye like to hear an auld sang?' That was how I met my first Ballad.

It was 'Captain Wedderburn's Courtship' (Child 46). I did not know its title then or for many years after. Harry did not trouble to announce a title; he went straight into the song, giving me the version I now recognize as Greig's,[1] though with a less extreme Aberdeenshire enunciation. Instead of beginning it:

> The Laird of Roslin's daughter walked through the wood her leen

he sang:

> The Earl o' Roslin's dochter gaed through the wids her lane

The tune he sang might possibly be No. 10 from Bronson's volume[2]; I do not remember it exactly enough to be sure of it. What I do remember is the way he sang it, standing easily and using not much more than a speaking rather than a singing voice. The local speech tended to the falsetto, so that Harry's heightened speaking voice was altogether a 'head' voice, clear in its enunciation, not quite nasal, produced without any strain. There were none of the emotional gurglings one sometimes hears in the renderings of people who think they can sing. It was a flat, impersonal voice.

At first the recurrent refrain at the end of every stanza, with its insistence on:

> 'We'll baith lie in ae bed, an' you'll lie neist the wa' '

made a faint ruffle of embarrassment in my feelings, but the unselfconscious directness with which Harry drove his way through the song cured me of that. Far from intruding itself, his personality vanished altogether; there was only a voice rhythmically telling a story to a tune.

He sang each line with a small break in the middle, like this:

> The Earl o' Roslin's dochter . . . gaed through the wids her lane.

[1] Greig, *Last Leaves of Aberdeen Ballads and Ballad Airs*, No. XIX

[2] Bertrand Harris Bronson, *The Traditional Tunes of the Child Ballads*, vol. I

He emphasized the syllable just before the caesura, so that when he sang:

> 'You will get to my suppér . . . a cherry withoot a stane'

I did not at first recognize the word 'suppér' and wondered for a moment what my 'sap-páh', which is what I thought I heard, could possibly be. On the second repetition:

> 'And you will get to my suppér . . . a chicken withoot a bane'

I did recognize it. My only other momentary misgiving was about the 'bird withoot a ga' ', which I took to be a bird 'withoot a ca' ', that is, a caw or call. I accepted the ballad, as it went on, with the simple directness Harry gave to it. My romantic young soul found nothing unlikely in a man's falling in love with a woman at first sight, and the shocking suddenness with which he proposed to put her in his bed, taken for granted in the ballad, was eventually taken for granted by me also. This effect, I am sure, is one of the reasons, if not the main reason, for the widespread vogue of this ballad in the North-East of Scotland. Greig recorded nine versions of it, and I should not be surprised to hear it sung today in a bothy, if there are still any bothies.

Besides the directness of the love story, the main reason for its popularity probably lies in the riddles it contains. Once upon a time the whole world, from far Cathay to the farthest North, loved a riddle. Guessing the answer to a riddle is the result of a collaboration between conscious and unconscious energies; if these combine successfully one gets a little shock of pleasure in the achievement, as anyone knows who has ever solved a difficult cross-word puzzle. Apparently random promptings from the unconscious help the gropings of conscious memory, and in the end the solution comes in an exhilarating flash. This exhilaration in earlier times seems to have been great, to judge from the ubiquity of riddles. Solving a riddle was enjoyed because it was the playing of a game, a game of percepts on the way to becoming concepts, and quickness of perception was as much prized as quickness of hand or foot. Child[1] says that ingenuity is one of the six transcendental virtues of Mahāyāna Buddhism; and it ranked high, in the early world, as evidence of natural ability, even as a sign of

[1] Child, vol. I, p. 11, footnote

favour from the gods. The man or woman who could keep open the lines of communication between the conscious and the unconscious self and interpret dreams or riddles was much honoured. In the wide extent of oral tradition we find that an ability to solve riddles saves many a hero or heroine from jeopardy, including, for instance, Oedipus faced by the Sphinx. Perhaps because it was the result of successful collaboration between mysterious parts of the self, it came to be a test of fitness for marriage. It could ensure success in the winning of a 'perilous princess', or, if the lady answered the riddles instead of posing them, it ensured the rescue of her father or lover from imminent disgrace and beheading. And one could outwit not only lethal human beings but supernatural apparitions by the power of the word, as we find in an old manuscript text, dating from 1450, of a ballad called 'Riddles Wisely Expounded'.

Thinking up riddles and posing them seems to be a step towards putting into words and consciously recognizing newly seen relationships, hitherto unguessed at, in the world around us. Perhaps we are now so habituated to simile and metaphor that we do not feel the fresh shock of recognition in solving riddles, outside of cross-word puzzles and Christmas crackers, to which lowly status we have reduced them. Yet I think that much of our most scientific research today depends on the posing and solving of the right riddles, with the requisite nimbleness of perception, and the ensuing shock of satisfaction, although it is also intellectual curiosity that impels us, not merely the fun of being quick-witted, of pinning down meanings and double meanings, of seeing a little way into mysteries.

In this ballad of Harry's the riddles had no dire penalties attached to them but they were still associated with fitness for matrimony, and they were old, traditional riddles, still carrying weight and giving pleasure.

I did not reflect on these things when I listened to Harry's song. I swallowed the ballad whole, not knowing that it was a Ballad. It was a new song of a novel kind; it was a love story; the riddles in it pleased me; and Harry was a friend of mine, so that I was receptive to anything he chose to sing. I think that I realized, even at the time, that I was having an unusual experience. A little later the second bachelor, Sandy, came swaggering away from the dance and said: '*I'll* sing ye a sang.' He postured and strutted and began:

> Come all ye listen to me,
> for I'm gaun to sing ye a sang,
> And if you'll all attention pay
> I'll not detain ye lang.
> Like a fool I married a wife,
> my fortune for to try,
> 'Twas the cause of all my strife,
> for she was the real Mackay.

On and on he went, thrusting his innuendos at us, jerking his thumb over his shoulder, fiddling his feet to and fro, never letting us forget for a moment that this was Sandy 'showing off'. The contrast between the style of this ditty and Harry's auld sang struck me disagreeably and emphasized the unusual quality of Harry's performance. I see now that I ought to have been thankful that I was introduced so clearly to the difference between one kind of oral tradition and another.

For both Harry's and Sandy's songs were products of oral tradition. Neither of them had ever possessed a song-book, nor was it then likely that they ever would. Sandy's song was in the pattern of the 'Come-all-ye's' brought to Scotland by Irish harvest labourers: Harry's had been passed on to him by other ploughmen, who had been receiving it for many generations from their forebears. I do not know whether either of them had ever looked into a song-book belonging to someone else, but as they read not even a daily newspaper and only rarely the local weekly, I incline to think that they had never studied a song-sheet of any kind; they learned their songs by ear, as the halflin played his melodeon.

What Harry could have got from no song-sheet, however, was the mode in which he sang his 'song'; similarly, Sandy's shufflings and jiggings were clearly imitated from the life, not taken from print. Harry sang his ballad as if sure of understanding and sympathy from his audience. There was no need for personal invitation, emphasis, or deprecation from him. Consequently, he himself faded out of the song as he sang it. The ballad needed only to sing itself. Sandy, on the other hand, sang as if unsure of his audience. He had to invite people to listen, to cajole them by deprecation, to nudge at their attention, to entertain them by clowning. This may have been partly a consequence of the song's origin; how could Irish labourers sing the songs of Zion in a strange land, as it were, except by buttonholing people? Together with the song Sandy had taken over the mode of singing it; together with the ballad, Harry had taken over the mode of singing it. One cannot separate a traditional song from the style in which it is sung.

The clowning tradition may be as old as the Ballad tradition, perhaps older, for unlike the latter it does not need a specially sympathetic audience; it can create its own sympathies on the spot, since these do not go so deep as the feelings shared by Ballad singers and listeners. It can induce belief, whereas the good Ballad feels no need to do that. The clowning song enters into the world of grown-up experience by trying to disarm its public, to win them over from possible hostility by laughter, while the Ballad enters into the grown-up world by drawing its listeners into itself on a current of assured common sympathy. These two extremes of oral tradition shade into each other through a long spectrum of nuances; one can mark the transitions, I think, by noting the gradual intrusion of the singer's personal ego as one nears the clowning end of the spectrum. Sandy was at the clowning end of oral tradition; his performance was highly personal. Harry was at the Ballad end of it; his performance was utterly impersonal. I do not think that this difference between their renderings arose from a difference of temperament alone: they sang other Ballads and songs, some of Sandy's verging on the bawdy, some of Harry's on the banal, but I retained my first clear impression of a difference in kind between the modes of impersonal and personal renderings.

I was lucky in having begun my acquaintance with Ballads through 'Captain Wedderburn's Courtship', a much better Ballad than some of the others Harry sang. It is not one of the 'great' Ballads, since it is neither tragic nor passionate; it has a happy ending and it may be relatively modern except for its cargo of riddles, which it tosses back and forth in a gamesome spirit. Yet it has immediately recognizable Ballad characteristics. One goes straight into the Ballad world with the first line:

The Earl o' Roslin's dochter gaed through the wids her lane.

In the Ballad world any young woman who walks by herself in the greenwood or among the broom-bushes is heading for trouble; she is bound to meet a young man whose intentions may or may not be honourable but are certainly frank. Any Ballad audience familiar with the convention would expect a young man to appear, and he does appear: Captain Wedderburn, a servant to the King. As is usual in Ballads, neither of the protagonists is particularized; the pretty lady remains a token figure, although a quick-witted one, matched by the quick-witted token figure of the Captain. The listeners are left, as usual, to fill in details from their own imaginations. Again, as in other Ballads, nothing that happens occasions surprise. One is supposed simply to accept it all. The young man may turn out to be a supernatural monster, or a ghost, or, as here, a soldier; the young woman may be raped or murdered or, as here, courted and married: anything may happen. A young woman who poses riddles to her would-be lover as a condition of marriage is presented as the most natural of figures. One does not ask whether that is what any young woman would naturally do. No comment is made on her actions, no explanation of why she should ask riddles; the listeners are assumed to need no explanations. I think one can take it as a law in Ballad-making that the audience is expected to have a natural ability to enter directly into any situation presented.

All these characteristics are common to Ballads and stamp 'Captain Wedderburn's Courtship' as belonging to the Ballad *genre*. The last verse, as sometimes happens, lets one down into daily life again, but does this by providing a comment from outside the story, which I incline to cavil at:

Little did that fair maid think,
  that morning when she raise,
That it would be the very last
  o' a' her maiden days.

Yet it is not so banal a conclusion as another version provides, which assures the listeners that the fair maid has beome 'Mrs Wedderburn'.

I now feel sure that Harry's unforgettable impersonal rendering of this song was delivered in the true Ballad style. I shall quote some evidence from other people, and then confirm my apparently rash conclusion by referring to the performance of a contemporary Ballad-singer, Jeannie Robertson of Aberdeen, who is, I think, a genius at Ballad-singing.

Olive Campbell and Cecil Sharp, when collecting English folk-songs from the Southern Appalachians, say this[1]:

> The mountain singers sing in very much the same manner as English folk-singers, in the same straightforward, direct manner, without any conscious attempt at expression, and with the even tone and clarity of enunciation with which all folk-song collectors are familiar. . . . When singing a ballad . . . he is merely relating a story in a particularly effective way which he has learned from his elders, his conscious attention being wholly concentrated on what he is singing and not upon the effect which he himself is producing.

Professor W. J. Entwistle in his book *European Balladry* says:

> Mr Neville Coghill has described to me his impression of ballads heard in the Blue Mountains of Virginia. They were sung to him without accompaniment, chorus or dance. The singers were all women who adopted a harsh, clear, nasal intonation completely devoid of expression . . . impersonal singing left the words of the ballad to do their own work.

Coming to more recent times, I found this in a book of Miss Honor Tracy's, *Silk Hats and no Breakfast*. She is describing street singers in Algeciras, Spain.

> The man . . . burst nasally into an interminable romantic ballad, the women supporting him with their hard, bird-like voices. On and on they went, with faces empty of all expression, a tone that never varied and a complete lack of self-consciousness, while the crowd listened avidly with the same utter, child-like absorption. Splats of rain fell on them all from time to time, but, spell-bound, they never stirred.

Being accustomed to the kind of entertainment where the

[1] *English Folk-songs from the Southern Appalachians*, N.Y. and London, 1917, pp. ix and x

individual performer strives to convey as much 'expression' as possible and to 'put himself across' to his public, all these observers were struck by the lack of this tendency in the Ballad-singer. 'Without any conscious attempt at expression', 'the conscious attention being wholly concentrated on what he is singing and not upon the effect he is producing', 'a clear intonation completely devoid of expression', 'with faces empty of all expression and a complete lack of self-consciousness'—these descriptions add up to the impersonal mode of singing, exactly as I heard it from Harry.

Child himself seems to have noted chiefly that the Ballad tunes were slow in tempo. He records of 'Earl Brand' (7), version *G*, from William Motherwell, that it was 'sung to a long, drawling, monotonous tune'. Of 'The Twa Sisters' (10), version *L*, a, he says the two four-line stanzas were sung 'to a slow, quaint strain'. Of 'Babylon' (14), version *B*, a, he reports that it was sung 'to a wild, melancholy old tune not in any collection'. Child's sources, William Motherwell, Jamieson *et al.*, who gave him these comments, were expressing their own tastes in describing tunes as quaint, monotonous, wild; we had better not depend on these statements for definitive evidence. But I do not wish to multiply instances, since I prefer to depend on my own experience in listening to Ballads, especially to the Ballad-singing of Jeannie Robertson.

I had never heard her before when one day I found myself listening to a record of her singing 'Lord Donald, my son'. This is version *B*, in Child, of 'Lord Randal' (12), and contains ten verses.

The immediate effect was unexpected and unusual. I was at once caught up into a timeless world—a world, at least, where time bore no relation to the clock, giving a curiously reassuring sense of endless duration. She was singing very slowly in a clear, high, true, impersonal voice. The tone of unhurried assurance would have soothed any infant like a lullaby, despite the tragic starkness of the words. This feeling of suspended, almost tranced duration lasted until the end of the song. She lingered over vowels more than would have seemed possible or necessary to an impatient modern consciousness. 'Wha-a-at li-ike we-ere thae fishies?' was a question not in any hurry to get an answer. One felt that the

story was unrolling so inevitably that hurrying it on would have been out of place.

Yet, if one considers only the words, this is an urgent story, and the slow rendering could seem at variance with the rest of it. The dying young man keeps telling his mother to make his bed soon, but the song flows on and on until he has verbally made his testament, in answer to his mother's deliberate questioning, and uncovered the treachery of his sweetheart. There it stops. The bed is never made and the young man never lies down to die. The situation is dramatic enough: a young man comes home to his mother after having been poisoned by his sweetheart: but the development of the theme is so leisurely that it is not sung dramatically. The drama is concentrated in the last verse, where the sweetheart is accused of murder and the long, leisurely build-up suddenly culminates in a silence, but Jeannie Robertson does not sing this last verse with dramatic force. There is merely a final silence, a sense of being cut off after so much assured duration, in itself a symbolic image of death. Nothing more need be added. It is a disturbingly effective performance.

The singer's voice is quite impersonal; she is merely the vehicle through which flows a remarkable sense of duration, almost of inevitable ceremony and ritual. The slow build-up works on one's feelings well beneath the level of consciousness. Behind the words and the tune lie spaces of silences in which one feels the presence of mysteries.

The mysteries thicken around the enigmatic figure of the Mother. She has at first a mother's care for her son; her immediate question: has he had his supper? lets us know that she would make supper for him if he needed it. Her persistent queries about the kind of 'fishies' he has eaten embody her anxiety for him. Yet when she suggests that he has been poisoned and he agrees with her: 'O yes, I am poisoned, Mother mak' my bed soon', the revelation elicits no comment at all. From this point onward she is caught up in something more important than the imminent death of her son, or her own personal feelings about that, which are never referred to. Some personal feeling is allowed to the son, because he has to betray the part his sweetheart has played, but it is the minimum of personal feeling. And the sweetheart, for all her criminality, is still referred to as the sweetheart; in another version she remains unalterably the truelove, although manifestly untrue. Private feelings have no interest for this Ballad-maker; like the mother he is drawn by something stronger, something so potent that it holds up the narrative, ignoring the hapless young man's plea that he wants to die in bed. This potent force is the claim of the family for its dues, its share in the dying man's possessions. That he should make his testament is much more important than that he should die in his bed. The kinship network blankets the individual members of the family; by comparison each of them seems to be insignificant, even the Mother, the primal functionary of the family, even the Son, who is dying; their personal feelings do not matter. The Testament must be made.

This intrusion of the testamentary theme occurs in every complete version of the Ballad, in 'Lord Randal' as well as 'Lord Donald'; it is omitted only in later versions, including one from Maine, U.S.A., where the son has dwindled into a dying child (croodlin' doo) and has no family possessions. It is found also in Finnish, Scandinavian, Spanish, French and other Continental versions of the story. As a narrative device, holding the listener in suspense while the various members of the family are named one after another until the villain is at last pounced on, it is effective, but it would not have been used in that way unless it were something which the listeners could accept as necessary, as an inevitable ceremony, not merely a trick of story-telling. It is apparently an accepted ritual, an integral part of a family death-bed scene. It occurs in other family stories, in 'The Cruel Brother' (11) where a daughter dies, and in 'Edward' (13): there are traces of it in 'Lizie Wan' (51), an incest story. As soon as the fundamental belief in its necessity begins to fail, it begins to look a little ridiculous; one then sees it merely as a trick, a story-telling device which lends itself to parody. Various parodies are found: the fox makes his will in a Danish song, the robin makes his in a Scottish song, the goat belonging to a bishop who has starved him makes his testament in a Czech song. To be taken seriously, the testamentary theme needs to be carried on a wave of traditional acceptance common to listeners and singer alike. In 'Lord Donald' it is taken seriously. And Jeannie Robertson sings the ballad in a way that conveys the full resonance of tradition behind the story. Her long, slow rhythms, her silences, conjure up the sense of timeless duration in which the weight of traditional feeling can make itself felt.

No printed copy of 'Lord Donald', however it were read, could convey this. The living singing voice is needed, and the long-drawn-out rendering. One has to travel slowly through a whole world of feeling to sense the implications behind the ballad. I hope I have now made it clear why I think that Jeannie Robertson of Aberdeen sings Ballads in what must be an authentic, high traditional style. Listening to her, one can begin to comprehend why the Ettrick Shepherd's mother, Margaret Laidlaw, Mrs Hogg, said to Sir Walter Scott, when he was preparing his Minstrelsy of the Scottish Border: 'There were never ane o' my sangs prentit till ye prentit them yoursel', an' ye hae spoilt them awthegither. They were made for singing an' no' for reading; but ye hae broken the charm now.'

What she called 'the charm', since it was a mystery she could not put a name to, was the slow impersonal underlying rhythm of traditional feeling, which carries with it vestiges of ancient beliefs and long-forgotten, or half-forgotten, rituals and ceremonies. To allow room and time for these a tragic Ballad must be sung as Jeannie Robertson sings it, in a slow, impersonal, unhurried, unregimented manner. The slowness is essential.

Full consciousness is purposive, focused to a point, and desires speed of movement, quick decisions, short-cuts to a goal. The underworld of feeling is by comparison unfocused; the eye of attention, as it were, is dilated because it is taking in a wider area of vibrations from deeper strata of experience. Consciously one may become aware of a feeling in an instantaneous flash; yet the feeling itself has been growing slowly for some time below the level of awareness, probably long before one registers its presence. Feelings can be embodied in imagined actions swiftly enough, as in dreams or reveries, but the feelings themselves may have taken nearly a lifetime to grow. One cannot travel fast through this underworld of feeling and be fully aware of it, just as one cannot travel in a fast car through a landscape and be as fully aware of it as one would be on foot. Clock-time with its counted minutes, its stress on speed, is for the conscious self, not for the underworld of feeling where the imagination takes its rise. Ballads belong to this imaginative underworld and the traditional rhythms of feeling behind their tunes and words need a longer wave-length than dancing songs, work songs, or gay entertainments. This is especially true of tragic Ballads.

I have heard 'The Wife of Usher's Well', a tragic Ballad, sung to a mechanical tonk-a-tonk on a guitar; even the gaps between the verses were filled in by a guitar obbligato in strictly measured time, an example of 'horror vacui', always, as J. Huizinga[1] says, 'a symptom of artistic decline'. The result was a travesty. Not because a guitar was used, but because it was used wrongly. It was not the instrument that was out of place, but the strictly measured and continuous beat to which it was played. Ballads need not be sung unaccompanied by an instrument; after all,

[1] J. Huizinga, *The Waning of the Middle Ages*, p. 228

very many years ago, Achilles, when Patroclus came to find him in his tent, was singing a Ballad to the phorminx. The minstrels who chanted the Homeric epics had stringed instruments; the mediaeval romancers had harps; the singers who perform Yugoslavian epic songs usually have each a *gusle*. There is no reason why a Ballad should not be accompanied by a fiddle or a guitar used with discretion, but that means not interfering with the long slow rhythms of feeling to which Jeannie Robertson gives such freedom; it means not pinning a Ballad down to a precise two-four beat.

Oral poetry everywhere is fluid in its tempo, as in everything else, even where it is embodied in syllabic verse. We do not know what liberties the singers took in sounding the many vowels in the majestic swing of a Homeric hexameter, but we do know that Yugoslav singers linger on long vowels and use flourishes of grace-notes in the wanderings and waverings of their melodies. We know that untutored human beings singing in lonely places, shepherds, for instance, let their voices wander and waver in apparently timeless modes according to the feeling that comes up their throats. Even in modern inhabited places unsophisticated people still fall into a slow rhythm when they are singing together without a conductor, whether hymns or sentimental airs are being sung. They will not be hurried: they will linger on every vowel even in the most falsely sentimental of songs: they will express their emotions in complete freedom from the strictly measured beat of counted time. We accord this freedom only to operatic singers, although within conventional limitations, because we expect strongly emotional singing in operas, but it is naturally claimed by all singers who give their feelings free vent. The slow rhythms of deep feeling will not be regimented: they cannot be measured by clock-time or a metronome. Nor, sometimes, can they be measured even by the rate of the human pulse. In the No plays of Japan, says Professor Empson, the presence of the supernatural is indicated by a tempo that is slower than the human heart-beat.

In extreme contrast to the unmeasured timeless underworld of feeling, our contemporary society is addicted to and conditioned by speed, measured by clock-time. The machine age in which we find ourselves trains us to live on the alert, with consciousness sharply focused; it is not easy for us to relax. So one becomes habituated to judging everything, even works of imagination, solely by the scrutinizing eye of focused consciousness—a prime cause of misunderstanding oral poetry, which needs to be felt more than scrutinized. One has to appreciate that oral poetry is both 'unlettered' and 'emotional', that the best way to understand it is through one's feelings. This proviso applies particularly to Ballads, which are more obviously unlettered and emotional than epic oral poetry.

The attitude of mind which has stigmatized 'emotional' as a dirty word is, I believe, on the way out, yet it still lingers in the air sufficiently to mislead people. I have met, for instance, a criticism of 'The Wife of Usher's Well' which dismisses her as a 'poor, deluded woman'. I have heard, as I indicated previously, a recording of the same ballad made by a young man with a guitar at a speed that can be described only as a fast mechanical tempo. Clearly there is a need to accustom people to the fact that Ballads are not to be approached as if they were written literature or pop songs. They belong to an ancient tradition of oral poetry and should be set in that perspective. To do this means appreciating something of the background from which Ballads emerge, and realizing a little how the underworld of feeling affects them and us. In the next two chapters I shall make an attempt to provide a perspective through which one may better understand Ballads and the effects they try to achieve.

BACKGROUNDS

3

BALLAD BACKGROUND I

The Underworld of Feeling. Gilgamesh, Homer, Norse Saga

IMAGINATION takes its rise in the underworld of feeling, which, like the sea, has tides and currents and is continually in motion. Imagined actions may form there and vanish again, trends of feeling may be discernible, but there are no concepts in that world, no categories; one might almost say no boundaries. In such a flowing medium a sense of personal identity must be difficult to come by. One has to emerge into some degree of consciousness to find that, and then chart oneself by reference to other people. Images must also have some relation to consciousness if they are to take coherent shape and be recognizable. In the underworld of feeling there is a sense of power, of rhythmic flow, of movement, of living energy, but only when it issues into consciousness, however dim, can all that energy find itself a name and a purpose.

Yet if we consider very early works of the human imagination, the fables and legends that come from the underworld of feeling, we can see that they do not reach far into consciousness. They lack the ability to analyse and divide into categories that draw clear lines of demarcation, or to trace logical connections between events, which is the work of the fully conscious mind. Men, animals, birds, trees and rivers appear to be all on the same footing, all intensely alive and aware of each other, all belonging to the same world in a common flow of feeling. There seems to be little or no turning back to reflective self-consciousness, as if the tides of human feeling ran out unchecked to fill the whole visible universe. In any fable every animal and bird, bush and tree, well and river is as much informed by human feelings and purposes as the human characters. They all use human speech; they all understand each other; they can all be malign or benevolent.

The whole world is personified in human terms, which are not recognized as exclusively human. It is an enchanting and, it seems now to us, an enchanted world. But it is perilous. For one's own protection one needs to come to terms not only with people, living or dead, but with every animal, bird or natural feature that one meets. It is a treacherous world, full of unpredictable movements and overbearing powers as well as unexpected allies.

This was the world our early forebears lived in, and it is still lived in by little children everywhere, which is to say that it persists somewhere in each of us. It is as ancient, I suppose, as the human race. It comes to light in every new generation before consciousness has grown strong enough to control it or explain it away; it lurks beneath the surface of life in every adult, however self-conscious. We are aware of it as a flux of emotion, very intense at times, and we feel that it 'comes up one's back', or 'rises in one's bosom', because it seems to come from below. That is why I have called it the underworld of feeling. From now on I propose to call it also the archaic world of feeling.

The long process of becoming self-conscious personalities, in which we are all involved, has developed conscious controls that keep in check this archaic world of feeling, so that it is less accessible to us now, when we are grown-up, than it used to be, hundreds or thousands of years ago. This is bound to affect our understanding of bygone ages. Yet we may find clues to bring us to a better understanding by looking into past works of imagination which should be able to tell us something at least about the archaic world of feeling as it was in their time, and help us to see in clearer perspective the oral poetry that has grown out of it. A few dips into that past will have to suffice here, before we look at our own Middle Ages, when the Ballads as we know them began to take shape.

Let us begin with an early work, the Epic of Gilgamesh, which comes from the Empire of Sumer, from the third millennium before Christ, between four and five thousand years ago. 'The most important elements in the story', we are told by Miss N. K. Sanders,[1] 'existed as separate poems in the older Sumerian literature and . . . probably were composed and recited long before

[1] *The Epic of Gilgamesh*, Penguin Classics, English version by N. K. Sanders, Introduction, p. 13

they were written down.' It has survived only because it was copied in cuneiform characters on clay tablets by Assyrians in Nineveh, also by Hittites in Anatolia, by Semites and Hurrians, evidence that it was widely known and popular in its time. These written versions are not primitive: the story of Gilgamesh came from a civilization long established in its city of Uruk in Mesopotamia.

First, we observe that the eponymous hero, Gilgamesh, was no ordinary, common man. He was the King of Uruk, and the son of a goddess. We are told that the great gods made him 'two-thirds god and one-third man'. This looks as if he belonged to a transition period between matriarchy and patriarchy, since he inherited two-thirds from his mother and one-third from his father. It would not have been possible in later patriarchal ages to assign so much credit to his mother for the making of him; the patriarchs believed, as many still do, that only sires matter. Mothers were still of the first importance in the days of Gilgamesh, and it is interesting to note that they continue to be of importance in much oral tradition, even in patriarchal times, right down to the Ballads and the present-day epics of Yugoslavia.

Next, we note that this is an age of great gods. The archaic world of feeling has emerged into consciousness sufficiently to shape into figures the immanent powers that once seemed diffused through everyone and everything. We are already far from primitive fables. Trees and animals do not talk any more; only great and overwhelming creatures like mountains, where the gods dwell, are addressed in human speech, or irresistible forces like the four winds of heaven. There is a goddess of creation, who made the world; there is a Sun-god, a goddess of Love and a War-god, besides a ruling god of the firmament and a Queen of the Netherworld of the Dead. The mother of Gilgamesh, Ninsun, wise as she is, belongs among the lesser deities, for the gods live in a hierarchical society. Authority radiates downwards.

The gods, however, no longer own and rule the Empire of Sumer, as once they did. There had been a time when the whole country was administered for the gods by their priests. That time is past; Sumer no longer belongs to the gods; it belongs to the

King. Gilgamesh is the ruler, and he does what he likes with the people. Yet Gilgamesh, the apex of the social pyramid, still has to be humble before the gods, since they decide his fate and are ultimately responsible for whatever he does. It seems that consciousness has not developed so far as to bring a sense of personal responsibility. Gilgamesh weeps, for instance, as he says to the Sun-God Shamash: 'If this enterprise is not to be accomplished, why did you move me, Shamash, with the restless desire to perform it?' Whatever impulses and passions rise in one's bosom have been set there by some god. One may reproach the god, but one takes his supremacy for granted. In much the same way the people of Uruk reproach Gilgamesh for governing them badly (No son is left to his father, for Gilgamesh takes them all; yet the King should be shepherd to his people), but take for granted his right to govern them. The hungry sheep may look up and not be fed, yet they do not question the fact that they are sheep, and that the King is their divinely appointed shepherd. In this archaic world of feeling, five thousand years ago, authoritative rule is assumed to be a natural exercise of god-given power. One can see that the archaic world, whatever stage of consciousness it has reached, is not yet very self-conscious. It is aware of existing powers and keenly aware of superior powers, but the ordinary people who live in it are barely aware of themselves. The common man can be only subject to superiors; he is himself of little account; he is not sufficiently conscious of himself to matter; he is not what we call a self-governing individual.

The one man who matters is the King. In the Epic of Gilgamesh, Gilgamesh himself becomes recognizably a personality, filled with restless desires and emotions that we can well understand. In his need to be rid of mortality, to overcome old age and death, he is not of Sumer only but of all time. One difference between him and us is that he believed it when he was told that a plant grew under the water, beside the far streams of Ocean, which would restore his lost youth to a man. So he found the plant and plucked it; but a serpent rose from the depths of the pool and snatched it away while he was bathing. It was the old serpent that became young and immortal. When Gilgamesh lost the plant, he wept; the tears ran down his face; yet he blamed neither the gods nor himself. 'I found a sign,' he said, 'and now I have lost it. Let us leave the boat on the bank and go.' The journeys he had made, the sorrows he had undergone, had brought him to a point where he touched civilized consciousness, as we understand it.

The imagination that constructed the Epic of Gilgamesh shaped in it another figure of great interest, a personification of that still older, fabulous world in which men and animals lived in close communion. The gods made Enkidu to be an intimate friend of Gilgamesh, his other self. Noble Enkidu, he is called; we can recognize in him the Noble Savage who still haunted men's imaginations thousands of years later, and whom in our day Rudyard Kipling re-created under the name of Mowgli. Enkidu, before the gods conspired to make him fall in with a harlot and become an adult man, 'ate grass in the hills with the gazelle and jostled with wild beasts at the water-holes'. He helped the beasts to escape traps; he was 'as strong as a star from heaven'. After he had lain with the woman, the wild beasts fled from him; he 'had grown weak, for wisdom was in him'. But she clothed him in half of her robes, and led him by the hand to where the shepherds lived. Here, instead of sucking the milk of wild animals, he learned to eat bread and drink wine, and became again strong and exultant. He went charging into Uruk to keep Gilgamesh from claiming his right to take a bride for her first night, the 'jus primae noctis' which persisted into Christian times, and they locked together in combat. Enkidu was thrown and acknowledged Gilgamesh as the stronger; their friendship was sealed.

Now Gilgamesh and Enkidu set out together on their great journey to Lebanon, to cut down the cedars, which were much needed in Uruk. That city of the low-lying river plains had palm-trees and reeds, but no timber. We note that this epic is full of movement, being made up of journeys and fighting, and that making a journey in those days was no light matter. A trapper who had met Enkidu in his wild state, for instance, was struck dumb with terror and when he went back to his home 'his face was altered like that of one who has made a long journey'. And Gilgamesh, in his second great adventure, says: 'Despair is in my heart and my face is the face of one who has made a long journey.' The best summary of the epic was made by Gilgamesh himself: 'I must travel an unknown road and fight a strange battle.'

The Land of the Cedars clearly belonged to the Sun-god: did he not descend over Lebanon every evening and probably sleep there? Gilgamesh and Enkidu had to make sure of his good-will. They sought guidance too from dreams. In the archaic world of feeling, dreams are of great import. It looks as if the lines of communication between the feeling self and the thinking self were wide open in these Sumerian times, so that warnings and prophecies could be easily conveyed from one to the other in dream symbols. Enkidu, as might be expected, since he personified a still older world less trammelled by consciousness, could expound all the dreams of Gilgamesh, and after due precautions, helped by Ninsun, the goddess mother, they both set out. What they had most to fear was another personification, the spirit of the cedar forest condensed into a huge and ferocious giant, Humbaba, who was its guardian. Enkidu already knew that forest; he said that its length was ten thousand leagues in every direction; he also knew about Humbaba, who was 'terrible to all flesh' and never slept. They encouraged each other by turns when they reached the mountain. Enkidu it was who thrust open the huge gate of the forest, so that his hand was never the same again, but after travelling more leagues and being shaken by more dreams, it was Gilgamesh who felled the first great cedar. Then came the fight with the giant Humbaba, in which Gilgamesh was moved by compassion and would have spared his life, but Enkidu, in the all-or-nothing absolute passion of archaic feeling, said: 'This Humbaba must die.' Gilgamesh listened to his words and thrust his sword into Humbaba's neck, while Enkidu struck the second blow. At the third blow Humbaba fell.

We come now to a strange episode. After they had felled and cleared the roots of the cedars 'as far as the banks of the Euphrates', Gilgamesh and Enkidu washed and rested. Gilgamesh changed into his royal robes and put on his crown, so that Ishtar the goddess of Love, who dwelt on that mountain, was struck by his beauty and invited him to become her lover. Gilgamesh refused her advances with scorn and cast up at her all the past lovers whom she had betrayed. Was he resentful because Ishtar was associated in legends with the deaths of earlier kings of Sumer? Ishtar complained to her father Anu and got him to make the Bull of Heaven to destroy Gilgamesh, threatening to smash in the bolts of Hell if he did not, so that all the dead would come out and 'outnumber the living'. The Bull fell on the earth and with his snorts killed hundreds of men, and more hundreds, but Enkidu dodged and seized it by the horns so that Gilgamesh, holding it by 'the thick of its tail' was able to thrust his sword between the nape and the horns and slay it. Then there was rejoicing in Uruk and the singing-girls chanted the glorious fame of Gilgamesh.

But Enkidu dreamed that the gods sat in council, and that Anu said: 'Because they have killed the Bull of Heaven and killed Humbaba, one of the two must die.' Enlil, his second-in-command, said: 'Enkidu must die.' Shamash, the Sun-god, protested, but was overborne. And so Enkidu fell sick. Before he died he cursed all who had brought him to this pass, beginning with the gate of the forest and ending with the harlot who had beguiled him. Yet Shamash reproved him and pointed out that he had gained the love of Gilgamesh, who would mourn him bitterly. Enkidu took back his curses and blessed the harlot, instead of ill-wishing her. Then he had a terrible dream about the Netherworld of the Dead, but Gilgamesh said: 'We must treasure the dream, whatever the terror.' He died, and Gilgamesh wept and sang a lament for him. Seven days and seven nights Gilgamesh wept; then he had a statue of Enkidu made in gold and lapis lazuli, and himself went into the wilderness to find out how a man could escape death and become immortal like the gods.

Now Enkidu had been, we are told, the King's 'other self'. It is therefore likely that in this epic Enkidu, a figure from an older, more archaic past, appears as a reminiscence of the substitute King who dies in the ancient rite of King-slaying surmised by scholars. Yet although it is the will of the gods that 'one of the two must die', which suggests the sacrificial rite, and that Enkidu should be the one, which again points to the use of a king's double in that rite, Enkidu is here more than the nominal shadow of the King: he is presented as a close friend, a beloved intimate of Gilgamesh, and it is real, personal grief that Gilgamesh feels for his loss. Old ritual is here transmuted into civilized human feeling. One gets an inkling of how remote to Sumer the ancient rite had become, how far the Sumerians had moved from their own primitive past. Enkidu's death remains mysterious; it is ordained by the gods; but it is no longer an obvious ritual sacrifice for the good of the people and the King.

The rest of the epic tells the story of Gilgamesh's journey through the wilderness, where he slays lions, through the terrible mountain of Mashu to the waters of death and across the Ocean, to find Utnapishtim, the Faraway, the one man who survived the Flood and was granted immortality together with his wife. We have Utnapishtim's account of the Flood and Gilgamesh's return home, where he dies and is lamented by his people.

This work of imagination from the archaic world, with its echoes of still more archaic beliefs and practices, certainly impressed its contemporaries. The Sumerians were apparently beginning to have a bad conscience about past ritual slayings, and in this epic they glossed over the brute facts and told a story which was in itself fascinating. I have given it much space because of its interest and because echoes and reverberations from it seem to be perceptible in Oral Tradition right through the Heroic Ages. It was not the more subtle, individual touches that were transmitted, as, for example, the change in the tone of Gilgamesh's utterances caused by the death of Enkidu; a remarkable instance of individual differentiation in a world where the individual person was still not of much importance. Before Enkidu died Gilgamesh was given to pious platitudes about death: 'as for us men, our days are numbered, our occupations are a breath of wind'; after Enkidu died the bitterness of his personal distress burst out: 'How can I rest, how can I be at peace? Despair is in my heart. What my brother is now, that shall I be when I am dead.' He was moved at a deep, passionate level, and it was this passion that reverberated through the ages. There may have been an element of guilt in Gilgamesh's despair; although it was not consciously recognized as guilt, its profound influence remained.

We find the same feeling much later in the *Iliad*, when the death of Patroclus changes the whole direction of Achilles' being. In both epics the death of a dear friend brings a passionate realization of what matters to a man. For Gilgamesh what mattered was the doom of mortality; he went solitary into the wilderness to find a way round that doom if he could. For Achilles what mattered was his need to revenge on Hector the death of Patroclus, since he blamed himself, not the gods, for letting Patroclus go out to fight without him. Here the element of personal guilt does emerge into consciousness. By comparison, Achilles felt that his anger with Agamemnon, which should have been controlled by a sense of necessity, was relatively unimportant. For both heroes, sons of goddesses, the death of a close friend evokes a moment of truth, of self-knowledge. Both, in a way, punish themselves by seeking death, Gilgamesh less consciously, Achilles more consciously.

In the *Odyssey*, which has more journeying than fighting, the resemblances to Gilgamesh are more diffused. Both epics give a description of the Netherworld of the Dead. Odysseus, like Gilgamesh, travels unknown roads, this time upon the sea, as befits the hero of a sea-going people, and fights battles as strange as any fought by Gilgamesh. The most pervasive resemblance, apart from the similar echoes of old practices and beliefs, lies in the relationship between gods and men, which in the *Iliad* and the *Odyssey*, as in Gilgamesh, determines the fate of mortals. Yet in the Greek epics the gods are already less remote than in the Sumerian world: there is more communication between gods and gods and between gods and men. The air is thick with gods, and especially goddesses, ascending and descending. In the Epic of Gilgamesh, by contrast, Shamash the Sun-god is snubbed by the other gods because they think that it is vulgar of him to let himself be seen daily by mortals. Gilgamesh too gives one an impression of lonely remoteness compared with the talkative Greek heroes; despite the ovations he receives in the streets of Uruk he seems a solitary figure, with no close friend but Enkidu. Even his mother, the goddess Ninsun, appears rarely, unlike Achilles' mother Thetis, who is always at hand to comfort her son. The Greek gods are authoritative, but much nearer to the human world, with the same passion for debate, the same quarrelsome sociability, as their Greek worshippers. And they begin to show signs of impatience because so much responsibility is foisted upon them. In the very beginning of the *Odyssey* Zeus protests: 'What things mortals blame the gods for. They say that their troubles come from us, but they themselves through their own follies increase their sorrows beyond what is decreed.' That such words should be put into the mouth of Zeus marks an advance towards human self-knowledge, as does the moment of truth for Achilles, when he looks inside himself, not outside, blaming himself and not the gods for the personal remissness that left Patroclus to die in battle without him. That these flashes of self-awareness belong to the Ionic rather than to the Mycenean world may be surmised but not established; at least, they point the way to the dramatic emergence in the seventh century B.C. of the Delphic oracle's advice: Know thyself.

As a social structure the Mycenean world was much like the Sumerian, although perhaps more complex, with authority radiating downwards. Agamemnon the overlord is supreme even over the many argumentative chieftains in his host. The archaic world of feeling with its insistence on authority, rank and status, still pervades the whole story, both in the *Iliad* and the *Odyssey*.

This resemblance in general background and style of themes—journeys and fightings—between the Epic of Gilgamesh and Homer may be felt, but one cannot prove that it is due at all to the influence of the former. The world of archaic feeling may naturally find expression in presenting movement of some kind, being itself so fluid and mobile. Something is always 'going on' in the underworld of feeling, and ongoings may therefore be expected in the imaginative works it produces. Yet the concentration on journeys and fightings should perhaps be remarked. One finds these themes, including journeys to the Netherworld of the Dead, recurring again and again through the Heroic Ages, in the Norse sagas, for instance; to this day journeys and fightings provide main *motifs* in Yugoslavian epics. One should remember, too, that known traditions have developed from other, older traditions which were long-continuing, although little or nothing is known about them, and probably largely ceremonial and ritual in purpose. In his book on Yugoslav epic singers Mr Albert B. Lord[1] says: 'Halting-places on journeys . . . both here and in Homer may deserve the emphasis given them . . . because the archetypal journey in epic was of a ceremonial nature and its stages were marked by significant events and meaningful encounters.' He also points out that 'return tales', where the hero returns home after long captivity or fighting 'seem to involve the death of someone close to the returning hero; in Yugoslav tradi-

[1] Albert B. Lord, *The Singer of Tales*, p. 109

tion this person is generally the hero's mother'.[1] One cannot prove that this tradition was influenced by the *Odyssey*, any more than that the *Odyssey* was influenced by Gilgamesh; but the recurrence of journeys involving deaths, or of returns from the Netherworld in which the hero is disguised (by the weeds of the Netherworld still clinging to him, Mr Lord suggests) before being recognized at home amounts to what looks like more than coincidence.

Another interesting comparison lies in the style of telling the tales, which seems to be a natural consequence of their oral composition. Anyone telling a story in Oral Tradition usually wishes the listeners to share it with him as an imaginative experience. He makes a journey, as it were, through the story and takes the listeners step by step along with him. The simplest way of doing this is by iteration; we employ this technique instinctively, for instance, in telling stories to children. The Epic of Gilgamesh, as it is the earliest epic we know, gives also the clearest examples of iterative technique. Here is an account of how Gilgamesh passed through the mountain of Mashu[2].

'When he had gone one league the darkness became thick around him, for there was no light, he could see nothing ahead and nothing behind him. After two leagues the darkness was thick and there was no light, he could see nothing ahead and nothing behind him. After three leagues the darkness was thick and there was no light, he could see nothing ahead and nothing behind him. After four leagues the darkness was thick' and so on, with exact iteration (which means journeying), through every single league, until: 'When he had gone eight leagues Gilgamesh gave a great cry, for the darkness was thick and he could see nothing ahead and nothing behind him. After nine leagues he felt the north wind on his face, but the darkness was thick and there was no light, he could see nothing ahead and nothing behind him. After ten leagues the end was near. After eleven leagues the dawn light appeared. At the end of twelve leagues the sun streamed out.'

In the same way, when Gilgamesh poled a boat across the waters of death we have to follow him pole by pole, until he has

[1] *Ibid.* p. 115
[2] *The Epic of Gilgamesh*, Penguin Classics, pp. 96-7

used and thrown away twelve, after which the narrator gives us a respite and tells us that Gilgamesh used up one hundred and twenty poles. The number twelve, by the way, seems a sacred and significant number to the Sumerians.

This iterative technique is not seeking to convey what we should call the facts, namely, that the mountain of Mashu was twelve leagues thick without a glimmer of light all the way through. These facts could have been compressed into one sentence, to make a short-cut such as consciousness likes to take through stories. What the story-teller was trying to convey was the *feeling* of experiencing that terrible journey: he was appealing directly to the emotions of his listeners rather than to their conscious, rationalizing, calculating minds. League by league he took them through it. The slow-motion repetition is in consonance with the nature of the imaginative underworld, which, as I ventured to say earlier, cannot be traversed fast if one is to be fully aware of one's surroundings.

Yet there are other ways of leading a listener step by step through an experience than by enumerating the milestones on his journey. One can instead linger over successive details, missing out nothing. This is the method more often employed in Homer than simple iteration, although iteration is also found. In the first book of the *Iliad*,[1] when Odysseus is commissioned to return Chryseis to her father, we are told that the ship carrying her came to land, and:

> Out they cast the anchor-stones and bound down the stern-ropes;
> Out they came themselves upon the surf-edge of the sea,
> Out they brought the hecatomb for far-darting Apollo;
> And out came Chryseis from the sea-faring ship.

Here simple, cumulative iteration is combined with successive detail: one can see it all happening and at the same time feel its significance. Simple iteration of lines and half-lines is diffused all through the *Iliad* and the *Odyssey*, not necessarily to lead the listener through an experience but to help the story-teller in composing his strictly syllabic metre. Whenever a ritual action recurs, like a sacrifice to the gods, the same lines are used time

[1] *Iliad*, I, 436-9

and again in the same order, with the same particularized detail; the description of the rite has become a formula. The epithet employed to describe a known figure similarly becomes a formula: far-darting Apollo, silver-footed Thetis, white-armed Hera. Formulae of welcome, of parting, of addressing one another, are repeated in the same way. According to Mr Lord, who bases the statement on work done by the late Milman Parry, the whole texture of the Homeric epics is felted together by a very large proportion of formular phrases that fit into the pattern of the hexameters; phrases that cover nearly every requirement of the story and have to be selected from his large store by the narrator as he goes along. I suspect that any metrical oral poetry makes use of formular phrases and verses to help the performer in his task: the Yugoslav epics do it, and so do the Ballads.

Outside the formula use, simple repetition is also employed in question-and-answer sequences. In the *Iliad*, Book VI, when Hector finds Andromache absent from the house, he asks the maids[1]:

> 'Has she gone somewhere to brothers' wives or
> husband's fair-robed sisters,
> Or to the shrine of Athena, where one and all
> the thick-tressed Trojan women are imploring the
> terrible goddess?'

and they give him back his exact words:

> 'She has not gone to brothers' wives or
> husband's fair-robed sisters,
> nor to the shrine of Athena, where one and all
> the thick-tressed Trojan women are imploring the
> terrible goddess.'

The same usage is common in the Ballads:

> 'O is your bairn to laird or loon,
> Or is it to your father's groom?'
>
> 'My bairn's na to laird or loon,
> Nor is it to my father's groom.'

One cannot say that this kind of repetition has been copied or

[1] Book VI, 378 *seqq.*

imitated from one oral poem to another. It arises naturally in the circumstances of oral composition; it gives the narrator a breathing-space, while he thinks what he is to say next. But it is not entirely unaffected by the desire to take the listener step by step through an experience: repetition can be depended on to deepen any impression.

The plenitude of homely detail in Homer, especially in the *Odyssey*, arises wholly from the desire to lead the listener step by step: it occurs wherever the action described is felt to be significant, wherever the listener is expected to enter fully into it and to remember its effect. Let us look at an example from the *Iliad*. When Achilles (Book XVIII) orders the dead body of Patroclus to be washed clean of blood, one follows each apparently trivial phase of the operation. No detail is left out. Not only is the three-footed cauldron set on the fire, water poured into it and wood kindled beneath until flames embrace the cauldron's belly, we are told that the water heated, and that when it bubbled in the cauldron then at last they washed him and anointed him with olive oil. The Homeric story-teller found it important not to short-cut the feeling here, but to let it have free flow, and so the water for Patroclus' lustration was heated up for five full hexameters (346-50). It was a solemn occasion. Where the flow of feeling is to be conveyed there is no niggling over details in Homer, whether obviously significant or not; we are supposed to re-live everything, even the anxious moments while we watch the pot till it boils.

In this style of story-telling, time is felt to be a process, not a momentary halt. I think this attitude is characteristic of works that are deeply immersed in the world of feeling, where everything seems to be a continuous present. Feelings do take shape, but it is a moving, flowing shape. The passage of time becomes literally a passage through which one advances, alert and aware of one's emotions. In the Epic of Gilgamesh and in Homer it is taken for granted that the listeners' feelings are engaged even more than their conscious attention.

Where words are the medium used in such a work, recapitulation of phrases, sentences or whole verses is a natural mode of presenting the journey through time. Where picture language is used, reduplication of figures suggests itself. This we find, for instance, in representations of gods in India, where the flowing movement of the arms through time is shown in simultaneous postures, so that one god may seem to have a dozen arms. The journeying of the imagination through time has left formal traces in languages like Greek and Latin; their structure preserves reduplications which shows that an action has not been momentary but a continuing process, reduplications which have been eventually reduced to a kind of stutter, but which derive from the same imaginative technique as the iterations in oral poetry. All these repetitions and reduplications arise from the immediacy with which an artist appeals to his listeners, or spectators, while he takes them step by step along with him in a shared experience of strong feeling.

The Ballads, coming so much later than Gilgamesh in the history of mankind, when consciousness was already taking short-cuts through the world of archaic feeling, do not use iteration at quite such length, but we can recognize in them the same style of utterance, which does not go in for curt statements like 'she picked three roses', but leads the listener to pick each rose separately, alongside the lady:

> 'she hadna pu'ed a rose, a rose,
> a double rose but only three.'

The Norse saga verses, by contrast with Gilgamesh and Homer, seem to have been ruthlessly pruned of feeling. One must remember that much of the saga verse has perished and been replaced by the prose versions of later narrators, clerks who may have excised phrases, verses, or whole passages that gave some play to feeling and so relieved the starkness of the tales. Yet some of the old verses survive, sandwiched between chunks of narrative prose, as in the Saga of King Heidrek, and in them one can sense that whatever feeling emerged into consciousness in the old Norse world was at once clipped down, except for a central shoot of warlike passion. The verse is clipped and taut as if produced under a strain of precisely this nature. There is no taking of the listener by the hand and leading him along; he is prodded along by emphasis. In the bare, taut metre the smallest repetition gives an effect of emphasis; a very strong emphasis simply repeats a phrase twice, the second time in reverse:

A bond-maid's child,
child of a bond-maid.

To find traces of repetitive technique in the use of alliteration may be fanciful, yet, where everything is clipped so ferociously, repetitions may well have been cut down to initial letters. Great ingenuity is shown in condensing metaphors into 'kennings' within these narrow limits; ships and swords, the most frequent symbols in this way of life, are given playful riddling equivalents, sometimes fantastically silly (a sword, for instance, can be a 'wound-giving leek'), that go a long way towards the recognition of concepts, even of abstract concepts, and might serve as material for intelligence tests. The play of ingenuity was apparently relished for its own sake, while any flow of feeling, except war-like feeling, was shunned as a weakness. Gilgamesh and Achilles could weep openly, but no Norseman in those old verses dared be caught shedding tears; that was for women only. In this war-like world, the repression of tender feeling, the sharpening of energies to lethal point and edge, must have put a great strain on everyone. As a relief, the champions drank deep and coped with the killings required of them by slackening all controls, gnawing the rims of their shields and going berserk. The habit of going berserk, in an uprush of violent passion, with the consequent lassitude when the berserk fit has passed, makes a rhythm of energies which is recognizably primitive, less civilized than Homer, older even than Sumer. The archaic world of feeling here has darkened, repressed as it is by a doom of violence in a terrorized ambience. There is no lack of violence in the Sumerian and Homeric epics, but the pressure of Fate is not so unrelenting, the need for human strength and endurance not so insistent as in the Norse verses, where the will to survive seems of necessity to be sharpened into a penetrating will to power. The fighting champions were embodiments of will-power; so also, it seems to me, were the poets, with the result that they were more ingenious than poetic in the kennings they constructed, which were a kind of verbal sword play.

Yet this dark, primitive world of fighting men fostered a stubborn independence of fighting spirit. The social structure, as one might expect in an archaic world, was authoritative, like the hierarchy of the gods; thralls and slaves, landless men, were despised; it was a deadly insult to call a man base-born. So much, however, depended on a man's nerve and will-power that a strong man of lowly status had a chance of being recognized as a champion, often a rebel champion. There were usually rebels in the Norse world, even rebels against the gods, and every strong man had a touchy sense of his own worth. The force of will-power and ready swords produced more aggressive heroes than one finds in Gilgamesh or in Homer. One cannot say that they were remarkable for self-knowledge; they might storm Valhalla and defy the gods to the limit of human endurance, but they did not look inside themselves for the means of changing events. It was easier to solve problems by slicing off heads or burning enemies alive.

King Heidrek, called the Wise, began as a rebel against his father, who gave him advice which he made a point of ignoring, and in time he rebelled against Odin. The old Norsemen distrusted Odin, although, or perhaps because, he was one of the supreme gods. All-Father he might be, but he was a treacherous deceiver who went about on earth in disguise, making mischief among men. He was one of the terrors that darkened the air in the Norse world; one never knew what he might be up to. Disguised as a certain Gestumblindi, an enemy of Heidrek's, he challenged the king to prove his alleged wisdom in a riddle-contest, and propounded thirty riddles to him, with a taunting formula repeated at the end of each. Heidrek answered each riddle, prefacing his responses with a polite formula, until he began to suspect, about the twenty-eighth riddle, who his antagonist was. At the thirtieth riddle he lashed out at the god with his sword and called him a vile rogue. Odin changed himself into a hawk and flew away, but his tail-feathers had been slashed off, which is why the hawk has had a short tail ever since.

This is a world not far removed from the fabulous. Magic and magical transformations are rife; there are bale-fires on barrows guarding the treasures of the dead; there are supernatural monsters in the sea. The long, dark winters must have helped to make it a tense world, and it was constricted within its tradition of slaughter as well. No wonder its old verses seem tense and constricted. Somewhere in the background were women who could be heard singing; perhaps it was war-songs they sang rather than lullabies, for they seem to be as power-hungry as the men and full of the same fighting spirit. (The Valkyrie name Gunnr, meaning battle, was common in kennings for women such as 'bed-battler', says Christopher Tolkien in his edition of King Heidrek's Saga.[1]) It was a violent, barbaric world and its influence spread wherever the Norsemen roved. In Ulster, which was largely Norse, the tales of the Ulster Cycle of mythology are quite different in tenor from those of the other Irish cycles. 'The central group of characters are not wizards but warriors who glory in their prowess and their unyielding endurance. It is not primarily intelligence but will-power and fearless action in the face of terrifying odds that are celebrated.'[2] The north of Scotland and the islands, including some of the western islands, were overrun by the Norsemen as late as the ninth century, so we may find a sub-stratum of Norse influence in various Scottish Ballads; we do, indeed, find Odin, disguised, of course, as a mischief-maker.

When these warriors broke out of their constrictions to plunder Europe, they were feared and execrated: their advance towards the more developed civilizations of the South, although in time they learned much, was not that of eager pupils. The bareness, the hardness of life in the frozen North, then unmitigated by scientific inventions, made them hungry for land and for the power which went with the ownership of land; wherever they settled they transmitted a passion for the owning of land and a devotion to its cultivation, as well as an independence of spirit in dealing with each other as proprietors. One cannot assess the extent of their influence among the Danes and Anglo-Saxons who raided and settled in Britain, but it was in all likelihood considerable. The Normans who conquered England in the eleventh century were still recognizably Norsemen, although they had been turned into Frenchmen as well and, even more remarkably, Christians.

The Anglo-Saxons whom they invaded were also Christians. What had happened to the archaic world of feeling when Christianity entered into it? Out of what kind of background in the Middle Ages did the Ballads arise? We shall find some answers to these questions if we look into our own Middle Ages.

[1] *King Heidrek's Saga*, p. 8, footnote 4
[2] Alwyn Rees and Brinley Rees, *Celtic Heritage*, p. 54

4

BALLAD BACKGROUND II

The Middle Ages

By the time Christianity reached Britain it had undergone various developments. The environment in which it had spread was the Roman Empire, not only a power-structure but the strongest power-structure in the known world. Authority in the Roman Empire radiated downwards; it did not spring up from below; it was very much in accord with the archaic world of feeling and desired to restore the lost aura of divinity to supreme rulers, as in the ancient Asian empires. A new religion spreading among common people and slaves was bound to cause uneasiness among their masters, not only because it seemed to by-pass the old gods—that was a general tendency—but because it ignored existing power-values. Once a slave began to think he had an immortal soul he might feel that he was as important as the next man. The Roman rulers, quite logically, tried to suppress Christianity because they believed it to be subversive, which, of course, it was. The teachings of Jesus, if closely followed, would have undermined all power-structures whatever. But Christianity, in the irrational way of underworld feeling, throve on martyrdom and persecution and began to organize itself into a Church.

Naturally, its ideas of organization were taken from those already 'in the air', and so the Church became an authoritative organization, a Church Militant. The more it spread, the more complex its organization, the more it needed men of authority to guide it, since many people prefer to shift responsibility for themselves on to other shoulders. It was an old habit of the human race to lay responsibility upon the gods, and many newly born Christian souls were glad to leave responsibility to their bishops. On the other hand, power-structures once in being tend to become self-perpetuating and self-elaborating. Christianity was now encountering not only simple believers in Palestine and Asia

Minor, but subtle intellectuals in Alexandria; its doctrines were being refined by intellectual analysis. Analysis splits things up and splinters them, and the Christian Church had to strengthen its organization and become more militant to keep down splinter-groups who would disrupt it into opposing sects. In its own firm refusal to worship the Roman Emperors it threatened to disrupt the Empire, and in the fourth century after Christ it was strong enough to obtain an Edict from Constantine which made it the official religion of Rome.

The Christianity that came to Britain was thus an official structure, a hierarchy, in which, nevertheless, humble men might rise to rank and power as Princes of the Church. Its authority radiated downwards, a pattern quite acceptable to the ordinary man who was accustomed to live in the archaic world of feeling. But it laid a new emphasis on the individual man and his responsibilities to himself. The tides of human feeling which in the archaic world had swept up towards the gods without turning back into self-examination, had now, as it were, been polarized; they reached up to Heaven but they also reached down to Hell. Christian doctrine insisted on a sense of personal guilt, original sin, to be punished by eternal hell hereafter, if one did not repent. Heaven was filled with Christ's love for the individual soul, Hell with individual retribution for personal sins. Both Heaven and Hell were organized hierarchically, in a way that any citizen could comprehend. Yet in a passionate and violent world, unused to a sense of personal guilt, the tides setting towards Hell seemed the stronger. Once Christendom was established over Europe, the fear of Hell, as Marc Bloch says, became a great social force in the Middle Ages.

The passions that surged in one's bosom could no longer be blamed on the gods. One had to know whether they came from Heaven or Hell, whether they were Virtues or Vices. For that, one needed, and got, the guidance of the Church. And one could pay for Masses or endow an Abbey to lighten one's trials after death. In that feudal world the Church itself became a great feudal landowner, profiting from endowments by princes and nobles and gentry and merchants, all of them taking for granted the old concept of authority transmitted through so many ages by the archaic world of feeling. The Middle Ages have been categorized as the Age of Faith; the very foundation of their faith was an acceptance of hierarchical authority, radiating from above.

As late as the fourteenth century, in 1381, when the labouring peasants of England rose in revolt against their miseries and the oppression of their landlords, the belief in hierarchical authority was still all-prevalent. The peasants were sure that if bad officers of the law, corrupt and encroaching Abbots, unjust overlords and knights could be got rid of, the King himself would see that they got justice. As Maurice Keen says[1]: 'The hierarchical principle was too deeply rooted in the medieval mind for men to conceive any kind of society without it. They even imposed it on sub-strata of their society: there were kings of minstrels and kings of jesters, and the heralds had an elaborate coronation ceremony for their Kings-of-Arms. When the peasants rose in revolt in 1381 John Lister had himself crowned their king in Norfolk.' Kings were a very old habit, not easily shed. Children had long, long been playing: 'I'm the King of the Castle'. It was not the hierarchical principle that the peasants revolted against, not even the existing hierarchical system: it was the wicked exploiters who usurped office and misused the system.

Christianity, within its authoritative framework, was also, paradoxically, concerned with the importance of the individual man even if it were chiefly his sins that came in question. And the individual man had to be weaned into Christianity at a deep level of feeling. The same Catholic authority which insisted firmly on the existence of Hell recommended bishops to go warily among pagan beliefs and superstitions, to adopt them into the Church and Christianize them where possible.[2] This very wise advice was followed for a time. At how deep a level it operated can be seen in the mediaeval Legends of the Saints. Here we are back in the archaic world of fable. Ravens and greyhounds brought food to the Saints in the wilderness; lions recognized and submitted to the power of holiness; flocks of birds sang hosannas at command. This was once more the archaic personified world, although its creatures, united now in the Divine Person as children of God, had been officially Christianized. The archaic world of feeling was given, as it were, a new lease of life under

[1] *The Outlaws of Mediaeval Legend*, Routledge & Kegan Paul, p. 93
[2] Pope Gregory the Great

new names. An ancient well with magical powers did not lose these when it became St Mary's Well; it could be resorted to with a better conscience than before. The Cross became a more potent talisman to subdue demons than any ancient magic. Being christened was a uniquely secure protection against evil spirits, witches or fairies. Into the perilous world of archaic feeling Christendom came at first as a new and more powerful magic, to counter the black magic of the past. Christianity prevailed by infiltration of this kind rather than by conquest, so that the people of the early Middle Ages lived in a resurgence of officially Christian but still largely archaic feeling, especially in Northern Europe, which was the last to be Christianized.

People expressed the new religion in terms already familiar to them. Christianity was to be newly learned, and the popular imagination seized upon it as fresh material for story-telling. The first Christian lesson-books were pictures, like strip-cartoons, which ran across Church walls and roofs presenting one episode after another, the Fall, Noah and the Flood, and, a great favourite, Daniel in the Lions' Den, which one can find also carved on a Pictish stone in remote Scotland. Then the prosperous guilds of the towns began to stage them in processions and mimes. The Wakefield cycle of Mystery Plays, for instance, showed 'the whole Christian story from the Creation to the Day of Judgement'. One gets the impression that whatever the upper ranks of society were doing, the lower ranks were excitedly absorbing Christianity, and that it was a Christianity very close to archaic feeling if not steeped in it, made up of magic, fables, miracles and enthralling stories, which helped new, tentative individuals in their reaching out for fresh experiences.

These mediaeval fables and legends must have been compiled by ecclesiastics, it could be argued; and how can one know that they correspond to deep levels of feeling in the populace? One can only guess that the monks and friars might have known what would appeal to their people, and that everyone liked saints to be accompanied by docile beasts. Animals were apparently 'in the air'. Until the late fifteenth century they figured largely as motifs in the exquisite silks coming from Italy, when they were superseded by a riot of plant motifs, which may have satisfied a Renaissance sense of wantonly luxuriating life. Animals peeped charmingly out of tapestries and were carved in unlikely spots in and on cathedrals. Animal fables abounded. Reynard the Fox was a widely popular figure in a French cycle of stories that came over to England; Dame Partlet, the hen, was a household word. Talking birds were accepted as a matter of course, and when Chaucer wrote his 'Parlement of Fowles' his subject was one that leapt naturally to contemporary minds. Presumably it was satisfying to believe that the animal world and animal passions belonging to the old pagan times were alike susceptible to Christian influence. Our Middle Ages were not yet burning cats and witches together as agents of the Devil.

The writers of the time, like the upper ranks of society, were beginning to wrestle with the new concepts of vice and virtue. Vices and Virtues in abstract form stalked through allegories, in which the populace were not interested; yet the Vice became a familiar comic figure in the town mimes. Writers drew extensively on symbols from the underworld of feeling to present novel ideas; when self-consciousness began to loom larger, they found it necessary to excuse this practice by claiming that what they wrote was all a 'dream'. The use of dreams as cover for underworld feeling shows that the archaic world was beginning to recede.

Yet it had not receded far even when the Elizabethan dramatists were at work. Many levels of archaic feeling went on persisting even into the Elizabethan age and beyond, since, as in all human movements, the advance towards greater self-consciousness was neither uniform nor systematic, and the new trend towards individualism which flowered in the Renaissance had not yet brought people in any number out of their archaic social structures. The old collective world which did not differentiate much between one human being and another, although it bound them all closely together, was still strong in Thomas Dekker, for instance, who, it has been said by a percipient critic,[1] lacked insight into individual desires, moods, and attitudes that make men unlike, while he had a quick sympathy for the suffering that makes men kin. It was possible even in Shakespeare's time for characters in plays to be referred to as mere functionaries instead of men with a Christian name, like *The Pedant* in *Love's*

[1] Una Ellis-Fermor, 'ThomasDekker', in *Shakespeare's Contemporaries*, p. 162

Labour Lost, or *The Braggart*. External marks of status and titles of office, rather than psychological qualities, were long held to differentiate one man from another. Sumptuary laws were passed to preserve differences in richness of dress between, say, courtiers and burgesses, because the kind of dress one wore and the number of one's retinue were very important as marking one's status. 'The quality' dressed in extravagant finery resembling the heraldic splendour of court cards. The packs of cards we use today came out of that self-same early mediaeval world, where rank and status counted for everything and the individual man, as such, for very little.

From this background the Ballads emerged, at a stage when the vernacular was in common use. How and when they began to take shape can be argued about, but not precisely established, since the earliest written texts we have are later in date than the songs themselves. Scholars are agreed, from internal and other evidence, that Ballads belong to the fourteenth and fifteenth centuries, and went on being composed until the seventeenth century and a little later. From internal evidence alone, from a study of the usages and beliefs familiar to Ballad-singers and listeners, the ascription of a definite starting-date to any Ballad would be difficult. People emerged from the Middle Ages at different times in different regions; an apparently fourteenth-century background might have survived until the fifteenth century in some part of England, and even later in parts of Scotland. The mediaeval background was far from being uniform or simultaneous throughout Britain; it was a moving, flowing process with its own eddies and backwaters. We ourselves can now perhaps see it in perspective, as the people who lived through these Middle Ages could not; we are beginning to realize that one cannot look at people and movements in the flat, since they are the resultants of continuous and perhaps continuing processes. But in the early Middle Ages even painters had not yet seen the need for perspective; hieratic pictures for the Church altars were painted in the flat, with clear, bright colours; that was how people saw themselves and others. We have still much to learn, but we have learned something about perspective. We can now see, for instance, as those who shaped them probably did not, that the Ballads belong to an ancient and honourable tradition of oral poetry. We can also see that emergence from the Middle Ages was a complex and varied process.

There are, in consequence, many definitions of the process. A historian, E. H. Carr, says that the mediaeval world finally broke up in the fifteenth and sixteenth centuries because new continents were discovered and the centre of gravity shifted from the Mediterranean to the Atlantic sea-boards, with a resulting increase of self-consciousness in human beings and an enlargement of self-knowledge. (An increase in self-consciousness and an enlargement of self-knowledge we have already noted as arising earlier from the doctrines of Christianity.) A man of letters, Professor W. J. Entwistle, has said that the end of mediaeval society came with the practice of writing, due in the West of Europe to 'humanism and the art of printing'. An economist might trace the break-up to the decay of the manorial system and the rise of tenant farmers, together with the development of mercantile interests in the towns, and of international finance. All these suppositions form part of the truth about the break-up of the Middle Ages and the emergence of what became our modern world. In this complex of movements the most we can do about dating the Ballads is to establish them within brackets of time, from a *terminus a quo* to a *terminus ad quem*. Even then we may be startled by the assertion of a Scotsman, John Allan,[1] that the farming people of North-Eastern Scotland were led out of the Middle Ages as late as 1713, when Alexander Grant of Monymusk introduced from Holland the use of turnips as a field crop for feeding cattle.

If this statement is true, if the farming populace in the North-East of Scotland were only just emerging from the Middle Ages in the early seventeen hundreds, it would go far to explain why Child said that the best Scottish Ballads came from the North, and why M. J. C. Hodgart has said that the Scottish versions have a richer content of folk-beliefs and pagan survivals. They might be less influenced, too, by the workings-over of broad-sheet sellers and literary intellectuals. For these reasons I propose in the next chapter to look into John Allan's statement and to begin studying the Ballads known to be then current in the North-Eastern Lowlands of Scotland.

[1] John Allan, *The N.E. Lowlands of Scotland*

5
Northern Scottish Background: The Fire of Frendraught

IN the North-Eastern Lowlands of Scotland, says John Allan, who is himself a farmer, there was always on the farms too narrow a margin between subsistence and hunger until turnips were introduced in the early seventeen hundreds for cattle-feeding. Before that there was little or nothing to feed cattle on during the hard winter, so that most of the beasts were killed and salted down at Martinmas. In those days seed-crops did not ripen so soon as they do now and the harvest had often not been gathered when the snow came and ruined it. Blackened fields were all too common. In the farm 'touns', he notes (that is to say in the farm enclosures and buildings), life must have been too often 'dark and damp and anxious'. When there was a good harvest, a rare occurrence, it was 'snatched from fate, not the rich and certain gift of fruitfulness'. In their damp, dark houses the people were always cold in winter, often hungry, and slept six in a bed on the floor. During the 'Seven Ill Years' of bitter winters at the end of the seventeenth century many of them starved to death.

There is evidence to confirm what Allan says about these living conditions. Thomas Pennant, for instance, an Englishman writing in 1769,[1] remarks about the houses on Deeside that they 'are shocking to humanity, being formed of loose stones and covered with parings of earth called *devots*; or with heath, broom or branches of fir'. He says that 'the fare of the inhabitants is equally mean; oatmeal, barley cakes, and potatoes are their usual food'. He did not, apparently, realize that the standard of living had begun to improve, thanks to the turnips which made it possible for people to have a chance of eating meat once in a while all the year round. By 1800 the farms were being energetic-

[1] Thomas Pennant, *Tour in Scotland*

ally cleared and better times were well on the way. Yet in 1769, according to him, living conditions were still what could be called mediaeval. In the records of the Monymusk estate there is mention of a house at Platecock which had 'neither door, nor window, nor lum'; presumably these facts were recorded because, it was felt, some betterment was needed. John Allan quotes a story about the laird of Waterton in Aberdeenshire who had arrested a defaulting tenant and confined him in his dungeon, but 'being a kindly man he soon decided that the criminal had been punished enough and ordered him set free. The servants reported that the prisoner refused to leave because the dungeon was more comfortable than his own house'.

It is not too much to infer that many of these houses could not have achieved even a bothy standard of comfort. The men and women who lived in them laboured all day in the fields or round the house. The women in especial worked hard, not only helping in the fields and barns but clothing their families in homespun, rearing chickens, milking cows, making butter, and, when a good harvest happened, brewing strong ale. Pennant says of them: 'The women are remarkably plain and early acquire an aged look. But they are more industrious than their husbands, and are the principal supporters of their families.' Yet these labouring people were not serfs. They were tenants, paying rent to lairds in a percentage of their produce, chickens, eggs, butter and various services.

In 1713 the lairds still had all their feudal powers, including the power of pit and gallows over criminals and defaulters. Issues between lairds and tenants, or between tenants and tenants, were judged by the lairds alone, in the courts of 'baron bailie'. The rural tenants thus had, apparently, few, if any, rights, hard duties and a notable lack of comforts. The Scottish Kirk, too, in the country districts tried to put down fornication and drunkenness as well as witch-craft. To us it seems that the rural populace led a bleak existence, and that they had nothing to sing about. Yet sing they did, and what they sang were Ballads.

Ballads were a part of their inheritance, an inheritance which they took for granted, like the sun and the moon and the seasons. The seasons of the year, like the Ballads, ran through their blood; the inclement winters might be 'cauld and mirk as ony Pit', but springtime, however belated, never failed to come and quicken them, as it quickened the silver birches. John Allan makes bold to say that nothing could repress the Scottish peasantry for long and that when spring came they made love in every thicket. The admonitions of the Kirk certainly did not penetrate very deep, if one is to judge by the Ballads, where fornication is accepted as natural, recurrent and inevitable. Witchcraft was eventually put down officially—the last of the alleged witches was burned at Dornoch as late as 1722—but fornication and drunkenness continued to flourish all through the eighteenth century. Day-to-day life is never so bleak as an abstract of it. The round of the farming seasons was not necessarily a monotonous iteration for these country people; no day would seem to them exactly like another, or like the same day in a previous year. And their main occupation was the fostering of vital growth, on the fields and in and about the houses, a deeply satisfying occupation, even if at times frustrating.

One supposes that they grumbled as farming people have always grumbled, but weather and living conditions alike are usually accepted in rural communities as a fate laid upon them by the arbitrary nature of things, not as a cause for envy and resentment. In any case, rural communities of that time were not competitive in our sense of the word; where all were struggling for bare subsistence, mutual help was as ready and unquestioned as hospitality in a desert. My late husband, who was born into a similar community in Orkney about a hundred and seventy years later, said of it[1]: 'The farmers did not know ambition and the petty torments of ambition; they did not realize what competition was . . .; they helped one another when help was required, following the old usage.' In such a society, whatever the living conditions and the climate, life may have been hard but did not necessarily seem bleak to those who lived it. Besides, human kindness tends to infiltrate even into the most oppressive social system. The laird of Waterton, for instance, whose prisoner would not leave his dungeon, merely replied to his servants: 'Well, just set the yett open and see that the bodie gets his diet regular.' We cannot doubt, either, that the interiors of the

[1] Edwin Muir, *An Autobiography*, p. 63. (The Hogarth Press)

'shocking' houses were vitalized by warm family feeling, being kept lively by the women who were 'the principal supporters of their families'.

They had need to be a vigorous and independent breed, these women, for their men were absent only too often on forays and feuds in the service of their lairds. The North-Eastern Lowlands were still a wild and turbulent area at that time because the great families who owned the land spent most of their lives in trying to get the better of each other. These gentry, still feudal barons like those of the fifteenth century in England, gave full rein to the absolute, violent passions that seem to accompany the possession of land in the archaic world of feeling. The civilization of Scotland did not penetrate far into these North-East regions: it seems to have been confined to Aberdeen and its immediate neighbourhood. So there was a salient difference between urban culture and the culture of these interior country districts. Yet even the towns, by our standards, were still mediaeval in some respects. If travellers from England were shocked in 1769 by the rural houses in Deeside, they were even more shocked somewhat earlier, for instance, by the condition of the streets in Edinburgh, the capital city.

A certain Joseph Taylor says of Edinburgh, writing in 1705: 'Every street shows the nastiness of the inhabitants, the excrements lye in heaps, and there is not above one house of Office in the Town, which may not improperly be called a house of Office itself. In a Morning the Scent was so offensive, that we were forc't to hold our Noses as we past the streets, and take care where we trod for fear of disobliging our shoes, and to walk in the middle at night, for fear of an accident to our heads. The Lodgings are as nasty as the streets. . . . Every room is well scented with a close stoole, and the Master, Mistress and Servants lye on a flour, like so many Swine in a Hogsty.' English visitors may have thought the Scots a peculiarly dirty people, but these were mediaeval conditions to be found also in contemporary Paris, if we are to believe Restif de la Bretonne; Paris, too, had the disconcerting habit of emptying chamber-pots into the street from a top floor. Indeed, the Edinburgh housewives had borrowed this custom from Paris, as is shown by the garbled French of the warning they shouted: Gardyloo! The countryside everywhere, even among its farmyard middens, was probably less noisome than any walled town.

Leaving our own hygienic prejudices aside, we can better judge how mediaeval those times still were by looking at two nearly contemporary works occasioned by the same event, one of them literary, the product of town culture, the other not, having been composed in the unlettered countryside. The event was the burning down of the Tower of Frendraught in Aberdeenshire, one October night in 1630. The country people made a Ballad about it, 'The Fire of Frendraught' (Child, 196); the town of Aberdeen, in the person of Arthur Johnson, the Rector of King's College there, produced two Latin poems in Ovidian couplets, one of them a complaint from a young noblewoman whose husband had been burned to death in Frendraught, the other a demand for the Government to inflict the most ferocious tortures on the fire-raisers. The Ballad was first partially written down, so far as we know, in 1794, and was later more completely recovered from oral tradition in 1825 and 1827; the Latin poems were published in Holland, in 1637 and again in 1642. The works of the Scottish Latin School, to which they belonged, were usually brought out somewhere in Europe, where they were admired by an international public, in itself a mediaeval survival. The townsman wrote out of a tradition of classical learning, the countryman composed verses out of a tradition of Ballad-making and singing. Why, we may ask, did either feel a need to record in verse the burning down of Frendraught Tower, since, in these turbulent times, the burning down of a great house was not uncommon?

The fate of Frendraught Tower was one of the unsolved mysteries of its day. I shall give a brief account of the known facts, since they provide as good a picture as any of what life was like in these parts at that time. There was a dispute between Crichton of Frendraught and Gordon of Rothiemay about fishing-rights pertaining to lands sold by Gordon to Crichton. The master of Frendraught took the quarrel to the Law Courts, got a decision in his favour and also had Rothiemay outlawed. Rothiemay, not at all legally minded, collected a band of wild fellows to harry Frendraught's lands in return. Frendraught at once procured a commission to arrest Rothiemay, and accompanied by various allies, including an uncle of his wife's who was a Gordon, set off to capture his adversary. In the ensuing fight Rothiemay was killed, and so was Frendraught's Gordon uncle. Then Rothiemay's son collected a posse of Highlanders from over the border to burn and ravage Crichton of Frendraught's lands. At this point Frendraught, feeling that the Law was perhaps not the best recourse against Highlanders, appealed for help to the most powerful magnate in the North-East, the Marquis of Huntly, chief of the Gordons, who was also a kinsman of his wife's. Huntly managed to bring about a settlement, according to which Frendraught paid compensation money to Rothiemay's family and to his uncle's family; everyone shook hands and all seemed well.

Yet one of Frendraught's allies, John Meldrum, who had been badly wounded in the affray, not being satisfied with what he got as compensation money, helped himself one night to two of Frendraught's best horses. Frendraught, feeling himself very much in the right, summoned him to court for the theft. Meldrum ignored the summons, so Frendraught procured a commission to arrest him. Meldrum was not found where he was looked for, at a place belonging to his brother-in-law, John Leslie, but one of the Crichtons accompanying Frendraught had 'hot words' with Leslie's son James; young Leslie was dangerously wounded. Most of the Leslies then rose in arms against the Crichtons. Frendraught again appealed to the Marquis, who sent at once for the Leslies. But the Leslies refused to be pacified until it should be known whether young James Leslie were to live or die. Huntly, aware that the Leslies had not gone home but were lying in wait for Frendraught, kept Frendraught beside him for two days and then sent one of his sons, Lord Melgum, together with young Rothiemay, to escort him safely to his own house. These two noblemen were entreated by Frendraught and his lady to stay as guests overnight and were lodged in the old Tower, a solid stone building with thick walls and barred windows. At about two in the morning the Tower went up in a blaze; the two young men and four of their servants were burnt to death, while the Frendraughts, in the adjoining dwelling-house, were unharmed.

The whole countryside seems to have assumed at once that Frendraught himself set fire to the Tower. One of his wife's uncles, Sir Robert Gordon, writing a History of these times, says:

'The rumour of this unhappy accident did speedily spread itself . . . some laying an aspersion upon Frendraught, as if he had wilfully destroyed his guests.'

Sir Robert Gordon shared what he called the suspicion of 'the most part' that the Leslies, with or without Meldrum, were the fire-raisers. But the whole Huntly clan and their friends took immediate vengeance on Frendraught, as a later state paper testifies: 'by frequent slaughters, herships and barbarous cruelties . . . also the whole tenants of his lands and domestics of his house have left his service, and himself, with the hazard of his life, has been forced to steal away under night and have his refuge to his Majesty's Council'.

Frendraught, safe in Edinburgh among the Lords in Secret Council, started 'a great action at law prosecuted . . . against the marquis', which his uncle, Sir Robert, tried to bring to arbitration. Huntly died before a decision was reached, so Frendraught went home again 'and there lived peaceably'. In 1634 John Meldrum was arrested and executed, very unjustly, as many thought.

It is a curiously tangled story, and perhaps if we draw out and look at one or two of the threads we may understand it better. The Lords of Secret Council in Edinburgh were Calvinists, and, to judge from the confidence with which Frendraught expected them to back up his legal processes, he was a Calvinist supporter. His wife, a Gordon, was suspected of being a 'secret Catholic', while the head of the Gordons, the Marquis of Huntly, was a professed Catholic, with a large Catholic following. The 'pretence of inquiry', as a Scottish historian, Hill Burton, called it, on the part of the Government, which exonerated Frendraught, arose, it was supposed, from the Government's wish to foster the Crichtons of Frendraught as a counterpoise to Huntly; it was also supposed that the death of Huntly's son was not unwelcome to the Edinburgh Lords. To this criss-cross of religious and political motivations may be added the fact that most of the gentry in and around the town of Aberdeen remained obstinately Episcopalian, with no love for the Calvinists.

This is where the Episcopalian Arthur Johnson comes in, with his Ovidian couplets. Like his friends he suspected the Government of being lukewarm in its search for the culprits, and he wrote his Latin poems to spur the Government into action against Frendraught, who was, he had no doubt, the fire-raiser. In this conviction he was in accord with the feeling of the countryside, but perhaps for different reasons. Being a doctor of medicine, and either invited or urged to inspect the bodies, he had gone to Frendraught himself and seen what was left of the Tower and the charred stumps of the victims. The horror of the sight genuinely shocked him, but he was even more shocked, in true mediaeval style, at finding the remains of the noblemen and the servants laid out on the same trestle in the stable quarters without discrimination of rank, exposed 'as a spectacle for the lowest vulgar', *imae spectacula plebi*. As for the Tower, he was sure that its burning was no accident. It was a massive stone structure, *saxea moles*. But a cellar opening beneath it had been widened and a hole made through which the incendiaries thrust their materials. 'All was pitch, sulphur, naphtha and bitumen'.

Both his poems are cries for vengeance, and although Frendraught is not expressly named in them, they leave one in no doubt that he is the culprit, the 'auctor'. The first poem professes to be a personal complaint from Lord Melgum's widow, Sophia Hay, daughter of the Earl of Errol. The second poem sets out to castigate the Government more directly and reminds them of their judicial duties and power to torture suspects. He adjures them to bring out the wheel, the staves, the machines to twist men's necks, the ropes, in order to save Scotland's honour and the glorious fabric of justice.

Arthur Johnson, to judge from the portrait included in the Dutch edition of these poems, was a genial, sociable man of the world, an educated, cultured representative of his time; he was certainly fluent and facile in the writing of Latin couplets. True, Porson would not have approved 'sed auctor ubi est?' as the close of a hexameter, any more than he approved a false quantity of Buchanan's, but Johnson's verses flowed easily enough. Presumably he had been trained in the mediaeval scholastic curriculum, which was a formal curriculum, learned by rote, a kind of intellectual game with counters that had no reference to contemporary life or language and taught one nothing about the fallacies in one's daily conduct, a purely cerebral education that left the imagination untouched.

In our days, unfortunately, torture has ceased to be a mediaeval curiosity, and perhaps we dare not call Johnson mediaeval simply because he approved the use of torture in the administration of justice. But it was a mediaeval attitude to take the torture of suspects for granted, as Johnson did. There is a striking contrast between his relatively ill-educated feelings and the elaboration of his conscious classical knowledge, a contrast marking a gap very like the gap between the Aberdeenshire countryside and Aberdeen. Scottish civilization was already becoming elaborately and consciously cerebral, thanks to Calvinism, with an excessive respect for cerebration rather than intelligence; the countryside was still deep in the world of archaic feeling, self-conscious only to a limited extent, aware of power and the forces of power, guided not by abstract concepts but by traditional feelings and stories in which passionate feelings, presented in episodes, were embodied.

Johnson shared in this archaic world of feeling but he was conscious enough and shrewd enough to know more than the rural populace about the forces then contending in Scotland. The contentions that were going on in their neighbourhood, on the other hand, presented no clear picture to the country people: they appeared merely as a succession of personal brawls. I have seen it stated that disturbed and brawling times are the ideal background for the production of Ballads; this statement, I think, needs qualification. One must have a nucleus of strong feeling round which to form a Ballad: the feeling may spring from pride of ancestry and the desire to celebrate ancestral heroic deeds, or from national pride, or from a deep partisan loyalty, or from personal passion, but a strong, unequivocal feeling there must be at the heart of a Ballad. The criss-cross of brawls in the north-eastern countryside of Scotland hardly allowed even for partisan loyalty: today's allies were too often tomorrow's enemies. Brawling by itself provides material for chronicles, not for Ballads, and Ballads which are merely chronicles are usually perfunctory Ballads: the news in them is stale to us and they seem dull.

What nucleus of feeling, then, did the countryside find round which to form their Ballad about Frendraught? Ancestral pride hardly came into it, nor did national pride, nor even the traditional hostility between Lowlanders and Highlanders. The people had no partisan loyalty to the Huntly family, who belonged elsewhere, or even to Rothiemay. But their sense of hospitality, the 'old usage', the tradition of unstinting and unquestioning service to incoming guests which they had inherited from their forebears, this deep feeling, taken for granted, had been outraged by the fate of Frendraught's guests, burnt to a cinder while the host and hostess remained unscathed. It was something that should not be. Around that conviction they made their Ballad, heightening the villainy of the Frendraughts and emphasizing the horror of the burning.

The reaction might not have been so violent had Frendraught been a popular man. His habit of calling in the Law to arrest people who 'countered' him, instead of meeting them man to man, as the countryside would have expected, could not have endeared him. His way of doing was that of a cold, self-righteous, legalistic mind, which strengthens the supposition that he was a Calvinist. Had he punched Rothiemay's head in the beginning of their dispute instead of having him outlawed he would have been more respected, even by Rothiemay, and probably none of the awful consequences would have followed. As things were, the reaction in the countryside was violent enough to make the Ballad crudely sensational in its eighteenth stanza.

The ballad is built up in the usual style, embodying the ruling feeling in episodes designed to express it. The technique of doing this is like that of dreams; one simply invents the appropriate situations and their details. Melgum and young Rothiemay could not climb out at a window, for instance, because of the bars: but why did nobody unlock the big door? Surely because the keys could not be found? And why could they not be found? Because one of the villainous Frendraughts had thrown them down the draw-well, of course. That the keys in fact were not in the draw-well did not matter. For a Ballad, as for dreams, myths, village gossip and other works of the imagination, facts are merely raw material to be worked over and, if inconvenient, discarded. To look for historical truth in a so-called historical Ballad is unrewarding. Any truth one may find is truth to a prevailing feeling, not to the facts.

The ballad, dealing as it does with recent events, is a chronicle Ballad, beginning in jog-trot chronicle style.

The eighteenth of October,
A dismal tale to hear
How good Lord John and Rothiemay
Was both burnt in the fire.

Frendraught, of course, simply asks for the alliterative adjective 'false', and so the lady of Frendraught, begging the guests to stay, is described succinctly as 'her false Frendraught' on the analogy of 'her ladyship'. A piece of traditional Ballad commonplace, inherited from an earlier time, is put in to get everyone to bed:

When mass was sung and bells were rung;

(which would hardly suit Frendraught's household)

And all men bound for bed,
Then good Lord John and Rothiemay
In one chamber were laid.

According to John Spalding, a contemporary historian, young Melgum was in a room on the ground floor, with his servant and page, while Rothiemay and his servants lay in the room above. One of Melgum's servants did escape, and, it is likely, Melgum might have escaped too had he not run upstairs to rouse Rothiemay and perhaps three more men in the top storey. The Tower had thick stone walls but it was full of old wooden panelling and beams: the fire must have roared up as in an incinerator; Spalding says: 'in a clap'. The staircase was blazing and no one could get down again. Rothiemay now takes the lead.

He did him to the wire-window,
As fast as he could gang;
Says, Wae to the hands put in the stancheons,
For out we'll never win.

When he stood at the wire-window,
Most doleful to be seen.
He did espy her, Lady Frendraught,
Who stood upon the green.

Cried, 'Mercy, mercy, Lady Frendraught,
Will ye not sink with sin?
For first your husband killed my father
And now you burn his son.'

O then out spake her, Lady Frendraught,
And loudly did she cry;
'It were great pity for good Lord John,
But none for Rothiemay;
But the keys are casten in the deep draw-well,
Ye cannot get away.'

Invention is now in full flow and so we have continuous dramatic dialogue. The Gordon servant who has escaped calls out:

'O loup, O loup, my dear master,
O loup and come to me.
I'll catch you in my arms two
But Rothiemay may lie.'

'The fish shall never swim in the flood,
Nor corn grow through the clay,
Nor the fiercest fire that ever was kindled
Twin me and Rothiemay.

'But I cannot loup, I cannot come,
I cannot win to thee;
My head's fast in the wire-window,
My feet burning from me.

'My eyes are seething in my head,
My flesh roasting also,
My bowels are boiling with my blood,
Is not that a woeful woe?'

This last woeful line is of a bathos that calls to mind some metrical versions of the Psalms and Paraphrases. I have already omitted one or two lines of that nature, which mark a working-over of the ballad by later Presbyterian interests. The dialogue goes on:

'Take here the rings from my white fingers,
That are so long and small,
And give them to my lady fair
Where she sits in her hall.'

We are then taken to Sophia Hay, as she receives the rings,

'O wae be to you, George Gordon,
An ill death may you die,
So safe and sound as you stand there,
And my lord bereaved from me.'

'I bad him loup, I bad him come,
I bad him loup to me;
I'd catch him in my arms two
A foot I should not flee.

'He threw me the rings from his white fingers
Which were so long and small,
To give to you, his lady fair,
Where you sat in your hall.'

Sophia Hay, Sophia Hay,
O bonny Sophia was her name,
Her waiting maid put on her cloaths
But I wot she tore them off again.

And aft she cried, 'Ohon! alas! alas!
A sair heart's ill to win;
I wan a sair heart when I married him,
And the day it's well returnd again.'

There was an older ballad extant which told of the misery of 'Young Tolquhon', the eldest son of Forbes of Tolquhon, when he was debarred from marrying Sophia Hay, his sweetheart, since she was given in marriage to Lord Melgum. Young Tolquhon pined and died unmarried, saying in his ballad:

'I wish her anes as sair a heart
As she's gien me the day.'

This is why Sophia Hay is made to speak of her 'sair heart' in the closing stanza, and so the story is rounded off.

There are five surviving variants of this ballad; the version here quoted is a collation of one printed in 1825 and another dated 1827. I think it had already been 'improved' by someone: 'I cannot', instead of the more likely 'I canna', for instance. It was first mentioned in 1794 by Ritson, who gave five stanzas of it. We can assume that it was popular, all the more because it was seized upon and used as propaganda both by Presbyterians and

Catholics. The Presbyterians infiltrated into the ballad itself, as in the seventh stanza of our version:

> 'O waken, waken, Rothiemay,
> O waken, brother dear,
> And turn you to our Saviour;
> There is strong treason here.'

or the ninth stanza of an 1832 version:

> 'Come let us praise the Lord our God,
> The fiftieth psalm and three;
> For the reek and smoke are us about,
> And there's fause treason tee.'

As Child says in a footnote: 'no doubt Lord John is taken for a Presbyterian'. Father Blakhal, a Catholic, went one better: he argued that Frendraught had burned Melgum out of theological malice 'for his zeal in defending and protecting the poor Catholics against the tyranny of our puritanical bishops and ministers'. God therefore bestowed on Melgum 'the grace . . . of persuading the Baron of Rothiemay to abjure the heresy of Calvin. . . . They two being at a window, and whilst their legs were burning, they did sing together *Te Deum*.'

I assume the Presbyterian infiltration because, in Ballads which have been traditional for a long time and are not chronicle Ballads, neither moral comment nor moral judgment on the protagonists is to be found, nor much direct reference to religious usage beyond the commonplace 'when mass was sung and bells were rung'. But in this ballad, which when it first came out was News, we can recognize the tone of popular news-sheets. The feeling behind it was of popular shock and outrage, so the Ballad-maker made it as sensational as he could. Later, when the public profession of Presbyterianism had become desirable in the country-side, the Ballad-singers of the day pandered to that necessity also.

It is perhaps worth noting that 'Lady Frendraught' bears all the weight of opprobrium in the ballad, and that her husband is mentioned in only one version, where Rothiemay's mother turns up to curse him. The woman of the house is expected to be the main carrier of the old usage, the tradition of hospitality, and so incurs the more blame when it is outraged.

A chronicle Ballad like this was the equivalent of a news-sheet. There was no great distance between it and its audience; the events described were recent and well known. This lack of distance alone made it difficult for the ballad to become good art. It has the appearance of having been hastily put together, with the help of Ballad commonplaces, like the 'white fingers that are so long and small', and 'an ill death may you die'. 'Will ye not sink with sin?' is an echo of the old rhyme:

> Edinburgh castle, towne and tower,
> God grant thou sink for sinne.
> And that even for the black dinner
> Earl Douglas gat therein.

It had to be cast in Ballad-form, because that was the tradition, perhaps the only tradition, for disseminating stories in the countryside. News-sheet prose had not yet been invented, as far as North-Eastern Scotland was concerned. We can take it for granted that there was a long, old Ballad tradition still prevailing in the countryside, familiar to everyone. And so, even this rhymed news-sheet, this chronicle Ballad, follows the Ballad conventions of dramatic dialogue, simple repetition, rapid changes of scene.

Perhaps it is not fair to assess the value of chronicle Ballads from this example of a relatively bad one. Ten years after the burning of Frendraught Tower, the house of Airlie was burned down by the Earl of Argyle, who had been granted by the Convention of Estates a 'commission of fire and sword' against the Earl of Airlie and other adherents of Charles I: the ballad (Child 199) to which this burning gave rise is a more endearing one than Frendraught. To begin with, it was formed round a different kind of emotion, one of approval and admiration and sorrow for the owners. The Bonnie Hoose o' Airlie would never have been so called had it not been well-liked by the country people around it. And the central theme of the ballad is the defiant courage shown by Lady Ogilvy, Airlie's daughter-in-law, which is admired. I may be wrong in thinking that disapproval and spite are bound to make a worse ballad than approval and admiration: the fact remains that The Bonnie Hoose o' Airlie is more singable and haunts the memory more than the other. This is partly due, I admit, to the double rhymes for Airlie, two long syllables, which recur in every verse and produce the haunting effect: the tune is also a better tune. The ballad is dramatic enough, but not melodramatic. It also begins more attractively:

It fell on a day, and a bonny simmer day,
When green grew aits and barley,
That there fell out a great dispute
Atween Argyle an' Airlie.

The Earl of Airlie at this time was in York with the King: the ballad puts Lady Ogilvy in charge of the House, which seems to be merely a piece of wishful thinking to allow the making of the song as people wanted it to be made. Montrose, at that time fighting for the Covenanters, had earlier spared the House and put a garrison into it: the vindictiveness of 'gley'd Argyle' (cross-eyed Argyle) against Airlie, a hereditary enemy, pushed him to destroy it. None of the family was in residence at the time.

The Lady looked ower her window sae hie,
An' O but she grat sairly
To see Argyle an' a' his men
Come to plunder the bonnie hoose o' Airlie.

'Come doon, come doon, Lady Ogilvie,' he cried,
Come doon an' kiss me fairly,
Or I swear by the hilt o' my gweed broadsword
'At I winna leave a stannin' stane in Airlie.'

'I winna come down, ye cruel Argyle,'

And so on, with the usual repetition of question and answer sequences, until the Lady asks Argyle to lead her to some dowie glen where she need not see the burning of Airlie. This he did not do.

He's taen her by the milk-white han'
But he didna lead her fairly:
He led her up to tap o' the hill
Faur she saw the burnin o' Airlie.

The smoke an' flame they rose sae hie,
The walls were blackened fairly,
An' the Lady laid her doon on the green to dee
When she saw the burnin' o' Airlie.

(This is Greig's version.)

There is a tender melancholy about this chronicle Ballad; perhaps it should not be called a chronicle Ballad, since the only authentic fact in it is that Argyle burned down the bonny house of Airlie. Even this fact is denied by Child (vol. IV, p. 55, footnote), but Alexander Keith, in his edition of Greig's *Last Leaves* (p. 123), says that Argyle was undoubtedly present at the burning of Airlie; apparently Child had mistaken the implications of a letter. Yet it expresses the feeling of the countryside about this historical fact, and so, in a way, serves as a chronicle, however fictional.

By this time I hope I have made it clear that it was the country people who were able to carry the Ballads, to sing them and pass them on, while the town people, governed by Calvinism, were learning to distrust the world of imagination. Works of imagination, outside the Bible, which was accepted as literal fact, were looked on as papistical deviltries. Respectable Scotsmen, therefore, shied away from the arts and went in for law, logic, philosophy or theology. The underworld of feeling, unless it escaped through the vent of religious zeal, had to keep very much under cover, and fictional imaginative works in especial were held to be so disreputable that years later, when imagination had come into fashion again, Walter Scott was for long ashamed of writing novels and published his first ones anonymously.

I propose now to look at the old, traditional Ballads which the North-Eastern Scottish countryside sang. They were still mediaeval enough, the country people, to carry a load of ancient magic and wishful thinking.

MATERIAL

6

Story Material: Hind Horn[1]

WHEN the Ballads were first made, wishful thinking had not yet fallen into disrepute and was freely drawn upon. The ballad about the Bonnie Hoose o' Airlie, for example, composed quite late in the history of Ballad-making, was still a fine example of wishful thinking, and followed, in this respect, a good old Ballad tradition. Wishful thinking, unless the term is a misnomer, ought to mean a collaboration between the wishful self in the underworld of feeling, and the conscious or thinking self; it does not mean merely the unfixed, vague wish-dream, which is a predominant force in the imaginative underworld but needs to be given shape by conscious purpose if it is to be called wishful thinking. Such a collaboration between the wishful and the thinking, shaping elements in human personality is an ancient usage of mankind, by no means peculiar to the Ballad-makers; for ages past it has brought dreams into action, provided new or traditional forms for energies seeking expression, invented children's games and created works of art. It is not an infallible guide, nor are its purposes always salutary, but it is of great importance in the make-up of human personality.

Peculiar to the Ballad-makers was the particular shape in which they cast their imaginative energies, the Ballad convention, with its short stanzas, singing rhythms and dramatic dialogue embodying phases in an action rather than presenting a logically connected narrative. The material which they cast into this form was often much older than the Ballads themselves, some of it very ancient, for the first Ballad-makers simply took whatever was 'in the air' and sang it into new shape.

Let us look at one of their themes, a favourite in the North of Scotland, the ballad of Hind Horn. Young Hind Horn falls in love with a princess who gives him a magic ring. He is forced to

[1] Child, 17

leave her for many years. According to one version of the ballad:

> The King an angry man was he,
> He sent young Hind Horn to the sea.

After a number of years, 'seven long years' in most of the versions, he sees that his ring is 'pale and wan', which means that the princess is in danger of being plighted to another man. Hind Horn sails back to his own country, exchanges cloaks with a beggar, and in this disguise turns up at the princess's wedding feast, where he makes himself known to her by dropping the ring into a drinking-cup. Then he sheds the beggar's cloak, eclipsing the rest of the company in splendour, and takes the place of the would-be bridegroom.

The extreme contrast between the beggar's rags and the splendour concealed beneath them heightens the hero's triumph, which is the climax, the end and aim of the story. As a simple success-story it is well fitted to encourage any unappreciated adventurer, for it says, in effect: See what the gods may send you, even though you appear to be a beggar.

Does it not seem familiar, this return of the hero, disguised as a beggar, after years of absence, just in time to stave off an unwanted marriage and claim the princess? It is the very story embodied in the *Odyssey*. The only element missing from the *Odyssey* is the magic ring, which may have been left out because the Greeks did not wear finger-rings, or because Odysseus was so well served by Pallas Athene that he had no need of one; or the ring itself may be a later interpolation. All the European versions —and there are many of them—contain the magic ring, which could have been picked up as the story travelled north. It is therefore an old story. But I think it is even more ancient than the *Odyssey*. The emphasis in this story lies not on the love-affair between the hero and the princess, but on the hero's triumph, on his achievement in rising from an apparently lowly condition to acknowledged and splendid status as a princess's consort, a near-king or a king. I suspect that it comes down from matriarchal times when marriage to a reigning princess carried with it dominion over armies, if not over her realms, and the status of king-consort. To claim not only a princess but a kingdom must have been a fortune much desired by adventurers of every sort; the possibility of it may well have inspired the wishful thinking of this story, shaped out of an ancient masculine wish-dream. If so, it is one of the oldest stories in the world.

By the time the tale was incorporated into the *Odyssey* patriarchy had displaced matriarchy among the Greeks, and the princess regnant was naturally displaced too, dwindled into a king's wife. In our ballad, and in many of the mediaeval Romances, she is a king's daughter. Yet what we may call the bones of the story remain the same. The emphasis still lies on the elevation and triumph of the hero after he has passed through many hardships and adventures: the main *motif* is triumph after ordeal. In the *Odyssey* the hardships are not only recounted but stressed: Odysseus has to keep encouraging himself by saying: 'Bear up, my heart, thou hast borne even worse evils than this.' His adventures are magical and varied, culled from many sources, and have a folk-tale atmosphere. In the mediaeval European romances the hero is hard beset among Saracens or Norse heathen, and the obstacles impeding his return are multiplied by intrigues. But the love-story, even in the romances, is not elaborated or much dwelt upon; this is not primarily a story of true love.

After the ordeal, the return in disguise is insisted upon in all versions. Beggar's weeds are the most usual, as in the *Odyssey* and our ballad; in the romances the hero sometimes disguises himself as a harper or strolling fiddler. Why this emphasis on disguise? In the early Middle Ages, when a man's status was proclaimed by the clothes he wore, it must have been easy for him both to feel and to be unrecognizable in clothes of a different mode, but the persistent recurrence of disguise in this story goes much farther back than the Middle Ages—besides, why must it be a beggar's disguise? The lowly disguise, of course, makes a dramatic contrast to the hero's final splendour and heightens the suspense of the recognition scene, yet one cannot help feeling that some other motivation once lay behind it. Mr A. B. Lord[1] may be right in suspecting an older form of the story in which the hero returns from a journey to the Underworld of the Dead, with the weeds of that strange country still clinging to him. Such a journey might well change a man's appearance. A journey to the Underworld of

[1] A. B. Lord, *op. cit.*

the Dead was also one of Odysseus' adventures. In the romances and in the ballad this undertone of meaning is not perceptible: the disguise is taken literally, as in the Yugoslavian epics, where it also persists.

But the conjunction of kingly figure and beggar seems to have pleased the human imagination so much that it keeps on cropping up, in *King Lear*, for instance. The ambivalence of the imaginative world, where the beggar is as the king, is shown in our day, neatly turned the other way round, by Yeats who sings about where 'the king is as the beggar'. Even when kings began to fade from the imagination of the Ballad-makers, several Ballads were composed about nobles disguised as beggars[1]; the princess becomes a farmer's or ale-house-keeper's daughter, who elopes with a beggar-man, only to discover that 'four-and-twenty belted knights' come riding over the hill whenever he blows his horn and that he is lord of a great castle, a turn of the theme verging upon the feminine wish-dream that takes shape in *Cinderella*. Or the princess becomes an Earl's lady who runs off with raggle-taggle gipsies. The story can be rotated to show many facets. It is also noteworthy that a song about the Gaberlunyie Man, a Scottish beggar-song, was generally believed to have been made by the King, James IV of Scotland. I do not know whether this belief has been proved a myth or not: it may well be one. In an old English *gest*, also, which we have in manuscripts dating from the thirteenth and fourteenth centuries, the hero is called 'King Horn'.

This *gest*, and a French and English romance about Horn, the latter two existing in fourteenth-century manuscripts, were, of course, 'in the air' when the ballad was made, but Child, rightly I think, denies that the oral tradition was necessarily derived from these manuscript versions. He says[2]: 'It is often assumed, without a misgiving, that oral tradition must needs be younger than anything that was committed to writing some centuries ago; but . . . there is certainly no antecedent probability of that kind.' Oral Tradition, we do know, has a longer reach than any written records; a story that goes back to the *Odyssey*, and perhaps be-

[1] Cf. 'The Jolly Beggar' (Child, 279); 'The Beggar-laddie' (Child, 280); 'Dugall Quin' (Child, 294)

[2] Child, vol. I, p. 193

yond it, need not have been copied from written mediaeval romances.

How the story reached the Ballad-makers we may never discover, but we do know what they made of it. The *gest* of King Horn runs to 1,550 short verses, the French romance is blown up into 5,250 verses, the later English romance has 100 twelve-line stanzas, but the longest version of the ballad, a Northern Scottish version, has 37 verses of two lines each, only 74 lines in all.[1] Yet nothing essential is omitted from the story; the introduction of the hero, his hardships, the princess, the magic tokens, the return, the exchange with the beggar, the recognition, the triumph, all these are mentioned and compressed into Ballad form. This version introduces Hind Horn in timeless, place-less vagueness:

> Hind Horn frank an' Hind Horn free,
> Whaur was ye born, in what kintrie?
>
> 'O, I was born in the forest sae free,
> An' a' my forbears before me.'

He goes on to say:

> 'Seven years I sair'd the King,
> Fae him I wat I gat naething.
>
> 'But one sight o' his daughter Jane,
> An' that was thro' a gay gold ring.'

Another Northern Scottish version, probably an earlier one, puts it like this:

> 'O seven years I served the King,
> And as for wages, I never gat nane,
>
> 'But ae sight o' his ae daughter,
> And that was through an augre bore.'

One glimpse through a peep-hole, bored by an auger, or made by a gay gold ring, could a courtship be minimized further? Apparently the courtship had simply to be played down even symbolically, being of little interest to the ballad. No explanation is offered of how the lady and Hind Horn came to be on such terms

[1] Greig, *Last Leaves*, *X*, a

as to let her give him love-tokens when he went away. The courtship is only glanced at. So are the hardships. Hind Horn was seven years in servitude to the King, and in one more line, in Greig's Aberdeenshire version only, we are told:

> Lang did he dwell aneath the grun'.

It is far-fetched, but not impossible, to explain this reference as a vague memory of that journey to the Underworld performed by Odysseus and surmised by Mr A. B. Lord. It may have come into the ballad by way of another legend, the subterranean dungeons in which Barbary pirates sometimes kept their Christian slaves. We are told no more. The ballad interest moves rapidly away not only from the courtship but from the hero's hardships. The magical love-tokens, however, are lingered upon, partly no doubt because they are needed to account for the hero's return in the nick of time, and partly because they are magical. The lady says:

> 'O I'll gie you a gay gold ring,
> But than a birdie sweet singin;'

('Than' is a dialect version of 'then'; 'but and', or 'but then', usually has the sense of 'as well as'.)

> 'As lang's your ring does keep its hue,
> Remember aye your love is true.
>
> 'As soon as your love loves a man,
> Your birdie will tak flight, an' it will flee hame.'

For seven years Hind Horn forgot to look at his ring or his bird: another sign that the love-story was of little interest to the Ballad-makers.

> An' when he lookit his ring upon,
> The gay gold ring it was pale and wan.
>
> An' when he opened his silver wain,
> His birdie had ta'en flight an' had flown hame.
>
> He hoisted up sails an' cam to lan',
> An' there he met an auld beggar man.

Interest now quickens. There are no less than eight verses of dialogue between Hind Horn and the beggar, a 'silly aul' man', silly in the sense of being decrepit. 'The morn's our young Queen's weddin' day,' is the great news the beggar has to tell. The title of 'Queen' given here to the princess suggests the aura of splendour surrounding her in matriarchal days. (I admit this matriarchal story to be mere supposition, but it seems to me a supposition that fits into what evidence we have.) Hind Horn, on hearing this news, proposes to exchange cloaks with the beggar, who is rather unwilling. Then comes a curiously moral verse:

> But pairt o' richt an' pairt by wrang
> The beggin' weed fae the beggar he wan.

This unusual comment, for a Ballad, occurs only in one other version, also from the North of Scotland:

> But part be right, and part be wrong,
> Frae the beggar man the cloak he wan.

Moral reflections are not made by the singer in early Ballads, so one is tempted to regard this as a later intrusion. The two Northern versions containing it, one quoted by Greig and the other by Child, are so like each other that they must be closely akin, and the intrusion should be taken as deriving from a single source.

The beggar now instructs Hind Horn how to behave as a beggar, to lean on his pike-staff like a decrepit old man, to beg from Peter and from Paul. This mysterious mode of begging occurs only in the Northern versions. In one of them, it is made a little more explicable by being called begging 'for St Peter' and 'for St Paul'.

> He sought meat for St Peter, he asked for St Paul,
> And he sought for the sake of Hynde Horn all.

There may have been mendicant brotherhoods operating under the names of these saints. (This, by the way, is the sole reference to Christian practices in any of the versions.) But although he sought 'meat' under this formula, Hind Horn

> Took nane frae Peter nor frae Paul,
> Nane frae the high nor low of them all.
>
> And frae them all he would take nane
> Until it came frae the bride's ain hand.

One version, feeling a need for someone to communicate the beggar's wish to the bride, inserts two commonplace verses which often recur in Ballads, about the porter who bows 'low down on his knee' and tells of a stranger at the gate. The other two Northern versions, and all the rest, ignore the presumed difficulty: the bride simply trips downstairs with a cup of wine for the beggar and gives it to him out of her own hand. He drops the ring into the cup, after emptying it. Now the tension mounts, with each terse line hurrying into the next.

'O whaur got ye that ring?' said she;
'Got ye it sailin' on the sea?

'Got ye't by sea, or got ye't by land,
Or got ye it on a droon't man's hand?'

'I got na't by sea, nor got i't by land,
Nor got I't on a droon't man's hand,
But I got it in my wooin' gay,
An' I'll gie't you on your weddin' day.'

Then comes the climax:

She tore the reid gowd fae her hair,
Says: 'I'll gang wi' you, love, for ever mair.'

He loot the clootit cloak doon fa'
An' he stood in reid gowd brisk and braw.

There is a more explicit ending given, along with its tune, by Greig:

He gaed butt thro' the kitchen an' ben thro' the ha'
An' in amo' the nobles, great an' sma,
He cuttit clootie cloaks an' he let them doon fa',
An' he was the brawest gentleman that was amo' them a'.

Odysseus, in fact, outshining the suitors. Child has a similar ending in another Northern Scottish version:

Atween the kitchen an' the ha
He loot his cloutie cloak down fa.

And wi' red gowd shone ower them a'
And frae the bridegroom the bride he sta.

HIND HORN

My husband, Edwin Muir, sang an old ballad at a concert in Orkney when he was four; he remembered only the end of the tune and the last four lines of the text:

> Then doon he loot his duddy cloots
> An' doon he loot them fa',
> An' he glittered in go-o-old,
> Far abune them a'.

'This,' he says in his Autobiography, 'gave me a great sense of glory'.[1]

Testimony like this, from personal experience, confirms that the aim of these beggar Ballads is to convey a feeling of triumphant exaltation. One must remember that a Ballad was sung, not read, to an audience deeply participating in its underlying feelings; the listeners' span of attention was not so long as among the Knights and ladies who heard the lengthy romances, but in all likelihood was more concentrated. To say that Hind Horn sets itself to awaken a sense of glory in the listeners is not too strong a statement. The emotional climax of the ballad, surrounding the ending like a nimbus of glory, is all that is left of the divine nimbus that once entirely enveloped oral tradition; in the archaic world the gods were always invoked as a matter of course at the beginning of a story and its development concerned them closely, but they have now vanished, and the Christian God, apparently, has not yet penetrated far into the imaginative world. Nothing is left but the bare bones of the tale, with a cloud of glorious feeling at the end of it. My husband, for instance, probably remembered only the last verse of his ballad because that was where the sense of glory inhered.

Hind Horn, except for its ending, may seem bare to us because we have grown accustomed to stories of romantic true love. Romance of that kind belongs to a more developed state of individual consciousness than is to be found in Hind Horn. The hero himself is merely a token figure and so is the princess. This may make it easier for an ordinary listener to enter imaginatively into the rôle of the hero, the beggarly figure who becomes a princess's consort; were he too particularized, identification with him would be more difficult. One can deduce that this ballad was

[1] Edwin Muir, *op. cit.*, p. 29

shaped before individual true-love came into fashion as an answer to the riddle of the cosmos, and before individuals were sure enough of themselves to draw moral conclusions from what they heard. Early Ballads of this kind, as I have mentioned, do not usually contain moral reflections by the singer, who remains impersonal, outside the Ballad story, the force of the traditional imagination still being much stronger than any one personality. The intrusion of comments by the singer, even such a slight intrusion as 'I wot', marks a later, more conscious working-over of Ballad material.

Moral reflections may occur in dialogue between protagonists in an early Ballad, but these are usually of a simple nature, ill-wishing or blessing someone for something said or done; they do not generalize; they reflect no systematic philosophy. This lack of system means a lack of conceptual thinking; because of this lack Ballads usually feel no need for logically connected narrative. Systematic thinking belongs to conscious life, while the underworld of the imagination flows only from one episode to another without explicit connection, so that imaginative action is always *ad hoc* action. It does not cross its bridges before it comes to them because it feels no need for bridges at all. It embodies situations as they occur, taking each on its own merits. In this way it often responds more exactly to the needs and implications of a situation than pre-conceived systematic theory, so that the best Ballads are as immediate and memorable as dreams.

The Ballad convention was first shaped by people in this early stage of conscious development. Once shaped, it was passed on and became traditional: it set a fashion which, because traditional, was little changed from age to age, even although the people who transmitted it had become more self-conscious than the first Ballad-makers. But we can perceive, through the convention, gradual changes in conscious grasp of the themes embodied and in their nature. Romantic true-love begins to come into the foreground, and so do families, especially the networks of family kinship, usually in opposition to the aspirations of romantic individuals. The struggles of the individual to emerge from family domination and the belief that true-love is stronger than death combine to produce a new set of Ballads, nearly all tragic.

There are other Ballads, meanwhile, marking the transition towards a preoccupation with romantic true-love. One of these is made by turning the theme of Hind Horn upside down. Instead of a man coming from overseas to claim a woman on the verge of marrying another, a woman comes from overseas to claim her forgetful lover on his wedding day. This is the ballad known in the North of Scotland as Young Beichan, a ballad with a happy ending, so popular that it was much worked over and can show in detail the kind of changes that happen to a Ballad in the course of time. It deserves a chapter to itself.

7
Story Material: Young Beichan[1]

YOUNG BEICHAN, being in form an inversion of Hind Horn, might be thought the later Ballad, but we have no recorded evidence for this assumption. Neither Ballad exists except in relatively late versions taken down towards the end of the eighteenth and the beginning of the nineteenth centuries. Indeed, three manuscripts of Young Beichan, dating from 1783 and 1791, are older than any of Hind Horn. And yet the theme of Hind Horn repeats a basic pattern found in the *Odyssey* while Young Beichan has folk-tale elements of dateless antiquity known to be current in every part of the world. Like many other Ballads these two rise out of impenetrable mists; which of their themes is the older can be rashly conjectured but not proved.

The folk-tale elements in Young Beichan belong to a constellation of stories in which a young woman, usually the daughter of a potentate, helps the hero to escape from her father's oppressions and is later deserted or forgotten by him. Hamish Henderson says[2]:

> 'The Girl as Helper in the Hero's Flight' is one of the most widely diffused of international folk-tale types. . . . Its classic prototype is the famous Greek myth of Jason and Medea. . . But . . . from Iceland to Madagascar and from the West Indies to Samoa have come versions of the same basic tale-type; it has been recorded among the Bushmen, the Eskimos, the Zulus and the American Indians. . . .

The girl who helps is usually skilled in magic, and belongs in turn to a wider constellation of stories in which a quick-witted woman comes to the rescue of her father or her lover or any hero in difficulties. (She is usually categorized as 'The Clever Lass', a term which seems to me like a pat of condescending approval.

[1] Child, 53

[2] *The Green Man of Knowledge*, Scottish Studies, vol. 2, No. 1, pp. 47-85, 1958

The so-called 'Clever Lass' was once, I am sure, a powerful priestess-magician whom one would not have dared to pat on the back.) The gravitational pull of these folk-tales has affected, indeed, may have caused, the simple inversion of the Hind Horn theme, and brings the woman's figure well into the foreground. In this ballad she sets out on a quest to find her forgetful hero, thus adding extra tension to the story.

An off-shoot of the same tale is to be found in the legend about Thomas á Becket's mother. According to the legend, Gilbert á Becket, or Beket, was captured and imprisoned by Saracens in the Holy Land. The only daughter of the Saracen prince Admiraud fell in love with Gilbert, as he served her father's table in his chains, and offered to become a Christian and marry him. Gilbert and his companions escaped, apparently without her help—at last, so the legend goes—leaving her consumed by love and grief. At last she went in quest of him, knowing only two English words: 'London' and 'Gilbert'. Pursued by jeering apprentices and wastrels, she walked the streets of London and stopped beside Gilbert's house, by pure chance, which is, after all, a kind of magic. She was recognized by his man and taken indoors. Eventually, after being baptized, she married her Gilbert. This legend, says Child, goes back to a date not much later than a century after the death of the saint, 'being found in a poetical narrative preserved in a manuscript of about 1300'. Allowing for the Christian colouring diffused through the tale and the omission of the lady's help in the escape of the Christians, the story is clearly based on the ancient constellation and was 'in the air' when our ballad took shape. The name Beichan, which is sometimes given as Bekie, is, as Child remarks, very close to Beket, and five versions of the ballad state formally that Bekie or Beichan was London-born. The legend affected the ballad, therefore, to some extent. But the ballad, as Child goes on to say, is not derived from the legend. Both the legend and the ballad come out of the same ancient tradition, and the ballad contains more of the original elements in the story than the legend. Yet it must be admitted that the *motif* of the woman's quest, which makes possible a happy ending, may have infiltrated into the ballad from the legend, although other sources are possible, since the quest was a generally popular *motif* in the Middle Ages. In the older folk-tales there is no happy ending: the patriarchal hero usually advances ruthlessly over the deserted, forgotten figure of the woman.

But however ancient and beyond conjecture the origins of the themes, the forms of the ballads as we have them are relatively modern and can be compared with each other. On examination it appears that Young Beichan has been more deliberately worked over than Hind Horn, so that even its earlier manuscript versions seem later in date than the earliest Hind Horn.

Let us look, for instance, at Child's *A* version, dated 1783. It is composed, like all the Beichan ballads, in conventional four-line stanzas, whereas Hind Horn is always given in two-line stanzas which in several versions are helped out by an interlined refrain and are probably older in form. There is no hint of a refrain in any of the Beichan ballads, unless the recurrence of the end-rhyme 'ie, y, ee, ea' in all versions but one is an attempt to mark the closing fall of each stanza by using one repeated vowel sound instead of a refrain. The recurrence of the 'ee' sound is apparently deliberate, not caused by a mere poverty of rhyme, so that in *The Loving Ballad of Lord Bateman*, an English rendering of the same story published in 1839 and illustrated by George Cruikshank, the word Northumberland is actually changed into Northumberlee. Perhaps it had become conventionally accepted among some Ballad-singers that -ee was the proper ending for a Ballad stanza? There are other rather late Ballads in which we find the same curious addiction to the -ee ending. (I cannot help thinking that it became a lasting convention for the less reputable reason that Ballad-singers found it an easy rhyme to match.)

Among the various versions of Hind Horn the intrusive 'I wot' occurs only once, while in this one Beichan manuscript it occurs twice, as well as a personal intrusion by the singer.

> 'She's landed at Young Bicham's gates,
> And I hop this day she sal be his bride.'

The hero is called Bicham, which seems to be a distortion of the more usual Beichan. There is no magic at all to ensure the timely arrival of the lady. And when 'Bicham's' bride's mother gets her daughter returned to her it is in these sophisticated terms:

> 'Take back your daughter, madam,' he says.

Although there is no written record of Hind Horn earlier than the eighteen-twenties, this line alone is enough to give the flavour of a period much later than any existing rendering of Hind Horn.

Child's *A* is a Scottish version, although it derives Bicham from London.

> In London city was Bicham born,
> He long'd strange countries for to see,
> But he was ta'en by a savage Moor,
> Who handled him right cruelly.
>
> For tho' his shoulder he put a bore,
> An thro' the bore has pitten a tree,
> An' he's gard him draw the carts o' wine,
> Where horse and oxen had wont to be.

The words 'pitten' for 'put' and 'gard' for 'caused' are Scottish forms. The Moor's 'ae daughter' is here called Shusy Pye, instead of Susie Pye, or Susie Pay as in other versions; in Scotland there are still people who say 'shir' for 'sir', aspirating the 's' as Middle Scots often did. In the Loving Ballad of Lord Bateman the lady's name is translated into Sophia, a more likely sobriquet, but that is a late interpolation by a literate scribe.

The romantic feeling in *A* (Young Bicham) is much more developed than in Hind Horn. After setting Young Bicham free and giving him

> a loaf o' good white bread
> But an' a flask o' Spanish wine

Shusy Pye bids him come back before seven years have an end and calls him 'love'. Then, without magical intervention,

> It was long or seven years had an end
> She longed fu sair her love to see;
> She's set her foot on good ship-board
> An turnd her back on her ain country.

When she lands, we are not told how, at Bicham's gates, she says to the porter:

> 'O has he taen a bonny bride,
> And has he clean forgotten me?
> An sighing said that gay lady,
> I wish I were in my ain country.'

These forlorn sentiments are in contrast to the bargaining with which the affair began.

> 'O hae ye ony lands or rents
> Or citys in your ain country
> Coud free you out of prison strong
> And coud maintain a lady free?'

Such bargaining does not sort well with romantic true-love, yet apparently has not impeded the growth of an authentic passion. None the less, Shusy Pye has had enough worldly shrewdness to equip herself with gold for the quest, so that she has a dowry with her. The porter tells Young Bicham:

> . . . on every finger she has a ring
> An on the mid-finger she has three,
> An there's as meikle goud aboon her brow
> As woud buy an earldom o lan to me.
>
> Then up it started Young Bicham,
> An swore so loud by Our Lady,
> 'It can be none but Shusy Pye
> That has come oer the sea to me.'

This mention of Our Lady is the sole Christian reference in Child's *A* version. But in Child's *E*, which is mostly derived from *A*, we find the so-called Age of Reason creeping in, together with the Presbyterian religious zeal of the Scots. For a more critical audience, accustomed to sermons logically expounded, the singer has introduced a chain of reasoning, deliberate explanations showing cause why things have happened. The statement in the first verse for instance,

> But he was taen by a savage Moor
> Who handled him right cruellie

is explained in an interpolated second verse:

> For he viewed the fashions of that land,
> Their way of worship viewed he,
> But to Mahound or Termagant
> Would Beichan never bend a knee.

This is copied in later versions and strengthened in Child's *H*.

He viewd the fashions of that land,
Their way of worship viewed he,
But unto onie of their stocks
He wadna sae much as bow a knee.

Which made him to be taken straight
And brought afore their hie jurie;
The savage Moor did speak upricht
And made him meikle ill to dree.

As if this were not enough, another verse assures us:

But Young Beichan was a Christian born
And still a Christian was he;
Which made them put him in prison strang
And cauld and hunger sair to dree,
And fed on nocht but bread and water,
Until the day that he mot dee.

The logician who made the interpolations in *E* was not likely to admit magic as a means of bringing Susy Pye to her lover in the nick of time, whatever old tales might suggest, yet he felt the need of a motivation, so he inserts two explanatory lines:

But long ere seven years had an end
She longd full sore her love to see,
For ever a voice within her breast
Said, 'Beichan has broke his vow to thee.'
So she's set her foot on good ship-board
And turnd her back on her own countrie.

(My italics)

He felt also the need for saving the young man's face as a romantic lover—an unexpected touch of human understanding—and so invents a dialogue between Susy Pye and a shepherd outside Beichan's gates.

There is a wedding in yonder hall
Has lasted these thirty days and three;
Young Beichan will not bed with his bride,
For love of one that's yond the sea.

This intrusion of the shepherd is nearly all that is left of the ballad in Child's *G*: it has lost its rational motivation and become an attractive interlude:

> O wha's aught a' yon flock o sheep,
> An wha's aught a' yon flock o kye?
> An wha's aught a' yon pretty castles
> That you sae often do pass bye?
>
> They're a' Lord Beekin's sheep,
> They're a' Lord Beekin's kye,
> They're a' Lord Beekin's castles,
> That you sae often do pass bye.

Here the singer has transformed the remembrance of a shepherd's being on the scene into a true Ballad repetition of items that cannot help singing themselves. The Age of Reason had little to do with this elaboration. But it added its own ideas of elegance to other selected episodes, notably the intrusion of the bride's mother as a speaking character in the story. She first enters the scene in Child's *B*, with relative simplicity, addressing the porter:

> Then up and spak the bride's mother:
> And O an ill deid may ye die!
> 'If ye didna except the bonny bride,
> Ye might hae ay excepted me.'

In Child's *D*, which comes from the North of Scotland and is dated 1802-3, her dialogue with the porter expands into two verses:

> Out spak the bride's mither
> An a haghty woman was she:
> 'If ye had na excepted the bonny brid,
> Ye might well ha excepted me.'
>
> 'No desparagment to you, madam,
> Nor non to her grace;
> The sole of yon lady's foot
> Is fairer than yer face.'

(Child's *D*, *Old Lady's Collection*, vol. I, p. 219.)

In *E* the mother recurs again, 'and an angry woman was she', but the porter's answer is less genteel:

'O hold your tongue, thou bride's mother,
Of all your folly let me be;
She's ten times fairer nor the bride
And all that's in your companie.'

By the time we come to Child's *N* version, the eighteenth-century elegance has become mere vituperation:

Out then spake the bride's mother,
I'm sure an angry woman was she;
'You're impudent and insolent,
For ye might excepted the bride and me.'

To which the porter retorts, with a fine appreciation of what constitutes beauty:

'Ye lie, ye lie, ye proud woman,
I'm sure sae loud as I hear you lie,
She has more gold on her body
Than would buy the lands, the bride and thee.'

This lamentable version was published in Falkirk, in 1815. It has lost the simplicity of the early Ballad and the terse rhythm of Ballad verse. Although it tries to keep traditional commonplace lines, it spoils them by unnecessary insertions, such as 'I'm sure'. The following is a characteristic travesty of Ballad tradition:

He had not served the savage Moor
A week, nay scarcely but only three.

The singer actually puts in, at one point:

Now we will leave young Susan Py
A while in her own country,
And will return to Young Bichen
Who is safe arrived in fair England.

He does not know the meaning of some expressions which he tries to use:

When she came to Young Bichen's gate
She chapped loudly at the pin.

Other versions agree that the lady 'tirled softly at the pin', which was not a knocker to 'chap', as *N* imagines, but a 'risp', an iron pin twirled scrapingly up and down, or 'tirled'. The understanding, the acceptance found in an audience familiar with the material presented, has been lost; the ballad has become the victim of literate and ignorant print, issued, not for an audience, but for a public.

There are two other versions, *C* and *M*, in which we find the country imagination actively at work improvising new episodes. These are also the versions that bring in the magic we have hitherto missed from the ancient story. Both of them come from Aberdeenshire.

Turkey or the Holy Land, which provide the usual setting for Beichan's captivity, are too far away for these Aberdeenshire singers; in Child's *C* the action is located in France, while in *M*, we are merely told that the hero went to a foreign land, and that the heroine 'saild on and further on' till she came to 'the water o Tay'. The Firth of Tay was perhaps as far south as people cared to look from Aberdeenshire.

The *C* manuscript, dated 1783, is a fine example of how a singer can enter imaginatively into a given story, taking the listeners with him, and linger over episodes in it where his feelings lead him to do so. The hero, called Young Bekie, has been imprisoned by the King of France because he has fallen in love with the King's 'ae daughter', Burd Isbel.

> An she has to the prison-house gane,
> To hear the prisoner's mane.

At this point the Balladist invents the song Young Bekie was singing in his cell.

> 'O gin a lady woud borrow me,
> At her stirrup-foot I woud rin;
> Or gin a widow wad borrow me,
> I would swear to be her son.
>
> 'Or gin a virgin woud borrow me,
> I woud wed her wi a ring,
> I'd gi her ha's, I'd gie her bowers,
> The bonny towrs o Linne.'

In the Yugoslav oral epics the hero, when captive in prison, usually attracts the attention of his captor's wife by shouting for days and nights on end, which seems to have been a recognized, conventional practice. Singing a wistful song seems a more sympathetic kind of prisoner's complaint; besides, it cuts out the need for unromantic bargaining probes, since it makes clear that the prisoner is a man of property. The lack of bargaining makes one all the readier to accept the tender feeling in the next three new stanzas.

> O barefoot, barefoot gaed she but,
> An barefoot came she ben;
> It was no for want o hose and shoone,
> Nor time to put them on.
>
> But a' for fear that her father dear
> Had heard her making din:
> She's stown the keys o the prison-house dor
> An latten the prisoner gang.
>
> O when she saw him, Young Bekie,
> Her heart was wondrous sair,
> For the mice but an the bold rottons
> Had eaten his yellow hair.

Earlier versions confine themselves to gifts of white bread and red wine, but *C* enters into more detail:

> She's gien him a shaver for his beard,
> A comber till his hair,
> Five hunder pound in his pocket,
> To spen an nae to spair.
>
> She's gien him a steed was good in need,
> An a saddle o royal bone,
> A leash o hounds o ae litter
> An Hector called one.

Nor does our imaginative Ballad-maker accept the conventional seven years' interval until the marriage; he says that they made a vow between them for three years, and only a twelvemonth elapses before Bekie is

> forc'd to marry a duke's daughter,
> Or than lose a' his land.

Bekie is here not allowed to be forgetful or callous; he is being constrained to the unwanted marriage.

> 'Ohon, alas!' says Young Bekie,
> 'I know not what to dee;
> For I canno win to Burd Isbel,
> An she kensnae to come to me.'

We are now exploring subjective emotional states which were beyond the scope of earlier Ballads: our token hero is assuming a living, suffering identity. The interest in romantic true-love has grown. And in outlining the lover's dilemma, the ballad also high-lights the necessary help suddenly provided by a magical figure, here called the Belly Blin.

The Belly Blin, or the Billie Blin, says Child,[1] 'presents himself in at least four Scottish ballads. . . . In all he is a serviceable household demon.' Child then goes on to suggest that he is an amalgam of two aspects of Odin, Bil-eygr, Odin benevolent, and Böl-eygr, Odin malevolent, mild-eyed and evil-eyed respectively. 'Originally,' says Child, '. . . . perhaps only the bad member of this mythical pair is blind; but it would not be at all strange that later tradition . . . should transfer blindness to the good-natured one, and give rise to the anomalous Billie Blind.' The bad Odin, he tells us, is found in Hrömund's saga as 'Blind the Bad' and also as 'Carl Blind'. This aspect of Odin is 'seen in the Ballad of "Earl Brand", masking as Old Carl Hood, "aye for ill and never for good".'

The Belly Blin, however, is kind to Burd Isbel.

> O it fell once upon a day
> Burd Isbel fell asleep,
> An up it starts the Belly Blin
> An stood at her bed-feet.

That impersonal usage 'up it starts' is worth a moment's consideration. We have met it already in *A*:

> Then up it started Young Bicham
> An sware so loud by Our Lady.

[1] Child, Introduction to *Gil Brenton* (5), vol. 1, p. 67

The effect produced is that of an instantaneous force arriving on the scene without conscious volition. The impersonal construction excludes any personal responsibility for the action, which comes from beyond conscious life, from somewhere else.

'O waken, waken, Burd Isbel,
How can you sleep so soun,
Whan this is Bekie's wedding day
An the marriage gaein on?'

The Belly Blin advises her to take two of her mother's 'marys' to keep her from 'thinking lang', and instructs her to dress them and herself in scarlet and in green, with girdles

'about your middles
Woud buy an earldome'

She is to go down to the sea-side where 'Hollans boats' will come rowing to her hand.

'Ye set your milk-white foot abord,
Cry, Hail ye, Domine,
An I shal be the steerer o't,
To row you oer the sea.'

In this magical way she is wafted across the sea and reaches Young Bekie's gate while the wedding is still going on. The usual porter, sweetened by the usual 'guineas three', runs upstairs to tell the king, the queen, and Young Bekie about the three fair maidens, one of whom wants speech with the bridegroom.

Then out it spake the bierly bride,
Was a' goud to the chin;
'Gin she be braw without,' she says,
'We's be as braw within.'

Then up it starts him, Young Bekie,
An the tears was in his ee:
'I'll lay my life it's Burd Isbel
Come oer the sea to me.'

He runs downstairs and kisses her tenderly. She reminds him of his vow, and of the gifts she bestowed on him.

'I gae you a steed was good in need,
An a saddle o royal bone,
A leash o hounds o ae litter,
An Hector called one.'

It was well kent what the lady said,
That it wasna a lee,
For at ilka word the lady spake,
The hound fell at her knee.

'Tak hame, tak hame your daughter dear,
A blessing gae her wi',
For I maun marry my Burd Isbel,
That's come oer the sea to me.'

That thin end of the family wedge, the bride's mother, does not appear at all, unless she is the person who makes a dignified protest in the next stanza, which is also the last:

'Is this the custom o your house,
Or the fashion o your lan,
To marry a maid in a May mornin
An send her back at even?'

The extra details put into this version far from impeding the action convey, very delicately, a sympathetic understanding of the emotions agitating the protagonists. The flow of feeling in the story is still the main thing, but it is more dwelt upon, more closely looked at, than in earlier Ballads. Romantic true love is beginning to be taken seriously. Yet how did *C* discover that magic belonged to this story? None of the aforementioned versions allows for the working of magic: the next version we shall consider, Child's *M*, has been largely copied from *C*, and could have adopted from *C* the intervention of a magical figure. It is not surprising that *C* should have brought in a Norse household demon, since there was an intimate commerce between Scandinavia and Aberdeenshire and Norse folk-tales were plentiful in the North of Scotland, but how did *C* come to be aware that this story needed a magician to bring the lady over? *C* has handled the traditional material with tact and great sensitivity, as well as with a feeling imagination: perhaps the imaginative gift in itself was enough to suggest that a magician was necessary; perhaps *C* knew one of the folk-tales from the ancient constellation, which could quite well have been current in the North of Scotland.

We should note here that whatever a Ballad-singer added to a story could not be copyright. Such an arrangement would have been alien to oral tradition. Every time a Ballad was sung it inevitably changed a little, according to the gifts or lack of gifts in the singer, and the changes went into the common stock. The tenor of the story remained the same; the details varied, the rhymes varied, the tune often varied: the common stock of episodes was freely drawn upon. No singer attempted to use fine words and phrases; his inner tact was devoted to setting forth an old story in familiar language in a traditional way, using traditional expressions which belonged to everyone, not to himself. It is a sign of degeneration in a Ballad when the Ballad-singer becomes a 'performer', showing off his abilities and obtruding his personality upon the song, very often introducing matter which is merely garrulous. By no means could one expect all Ballad-singers to be artists like the unknown transmitter of *C*.

This becomes evident when one looks at Child's *M*, a version which takes over the inventions of *C*, but spoils them by insensitive and needless enlargement. The prisoner's song gets an extra introductory verse, and has a showy legal word 'infeft' substituted for *C*'s simple statement:

> 'I'd gi' her ha's, I'd gie her bowers,
> The bonny towrs o Linne.'

M makes him sing grandly, almost like an operatic hero:

> 'I'd wed her wi a ring,
> Infeft her wi the ha's and bowers
> O the bonny towers o Linne.'

The *D* manuscript, which has also taken over some of C's inventions, including the song, makes the prisoner repeat it at the lady's request, a trick adopted by *M*, which omits no chance of spinning out the ballad to greater length and actually keeps it going for no less than fifty-four stanzas of four lines each. This inordinate length might be the result of including all the verses in the common stock known to the neighbourhood, but so many of the interpolated stanzas are garrulous or irrelevant to the main line of the story that a certain self-complacency in the singer is indicated.

Young Beichan has here become Young Bondwell, and Burd Isbel is changed into Dame Essels. The tender little verses about the lady softly going barefoot to keep from awakening her father have been left out, but the singer has noted the entrance of the father as a character and brings in five verses about him a little later. The 'shaver' and the 'comber' are omitted from the gifts; the 'five hunder pound' are scaled down to 'a hunder pund o pennies round', which might indicate an earlier date but, I think, merely points to a poverty-stricken audience who would think a hundred pounds of pennies a sufficiently princely sum. Two gos-hawks are added to the leash of hounds, and the name of one hound is changed from Hector to Cain, a more Scriptural, or even witch-like, but less appropriate name. In a good verse couched in familiar vernacular:

> When mony days were past and gane
> Dame Essels thought fell lang,
> And she is to her lonely bower
> To shorten her wi a sang.

The use of *short* in current phrases where we use only *long* (i.e. long ago) can still be heard in the North of Scotland and in Orkney, where people will say: 'I saw him short ago.'

> The sang had such a melody
> It lulld her fast asleep;
> Up starts a woman, clad in green,
> And stood at her bed-feet.

Green is, of course, the fairy colour. This fairy woman gives Dame Essels the same instructions as the Belly Blin gave Burd Isbel, in terms somewhat more vague and pretentious:

> 'And ye'll put girdles about their middles,
> Sae costly, rich and rare.'

The same magic ship will come sailing in:

> 'Ye'll take a wand into your hand,
> Ye'll stroke her round about,
> And ye'll take God your pilot to be,
> To drown ye'll take nae doubt.'

At this point the singer chooses to bring in Dame Essels's father, in verses mostly borrowed from another Ballad:

> Then up it raise her Dame Essels,
> Sought water to wash her hands,
> But aye the faster that she washed
> The tears they trickling ran.
>
> Then in it came her father dear,
> And in the floor steps he:
> 'What ails Dame Essels, my daughter dear,
> Ye weep sae bitterlie?
>
> 'Want ye a small fish frae the flood,
> Or turtle frae the sea?
> Or is there man in a' my realm
> This day has offended thee?'
>
> 'I want nae small fish frae the flood,
> Nor turtle frae the sea;
> But Young Bondwell, your ain prisoner,
> This day has offended me.'
>
> Her father turned him round about,
> A solemn oath sware he:
> 'If this be true ye tell me now
> High hanged he shall be.
>
> 'To-morrow morning he shall be
> Hung high upon a tree':
> Dame Essels whispered to hersel,
> 'Father, ye've made a lie.'

One cannot but think that this attempt to heighten the tension is clumsy and misplaced, besides setting Dame Essels, sly creature, in a poor light. After this interlude, Dame Essels takes her maids (not her 'marys') with her and sails away. The singer now spins out every part of the story in the flattest of flat verse.

The Ballad convention of short stanzas, in short lines, with the 'plot' carried on by dialogue, lends itself to garrulous verses once the principle is accepted that brand-new material may be added to an old story. It is as easy to keep on adding verses that say very little as it is to keep on repeating 'said he' and 'said she' in village gossip. For example:

So they saild on and further on,
Till to the water o Tay;
There they spied a bonny little boy,
Was watering his steeds sae gay.

'What news, what news, my little boy,
What news hae ye to me?
Are there any weddings in this place,
Or any gaun to be?'

'There is a wedding in this place,
A wedding very soon;
The morn's the young squire's wedding day,
In the bonny towers of Linne.'

O then she walked along the way
To see what coud be seen,
And there she saw the proud porter,
Drest in a mantle green.

'What news, what news, porter?' she said,
'What news hae ye to me?
Are there any weddings in this place
Or any gaun to be?'

'There is a wedding in this place,
A wedding very soon.'

and so on, and so on.

One must take into account the bad verses in Ballads, as well as the good, to arrive at a just estimate of their nature and function. Lengthy garrulity like this shows that the individual personality of the singer is coming more and more into the foreground so that it intrudes upon the traditional stories, loosening and often spoiling them. Old, traditional versions are terse and shapely, as this version is not. The drama they embody is all the more effective for being compressed, and all the less effective for being teased out and added to by self-important singers. Not everyone is a poet by instinct. In describing how Dame Essels is recognized by her hounds, for instance, *M* says:

'O Cain! O Cain!' the lady cried,
And Cain did her ken;

They baith flappd round the lady's knee
Like a couple o armed men.

One must put *M* down as a poetaster, and a bad one at that.

Yet the bad interpolations of *M* and the good interpolations of *C* both bear witness to the fact that the ordinary people of the countryside lived through their Ballads, taking them into themselves and giving them out again coloured to some extent by their own habits and feelings. Dame Essels, for example, stole the keys of the prison

where under the bed they lay.

Hind Horn

Gaed butt thro' the kitchen an' ben thro' the ha'.

These details are put in by people who have only two rooms, a but and a ben, and keep their private possessions under their beds, the ordinary labouring people of an agricultural countryside. Can we, then, assume that these ordinary people were capable of the fine shades of feeling to be found in the *C* version of Young Beichan? I do not see that we can do anything else. The evidence is there. The individuals beginning to emerge in the countryside during the eighteenth century, impelled by forces they were unaware of, following the trend of their times, were men and women who might be called illiterate but had sensitive feelings inherited from generations of Ballad-singing forebears. The Ballads kept doors open for them into a wider world than every-day experience. As they listened, they translated the themes into familiar terms of local life, but that did not mean that all their interests were narrowly parochial. The Ballads, or, at least, most of the Ballads, were not parochial in theme; moreover, the Ballad stories brought with them, embedded in their material, recognizable vestiges of beliefs and customs from the past of mankind, providing some depth of background for an audience that had no instruction in formal history or geography.

I do not wish to theorize about what the country people may or may not have learned from the Ballads: it is better to look into the Ballads themselves and see what is there. I propose now to consider the magical elements found in many Ballads.

8

Story Material: Magic. Tam Lin[1]

IN Hind Horn the princess supplies the magic ring and the magic singing-bird; it is taken as a matter of course that she should be able to do so. But in Young Beichan the magic is brought in from outside. 'Up it starts' the Belly Blin or the woman in green, at the bed-foot, arriving suddenly from some area beyond the focus of conscious life. The Belly Blin is a Norse demon, the woman in green a fairy.

Fairies in the Scottish Ballads are not the consciously prettified little creatures found elsewhere; they are Powers, coming from the utter darkness of the surrounding unknown, from beyond even the relatively dark unfocused world of sleep and the dreaming imagination. In the ballad of Tam Lin their magic manifests itself 'at the mirk and midnight hour' like flashes of angry lightning. Nor is the Belly Blin a happily domesticated spirit like the English Puck; he belongs to the old Norse world of bale-fires and savage revenges, although he can be helpful when he likes. The Ballads themselves give us some idea of where these Powers come from. Everyone knows about the information given to Thomas the Rhymer by the Queen of Elfland (Child, 37):

> 'O see not ye yon narrow road
> So thick beset wi thorns an briars?
> That is the path of righteousness,
> Tho after it but few enquires.
>
> 'And see not ye that braid, braid road,
> That lies across yon lillie leven?
> That is the path of wickedness,
> Tho some call it the road to heaven.
>
> 'And see not ye that bonny road
> Which winds about the fernie brae?
> That is the road to fair Elfland
> Where you and I this night maun gae.'

[1] Child, 39

Yet perhaps not everyone has realized that the untamed wildness of the fernie brae leads into a part of the ancient world as it was before the coming of Christianity, full of archaic forces and strange portents, a surviving enclave of immemorially old Powers. The Christian Heaven apparently ignores this remnant of the archaic past, but Hell encroaches upon it in a sinister way. Tam Lin, who was caught and taken there by the fairies, tells us:

> 'And pleasant is the fairy land,
> But, an eerie tale to tell,
> Ay at the end of seven years
> We pay a tiend to hell;
> I am sae fair and fu o flesh,
> I'm feard it be mysel.'

A refuge from orthodox belief which has to pay tithes to Hell and is therefore tributary to the Devil is but a precarious stronghold. Yet there it is, according to the Ballads, another dimension added to the imaginative world of the Scots, a wild enclave from which anything may come, fairies, Norse demons, Pictish water-goddesses, unpredictable and magical. Because this uncanny region haunted the back of their minds, country people in Scotland were deeply anxious to be christened, or 'sained', since christening was a protection against its power; though if the rite were carelessly done the protection did not avail. Tam Lin, for instance, was snatched away in spite of his having been christened, because his step-mother had been careless. In one version of the ballad he accounts for his fate:

> 'My step-mother put on my claithes,
> An ill, ill sained she me.'

There were recognized times in the year when this archaic world could penetrate into middle earth, cracks in Time, as it were, through which the uncanny powers could come. That the dividing or boundary line between one dispensation and another could let in other-worldly dangers was a widespread ancient belief. Law and order might prevail right up to a boundary line and might be reconstituted again at the other side of it, but on the boundary line itself law was abrogated and the forces of chaos, of misrule, struggled to assert themselves. Mischief and lawless turbulence could be expected, for instance, in the crack of Time between the death of a King and the crowning of his successor, or between the death of the Old Year and the arrival of the New. On such occasions one took the precaution of holding propitiatory rites, or boldly communicated with the uncanny powers by venturing on divinations of the future, as may still be done during the Twelve Days of Christmas in England or the eve of Hogmanay in Scotland. The most ominous crack of all, even more dangerous than that between the Old Year and the New, was the one that opened between the end of summer and the beginning of winter, since it marked the coming of the dark months and at the same time was well known to let the souls of the dead return temporarily to the land of the living. This sinister boundary, coming between the last day of October and the first day of November, was called by a propitiatory name, Hallowe'en. In Scotland it still has an uncanny feeling.

The corresponding crack between the end of winter and the beginning of summer, the eve of May, is also ominous and has its own peculiar rites and divinations, but it is a more hopeful, a happier interruption of the established order, since it marks the coming of light, not of darkness, of life rather than death. Hallowe'en, however, is haunted by death. With bated breath one ventures into the dark of the kailyard, or, worse, the churchyard, to commune with infernal powers and discover one's future sweetheart, even though one knows that a sudden apparition may be only a 'guiser', a young man with blackened face and turnip lantern impersonating a spirit.

Not only the great cracks opening between recognized stretches of Time are suspect; smaller boundaries on earth have to be ritually purified and re-defined (as in the beating of town and county bounds); even the domestic threshold is a possibly dangerous boundary. In the North-East of Scotland, when I was young, prudent housewives still chalked patterns of rowan berries and other defensive symbols on their doorsteps, and a prudent bridegroom would lift his bride over the threshold of the new home. Some vestige of the old belief caused us children to step carefully over the dividing lines between paving-stones. Ghosts were known to prefer stiles as a haunting-place, and unhallowed corpses, such as suicides and unchristened children, were supposed to be buried along boundary lines.

Hallowe'en, then, is a peculiarly ominous evening, when fairy folk may well be expected to appear on earth, and in the ballad of Tam Lin it is on Hallowe'en that the heroine, sometimes called Janet and sometimes Lady Margaret, rescues him from their enchantments.

The ballad begins gaily enough with the usual greenwood episode. We are told that Tam Lin was held in honour among the fairies, and that may be why they allowed him to visit the greenwood from time to time, where he met Janet. In any case, the greenwood is a kind of annexe to the archaic world, still haunted by the aura of ancient fertility cults. Seduction usually happens when a Ballad heroine visits the greenwood, and invariably results in pregnancy. The greenwood, tall-growing rye, and broom-bushes all have erotic overtones both in the Ballads and in folk-song.

The Aberdeenshire versions of this ballad (Child's 39*D* and *G*, Greig's XV) describe the seduction in forthright style:

> He's taen her by the milk-white hand,
> And by the grass-green sleeve,
> And laid her low on gude greenwood,
> At her he spierd nae leave.
>
> When he had got his wills of her,
> His wills as he had taen,
> He's taen her by the middle sma,
> Set her to feet again.

Variants of these two stanzas recur in other North-Eastern Ballads[1] as a commonplace for describing seduction and slip past smoothly as if literal meaning had long been drained out of them. The young woman is presented as a passive victim who meekly turns round after being set on her feet to ask the name of her ravisher. But in 'Tam Lin' the young woman, as we shall find, has a more than ordinary share of spirit and courage, so that this assumption of passive helplessness must be taken as a mere convention. Sir Walter Scott boggled at the verses: in the rendering of Tam Lin his *Minstrelsy of the Scottish Border* produces coy alternatives, which were never composed in any Scottish countryside:

[1] Cf. Child, 52 and Greig, XXI, Greig, XLIII, Greig, LXVIII

He's taen her by the milk-white hand,
Among the leaves sae green,
And what they did I cannot tell,
The green leaves were between.

He's taen her by the milk-white hand
Among the roses red,
And what they did I cannot say,
She ne'er returnd a maid.

Janet did not discover her 'true-love's' name on this occasion, for when she turned to ask the usual question:

Naething heard she nor naething saw,
As a' the woods grew dim.

No wonder she thought that her lover was a fairy. She informed her father:

'If my love were an earthly knight,
As he's an elfin grey,
I wad na gie my ain true love
For nae lord that ye hae.

'The steed that my true-love rides on
Is lighter than the wind;
Wi siller he is shod before,
Wi burnin gowd behind.'

This latter verse is a commonplace used to convey a sense of magical splendour. The fairies were felt to be splendid creatures, splendidly accoutred, like True Thomas's Queen of Elfland, whose

skirt was of the grass-green silk,
Her mantel of the velvet fine,
At ilka tett of her horse's mane
Hung fifty silver bells and nine.

The ballad does not tell us how Janet discovered her lover's name, but when she appears in the greenwood again, heavy with child, she knows what he is called. This time he accuses her of being in the greenwood to pick some herb that would kill 'the bonny bairn that we got us between', a suggestion Janet does not trouble to deny. The ancient greenwood, indeed, must have harboured many expedients either to further or to prevent childbirth. What preoccupies Janet is the old fear about not being christened.

> 'O tell me, tell me, Tam Lin' she says,
> 'For's sake that died on tree,
> If eer ye was in holy chapel
> Or Christendom did see?'

So Tam Lin tells her his story. In the southern Scottish versions he claims to be 'Roxbrugh's grandson'; in the northern versions he is the eldest son of the Laird of Foulis, or of Lord Forbes. By a coincidence, which comes too pat to be mere coincidence, they have met on the eve of Hallowe'en, and he begs her to rescue him that very night from the Fairy People and instructs her what to do.

In Scotland November was known as the Black Month; it was a glumly dark time of year. What Tam Lin proposed to his lady amounted to a severe trial of nerve. Sir Walter Scott, in volume two of his *Minstrelsy*, relates a tradition about a farmer in the Lothians whose wife had been carried off by the fairies; he set out on Hallowe'en to rescue her, but when the fairy train came past lost his nerve and lay low among the furze, so that he lost his wife too, forever. Janet was made of different metal. Tam Lin tells her:

> 'Just at the mirk and midnight hour
> The fairy folk will ride,
> And they that wad their true-love win,
> At Miles Cross they maun bide.
>
> . . . . .
>
> 'O first let pass the black, lady,
> And syne let pass the brown,
> But quickly run to the milk-white steed,
> Pu ye his rider down.
>
> . . . . .
>
> 'They'll turn me in your arms, lady,
> Into an esk and adder;
> But hold me fast and fear me not,
> I am your bairn's father.

'They'll turn me to a bear sae grim,
And then a lion bold;
But hold me fast and fear me not,
As ye shall love your child.

'Again they'll turn me in your arms
Into the burning gleed;
Then throw me into well water,
O throw me in wi speed.

'And then I'll be your ain true-love,
I'll turn a naked knight;
Then cover me wi your green mantle,
And cover me out o sight.'

Here is high magic, very old, as practised by pagan priests and sorcerers for thousands of years past. Magical transformations of this kind were reported by Apollodorus, for instance, from much earlier traditions. In Greek mythology they are well embodied, and even in the early eighteen hundreds still survived in a Cretan story[1] very like that told by Apollodorus; they are found in the Arabian Nights' Tales, in India and in most Asiatic countries. This ballad preserves even a necessary part of the technique, the throwing of Tam Lin last of all into well-water, or, as another version has it:

'First dip me in a stand o milk,
And then a stand o' water;
Haud me fast, let me na gae,
I'll be your bairnie's father.'

To regain human shape, or to lose it, one must pass through a liquid, sometimes milk but generally water. There is an intimate connection between most magical practices and water, wells, springs or rivers: water is traditionally holy.

Janet undertook the task.

Gloomy, gloomy was the night,
And eerie was the way,
As fair Janet in her green mantle
To Miles Cross she did gae.

[1] See Child, vol. 1, p. 337

About the dead hour o the night
She heard the bridles ring;
And Janet was as glad o that
As any earthly thing.

One can almost hear Janet's heart-beats stop and go on again. This flash of pure imagination conveys all the terrors of that night. It first occurs in a version communicated by Robert Burns, and may well have been put in by him: it comes out of the same imaginative underworld as the feeling in all good Ballads. The kind of fanciful detail provided by conscious cerebration, on the other hand, can be seen in other stanzas supplied to Walter Scott by 'a gentleman residing near Langholm', describing the fairy train:

Their oaten pipes blew wondrous shrill,
The hemlock small blew clear,
And louder notes from hemlock large
And bog-reed, struck the ear;
But solemn sounds, or sober thoughts,
The fairies cannot bear.

. . . . .

Fair Janet stood, with mind unmoved,
The dreary heath upon,
And louder, louder waxd the sound
As they came riding on.

This is not in the Ballad world at all: the contrast is extreme. The gentleman from Langholm was looking at the scene from outside, as a spectator. All his consciously thought-up details, categorized and enumerated, do not evoke the depth of intimate feeling conveyed in the simple statement:

About the dead hour o the night,
She heard the bridles ring;
And Janet was as glad o that
As any earthly thing.

Following instructions exactly, Janet pulled Tam Lin down from his horse and the angry fairies transformed him as he had predicted. But she held on. One of the versions, dating from 1825, brings in name-magic too.

But she held him fast, let him not go,
And cried aye 'Young Tamlin',

Then she 'wrapt him in her green mantle',

And sae her true-love won.

Up then spake the Queen o Fairies,
Out o a bush o broom;
'She that has borrowed young Tamlane
Has gotten a stately groom.'

Up then spake the Queen o Fairies,
Out o a bush o rye;
'She's taen awa the bonniest knight
In a my cumpanie.'

'But had I kend, Tam Lin,' she says,
'What now this night I see,
I wad hae taen out thy twa grey een.
And put in twa een o tree.'

Most of the versions, nearly all from the South of Scotland, finish the ballad here, with the Fairy Queen's recriminations. But two Northern versions break into admiring commendation of the spirited heroine. Child's 39*G* says:

She borrowed her love at mirk midnight,
Bore her young son ere day,
And though ye'd search the warld wide,
Ye'll nae find sic a may.

A probably older version of Greig's (*Last Leaves*, XV), puts it this way:

But wasna she a lady wight,
A lady wight an' keen,
She borrowed her love at mark midnight
An bore her son at neen.

There is a Norse flavour about such frank appreciation of courage and will-power. Aberdeenshire did not go in for swooning female sensibility. Nor did it lift an admonitory finger to warn young ladies from the greenwood, as the Southern versions do. Greig's XV goes straight into the story, in traditional Ballad style.

Lady Margaret sits intil her bower.

Many Ballad heroines open a story thus by sitting in their bowers. In 'Lady Isabel and the Elf-Knight' (Child, 4):

> Fair lady Isabel sits in her bower sewing,
> Aye as the gowans grow gay,
> There she heard an elf-knight blawing his horn,
> The first morning in May.

In 'Hind Etin' (Child, 41):

> Lady Margaret sits in her bower door,
> Sewing at her silken seam;
> She heard a note in Elmond's wood
> And wishd she there had been.
>
> She loot the seam fa frae her side,
> And the needle to her tae,
> And she is on to Elmond's wood
> As fast as she could gae.

Or there is 'The King's Dochter Lady Jean' (Child, 52):

> The King's young dochter was sitting in her window,
> Sewing at her silken seam;
> She lookt out of the bow-window
> And she saw the leaves growing green, my luve,
> And she saw the leaves growing green.
>
> She stuck her needle into her sleeve,
> Her seam down by her tae,
> And she is awa to the merrie green-wood
> To pu the nit and slae.

That is how a Ballad heroine takes to the greenwood, on impulse, dropping her needle and her seam, running fast. Janet, too, has a credible prologue to her adventure with Tam Lin.

> Janet has kilted her green kirtle
> A little aboon her knee,
> And she has broded her yellow hair
> A little aboon her bree,
> And she's awa to Carterhaugh,
> As fast as she can hie.

This should be the first, but is only the third stanza in Child's *A*, being preceded by two admonitory verses:

O, I forbid you, maidens a',
That wear gowd on your hair,
To come or gae by Carterhaugh
For young Tam Lin is there.

There's nane that gaes by Carterhaugh
But they leave him a wad,
Either their rings, or green mantles,
Or else their maidenhead.

It is Robert Burns's communicated version that contains the prefatory admonition, copied later by all the other versions except two from the North. I incline to think that it was due to Burns himself: its tone belongs to the second half of the eighteenth century rather than to earlier times.

To what earlier times, then, does the ballad of Tam Lin belong? It is found only in Scotland, nowhere else. As far back as 1549, in *The Complaynt of Scotland,* mention is made of what may be a ballad of Tam Lin, though it does not sound like the ballad we have today. Among a list of popular tales, songs and dances there is quoted a 'Tale of the zong tamlene and of the bald braband'. If this was a kind of Robin Hood adventure in the greenwood, involving Young Tamlene and a Bold Braband, all trace of it has been lost. The term 'Young Tamlin' certainly occurs in one of our versions, where the heroine is enjoined to keep calling on him by name while the transformations go on. 'Young Thomlin' is also quoted in Forbes's *Aberdeen Cantus* as a refrain in a merry dance:

The pyper's drone was out of tune,
Sing Young Thomlin,
Be merry, be merry, and twise so merrie
With the light of the moon.

If Young Tamlin was a bogey of the greenwood, he was at that time a merry bogey. He must have been well-known as some kind of comic character, for in 1557-1558 there was licensed a ballad (Stationers' Register A, leaf 22) in England of which this is one verse:

Tom a lin and his wife, and his wives mother,
They went over a bridge all three together;
The bridge was broken, and they fell in:
'The Devil go with all!' quoth Tom a lin.

A Scotsman, Mr Halliwell-Phillips, who published in 1849 *Popular Rhymes and Nursery Tales* says: 'An immense variety of songs and catches relating to Tommy Linn are known throughout the country'.

So we have a traditionally gay Tam Lin, associated with mirth and perhaps with seduction in the greenwood, which might account for these admonitory verses. But no hint is given in *The Complaynt of Scotland* or elsewhere that he has any connection with Fairyland or transformation magic, both of which are found independently of him and of each other in various Ballads. In Child's 44 (The Twa Magicians), a Northern Ballad, a coal-black smith, for instance, pursues a proud unwilling lady through eight transformations before getting the better of her, following a well-worn tradition of transformation contests in Europe and in Asia that may derive, it is said, from magical contests between Buddhist and Brahman saints.[1] I suspect that the legend of transformation magic is older than this, older even than Proteus, going back to the time when a priest-king in some tribal emergency managed to substitute a bull or a ram for sacrifice instead of himself, and was credited with having transformed himself into the animal. In the archaic world of feeling such a transformation would be highly credible, indeed necessary, to explain a departure from precedent. The European traditions are more playful than a contest between rival saints would suggest; they all involve an evasive lady and a persistent suitor. The Scottish coal-black smith has a humorous flavour about him, well shown in the recurrent refrain:

O bide, lady, bide,
  And aye he bade her bide;
The rusty smith your leman shall be,
  For a' your muckle pride.

The gay Tam Lin and this playful transformation magic might well have gravitated towards each other, but the ballad we have

[1] Cf. Child, vol. 1, p. 402, footnote

is more like a Hallowe'en hair-raiser than a playful wooing. Some unknown genius knitted the story together as we have it, at some later date than 1549. I have wondered how much of it was in the air when Robert Burns 'communicated' it. The many variations from his original communication were written down later: for all we know he might have knitted it together himself. And yet, as a poet, he would be likely to leave traditional verses untampered with. Much of the material in this ballad, as in the Scottish Ballad world generally, came a good while earlier from France, the great centre of luxury and ceremonial. The Queen of Elfland's silver bells, for instance, reflect occasions like the entry of Louis XI into Paris in 1461, when the horses of his great nobles were ornamented with large silver bells, while the retinue of four-and-twenty ladies that mark Janet's rank as a noblewoman also come from France's fifteenth-century habits. 'Philippe de Ravestein takes the field with four and twenty noblemen . . . all dressed up as shepherds.'[1] The transformation magic, in the guise of a playful wooing, was well known all over France, especially south of the Loire, having apparently come from southern Europe, where it was widespread. One must remember that until the time of Mary, Queen of Scots, Scotland and France were intimately bound together and that French influence then naturally pervaded Lowland Scotland. It is more than likely that gay Tam Lin, the transformation magic, and the existence of Elfland were all 'in the air' as popular pre-Reformation traditions long before Burns was born. The Scottish genius knitted them together into an eerie ballad, which, of course, is not found elsewhere.

The fact that commonplace verses such as those that describe seduction, for instance, or the retinue of a noble lady, have been drained of literal meaning also suggests an old tradition. A retinue of four-and-twenty has become merely a convention, as can be seen in Hind Etin Child, 41*C*), second stanza:

> Four an twenty fair ladies
> Put on this lady's sheen,
> And as mony young gentlemen
> Did lead her ower the green.

[1] J. Huizinga, *The Waning of the Middle Ages*, p. 123

The lady's 'sheen' does not refer to resplendent clothing; it is good Aberdeenshire for 'shoon', shoes.

Janet is a noblewoman of high rank: her father has a castle and attendant knights. In the North she becomes Lady Margaret, a king's daughter. This is also a sign of old tradition, harking back thousands of years to the time when next to the gods kings and noblemen, inspired if not appointed by the gods themselves, were the exemplars for ordinary people in a hierarchical society. The archaic world of feeling seems to be unequivocally hierarchical and preserves, according to precedent, traditional distinctions of rank. I have seen it stated that in such a society nothing seems real to people unless and until it is known to have precedents, and this seems likely. What is novel, what is not enjoined by tradition, cannot be valid at all; it hardly exists; it has to be imposed by a strong personality, a kind of hero-king acting with the authority of the gods, before it can be accepted. The archaic world of feeling recognizes power, and the successes obtained by power, as being godlike, and will not accept anything less. When one considers how fluid and unstable the underworld of imagination is, one can more easily understand that it is strongly drawn towards any display of secure and confident power. It may be that the more imaginative and steeped in archaic feeling people are, the more they are susceptible to totalitarian systems that claim to represent the will of the gods.

In Scotland, certainly, there was no lack of imaginative vitality before the Reformation. The Calvinist Reformers, who were totalitarian on principle and by temperament, recognized the strength of the ancient world of archaic feeling, which had to be dragooned by force into their religious system, and did their rigorous best to extirpate any imaginative expression outside their own prescriptions. The Ballad World was an enemy. As early as 1533, for instance, a proclamation was issued to suppress 'fond books, ballad, rhimes and other lewd treatises'. An attempt was then made to 'godlify' Ballads, by composing new verses for old and well-known tunes. Yet the old Ballads went on surviving until they were written down in the eighteenth and nineteenth centuries, still carrying with them pre-Reformation traditions. Not only did they survive, they went on being composed. Tam Lin must have been composed in its present form at some time after the Reformation. Perhaps the existence of Elfland and Norse demons, in that enclave from which the uncanny Powers emerged on Hallowe'en, preserved for the Scots a back-door escape from the encroaching rigours of a totalitarian religion. In one version of Tam Lin, dated 1769, Tam Lin says:

> O pleasant is the fairy land,
> How happy there to dwell!
> But ay at every seven years end
> We're a' dung down to hell.

According to Calvinism most people, except the few Elect, were due to be 'dung down to hell' anyhow, and the country people in the North-East of Scotland may have preferred to take the risks of fairyland.

Tam Lin himself remains a puzzling figure. A fragment of an old ballad, called Burd Helen and Young Tamlane (Child, 28), has, as Child says, 'no apparent relevance to what is elsewhere handed down concerning Tamlane, or with the story of any other ballad'. Here Tamlane is a heartless seducer who refuses to 'rock' his young son; the last verse says:

> Young Tamlane to the seas he's gane,
> And a' women's curse in his company's gane.

This Young Tamlane seems a greenwood bogey who is not at all merry. Perhaps the fragment (five couplets in all) comes from an earlier, cruder version of his activities.

The older forms of his name, Tom a Lin, Thom o Lin, present Lin as a place-name, and as a place-name it appears in various other Ballads, e.g. The bonny towers of Linne (Young Beichan), The Heir of Linne (Child, 267). Child called it 'a stock ballad-locality'. There is a Loch Linnhe in western Scotland, and a tradition that some clans of supposed Viking descent were known as Lochlannach, people coming from Loch Linn. Yet the Dé Danann gods in Ireland also came from Loch Linn. Was Loch Linn the place where they last paused on their journey westward? Or was Loch Linn a Pictish name, or a Norwegian name, or even a name from Celtic Europe? A blur of ancient meaning obscures the name of Linn which these scraps of information and surmise cannot focus into clarity. The probability is that the figure of Tam

Lin in our ballad has been furbished up from some forgotten legend. Perhaps this was Norse in origin, as the ballad seems Norse in spirit. Tam Lin and Janet were none the worse of their peculiar experiences because they had the strength of spirit, will and courage that belonged to the old Norse world. Janet's anxiety about christening and Tam Lin's assertion that he had been 'ill sained' show an archaic magical cast of feeling belonging to the old gods rather than to Christianity. A later Presbyterian infiltration into the ballad, which makes Janet carry a Bible with her to Miles Cross, embroiders but does not destroy this basic attitude.

9

Story Material: Magic and Family Authority

THE High Magic practised in 'Tam Lin' by the fairies is supplemented in the Ballad world by a more everyday, domestic magic practised by the mothers of families in the exercise of family authority. Like the princess in 'Hind Horn', Ballad mothers have at hand magical skills which are taken for granted by everyone. Magic seems to be a feminine prerogative, and a mother who uses it is never called to account, however ruthless her actions: she has an unquestioned right to control and interfere with the love-affairs of her children. Family Authority here is a law to itself, an absolute authority, exercised by mothers with absolute power.

Possibly the mothers' absolute power, as well as their skill in magic, derives from an older tradition, a climate of belief left in the air by the matriarchal Picts. These Picts, an elusive but authentic aggregate of peoples, were absorbed into the Kingdom of Scotland round about A.D. 843 and later overrun, in the north of Scotland, by the Norse; yet climates of belief have been known to persist for longer than seven or eight hundred years, especially in rural communities, and it is not unlikely that strong elements of Pictish belief went on lingering in Scotland for many generations. At any rate, the mothers who use magic in the Ballads behave like unquestioned matriarchs.

The ballad called 'Willie's Lady' (Child, 6) or 'Simon's Lady' (Greig, III), both titles coming from Aberdeenshire, shows a mother putting spells upon her son's wife, whom she mislikes, to prevent the first child from being born. The pregnant woman sends her mother-in-law an appealing message:

> 'How good a gift to her I'll gie,
> Gin she will let me lichter be.'

An uncompromising answer comes back:

> 'Your lady shall never be lichter
> An' her bower shall never be brichter.
>
> But marry ye yon bonnie may,'

or, as Child's version has it:

> 'But she shall die and turn to clay
> And ye shall wed another may.'

The son vows that he will never wed another may. This deadlock is broken by the kind intervention of the Belly Blind, or Billy Blin':

> Then oot it spak the Billy Blin
> That sat upon the binkie en'.

His advice to the son is to buy 'a loaf of wax' in the market-place, to shape it 'bairn and bairnly-like', with two glass eyes, and then to invite his mother to the christening.

> 'And do you stand a little fore-bye,
> And listen weel what she shall say.'

Presumably it was the custom to hold the infant in one's arms while issuing such an invitation. The matriarch, at any rate, is deceived and in her rage gives away her secrets:

> 'Oh, wha has loosed the nine witch knots
> That was amo that ladie's locks?
>
> 'And wha has taen oot the kaims of care
> That hangs amo that ladie's hair?
>
> 'And wha's taen down the bush o' woodbine
> That hang atween her bower and mine?
>
> 'And wha has killed the master kid
> That ran beneath that ladie's bed?
>
> 'And wha has loosed her left-foot shee,
> And lotten that ladie lichter be?'

It does not take the husband long to do all these things, for his wife's bower and his mother's are clearly next door to each other, in the same house, with a bush of woodbine hanging between them.

Greig's version of the ballad, 'Simon's Lady', provides a different list of magical spells.

> 'Wae worth the han's that brak the ban's
> That I had on his lady's arms:
>
> 'Wae worth the key that opened the lock
> That I had on his lady's bed-stock:
>
> 'Wae worth the knife that killed the ted
> That I'd aneath his lady's bed.'

When these various spells are undone, a 'braw young son' is born, and so the matriarch is slily outwitted. But she is not censured, even although the household has a patriarchal structure as we know, because Willie, we are told in the first verse,

> woo'd a wife and brought her hame

whereas in a matriarchy he would have gone to live in his wife's home.

The magical practices in this ballad are based on sympathetic magic, which must have been in the air not only when it was first composed but during its continued transmission, since there are so many varying spells, apparently all well known. What is in the air, making a climate of belief, is very much alive. It takes more than one wind of change to disperse a climate of belief. There are possibly still people in remote corners of Scotland who believe that a woman is helped in delivering her child by having all knots in the house unloosed and all cupboards or drawers unlocked. One cannot therefore say that this is an old ballad because of its magical contents, although one can surmise that it is fairly old because it is sung in couplets, not in four-line stanzas, in the style of Hind Horn and other early Ballads. Nor can one ascribe a possible date to it because it shows matriarchal elements lingering on in a patriarchal society: to this very day in parts of Scotland there is a strong matriarchal bias in family life. A mother's authority in her family is an ancient and enduring habit. One can only note that magic fades out of later Ballads, so that mothers have recourse to other means when they want to domineer over their children.

Meanwhile, in early Ballads, mothers have no lack of magical skills at their disposal. A bride in the Ballad world cannot hope to escape the magical inquisition of her mother-in-law, since in a patriarchal society, where children inherit name and property from their fathers, bastardy becomes a stigma and a bride's virginity an essential. The older woman would set out a golden chair, for instance, in which only a virgin could sit at ease for any length of time. She would provide enchanted pillows and sheets which could tell the bridegroom whether the partner in his bed were a maid or not. If she were not, the penalty could be brutal.

> 'Seven King's daughters has our king wedded,
> An seven King's daughters has our King bedded,'

confides the helpful page in 'Gil Brenton' (Child, 5), as he is escorting the King's eighth bride to her new home,

> 'But he's cutted the paps frae their breast-bane
> An sent them mourning hame again.'

After this warning the page goes on to advise the new bride to sit quiet all day in the golden chair, no matter how she feels, and if she be not a maid, as her tears seem to betray, that she should bribe one of her bower-women to take her place in the King's bed. This she does. The enchanted bed-clothes tell the bridegroom:

> 'It's nae a maid that you ha' wedded,
> But it's a maid that you ha' bedded.
> . . . . .
> 'Your lady's in her bigly bowr
> An for you she drees mony sharp showr.'

(I think that 'showr', here, must be related to the German 'Schauer', a shudder; it cannot mean 'rain'.)

Another variant says:

> 'But your bonnie bride is in her bower
> Dreeing the mother's trying hour.'

The disgruntled bridegroom leaps out of bed and rushes to his mother:

> 'I am the most unhappy man
> That ever was in christened lan'.
>
> 'I woo'd a maiden meek an' mild,
> And I've marryed a woman great wi' child.'

The strength of the 'auld queen' is emphasized when she is described battering her way into her new daughter's bower.

> The auld queen, she was stark an' strang;
> She gard the door flee off the ban.
>
> The auld queen, she was stark an' steer;
> She gard the door lye i the fleer.

Her first question is sharp and authoriattive:

> 'O is your bairn to laird or loon?
> Or is it to your father's groom?'

The bride tells a familiar story, how she met with a stranger in the greenwood who appeared to be 'some Kingis son' and gave her tokens before leaving her. The old queen, on hearing what these tokens are, ransacks the young woman's coffer to find them and recognizes them as her son's. Being a just matriarch, she now comforts her daughter-in-law and goes off to 'parley' with her son, so that there is a happy ending. Yet the strongest impression made by the ballad is that of the mother's unquestioned power.

A mother's curse is a potent spell. In a ballad called 'The Mother's Malison' (Child, 216, and Greig, LXVII) a son who loves the wrong girl is so unmanned by his mother's curse that he lets himself drown in a river,

> His brother stood upon the bank,
> Says 'Fye, man, will ye droon?
> O turn ye to your high horse head
> An' learn how to soom.'
>
> 'How can I turn to my high horse head
> An' learn how to soom?
> For I've got my mother's malison,
> And it's here that I maun droon.'

In a fit of passion a mother may not only curse her son but use sleight-of-hand to poison him, as happens to Prince Robert (Child, 87), because he has married the wrong wife and, perhaps even worse, put forward this plea:

> 'It is the fashion in oor countrie, mither,
> I dinna ken what it is here,
> To like your wife better than your mither . . .'

Yet the Ballads shrink from ascribing to mothers the most spectacular magic of all, shape-shifting, which is always performed by a step-mother or a witch outside the family. Step-mothers are bad women. Anyone 'witched to a ghastly shape' owes it to some 'stepdame's skill' ('King Henry', Child, 32). A commonplace verse about step-mothers begins several grisly songs; in 'Kemp Owyne', for instance (Child, 34), where a step-daughter is thrown into the sea in the shape of a 'savage beast', the first stanza runs:

> Her mother died when she was young,
> Which gave her cause to make great moan;
> Her father married the warst woman
> That ever lived in Christendom.

The ballad about another step-mother who changes her step-son and step-daughter into 'The Laily Worm and the Machrel of the Sea' (Child, 36) has a similar introduction:

> 'I was but seven years auld
> When my mither she did die;
> My father married the ae warst woman
> The warld did ever see.'

This laying of odium on step-mothers may mask some rebellion against the power of mother-figures, a rebellion which does not yet dare come into the open. But in any case transformation magic goes beyond the scope of domestic spells; it belongs to the supernatural enclave where fairies and water-goddesses belong, to which a step-mother who is a witch is more likely to have recourse than a mother. A mother may be cruel; she may even poison her offspring; but she is less ready than a step-mother to change their human shape, the shape in which she has borne them.

Domestic magic includes, as a matter of course, talking birds who not only speak but carry letters and other messages, like the 'Gay Goshawk' (Child, 96).

> 'O well's me o my gay goss-hawk
> That he can speak and flee;
> He'll carry a letter to my love,
> Bring anither back to me.'

The alleged Age of Reason, the eighteenth century, as Child notes, changed this goshawk into a parrot, when facts, so-called, were gaining more prestige than imagination did. (I can still remember from my young days the reverence with which one Scotsman used to say to another: 'Man, is that a fac'?') Yet a continuous and persistent climate of belief brought into a Jacobite song, during the eighteenth century itself, a talking bird which was no parrot, a wee bird the burden of whose song was: 'Waes me for Prince Charlie', a bird that came straight out of the Ballad world, as also did Prince Charlie, that 'Kingis son'.

Climates of belief, persistent though they are, can let traditions fade, sometimes until only tenuous traces are left. The Billie Blin', for instance, the Norse household demon also called the Belly Blind, becomes 'an auld belly-blind man' in the Ballad 'The Knight and Shepherd's Daughter' (Child, 110, Version *D*), although he performs the same kind of function as the original figure, that is to say: intervening kindly to resolve a problem. The magical golden chair of the matriarchs, still doing its fell work in Greig, IX, a version of Leesome Brand (Child, 15):

> 'The morn is the day,' she said,
> 'I in my father's court maun stan',
> An I'll be set in a chair o gowd,
> To see gin I be maid or nane.'

has lost its significance in two versions of Lady Maisry (Child, 65) which tell us:

> An her mither sits in her gowden chair
> To see her dochter burn.

The golden chair has become merely a mother's chair of state, retaining only a vague ceremonial connection with her. The same sense of forgotten significance haunts that implement of domestic magic, the comb, which seems to be more than merely a 'weaving comb'. In 'Willie's Lady', nine witch knots in her hair and 'kaims of care' are among the magic spells that bind the pregnant wife; the combs which in any rational interpretation should have been able to untangle the witch knots are adding a sinister power of their own, left unexplained. Whatever that power may be, it brings combs into so many Ballads that one begins to wonder why they are so frequent. A simple use of combs as the equivalent of the maiden's wreath or green chaplet in European tradition needs no accounting for, except for the insistence on their being golden combs. Fair Annie (Child, 62), a heart-broken concubine making ready to welcome her lover's bride, sets

> A kaim o gowd upon her hair
> As maiden she had been.

The 'reid gowd' which Hind Horn's princess tears from her hair is presumably her maiden comb or combs. The admonitory verse tacked on to Tam Lin:

> 'O, I forbid you, maidens a'
> That wear gowd on your hair,'

refers clearly to this alliance between golden combs and maidens. Yet 'golden' and 'silver' were adjectives used in the Ballad world to convey magical significance. Otherwise, if one is to descend to realism, there could not have been golden combs enough in Scotland to deck all the maidens, one would think. These maiden combs of gold suggest forgotten magic. And what is to be made of the 'red river' comb in 'The Lass of Roch Royal' (Child, 76, version *A*) or the 'tabean brirben kame' in version *B* of the same ballad? These ambiguous combs are rationalized, in a later rendering, into a 'new-made silver kaim', yet in other renderings they remain ambiguous as ever although turned into a 'brown berry' comb or 'a fine rispen kame'. In another version there is a 'haw bayberry' comb, which, it has been suggested, might be a High Barbary comb.

There is a blur of forgotten meaning around these combs, yet they keep on recurring. Combing hair is a service rendered to each other by various Ballad sweethearts; this may strike one as odd but hardly important. The oddness increases, however, in Child, 35, where the ugly witch Allison Gross, wishing to overmaster her victim, takes his head on her knee and combs his hair. According to Child, also,[1] in some German and Scandinavian Ballads the maiden victim offers to 'red' or comb the villain's hair, in a last attempt to get him into her power. A comb begins to look like a sinister weapon. Perhaps Delilah used one on

[1] Child, vol. I, p. 25, footnote

Samson before reaching for the shears. None the less, in this Aberdeenshire ballad about Allison Gross, after she has changed her victim into 'an ugly worm', that is to say, a serpent, 'toddling' around a tree, he goes on to relate:

> 'An ay, on ilka Saturdays nicht,
> My sister Maisry came to me,
>
> 'Wi silver bason an silver kemb
> To kemb my heady upon her knee.'

The combing here, which seems superfluous for a serpent, is presented as a sign of affection, perhaps some kind of symbolic ritual. In the very next Child Ballad (36), this ritual combing again appears, after the wicked step-mother has changed a brother and sister into the Laily Worm and the Machrel of the Sea.

> 'For she has made me the laily worm
> That lies at the fit o the tree,
> And my sister Masery she's made
> The machrel of the sea.
> An every Saturday at noon
> The machrel comes to me,
> An she takes my laily head
> An lays it on her knee,
> She kaims it wi a siller kaim
> An washes't in the sea.'

That silver comb is brought by a maiden shaped like a fish, a maiden from the sea. One begins to remember that a mermaid, by convention, always has a comb and a glass in her hand. Sister Maisry's silver bason could have functioned as a hand-glass if it were filled with clear water. What is the significance of the sea-maiden, the comb, and, possibly, the glass?

An unlooked-for answer comes to this question, although the answer itself is baffling. In Aberdeenshire (and these two Ballads, Child 35 and 36, come from Aberdeenshire) there is, in Garioch, a Pictish stone still known as the Maiden Stone; on it there is sculptured a large serpent, a hand-glass and a comb. Pictish stones, with various symbols upon them, are mainly found through the eastern half of Scotland from the Firth of Forth, (beside the Pentland, or Pictland Hills) northwards as far as Shetland. I shall not comment upon the other symbols to be found on them, but shall restrict myself to the conjunctions of comb and hand-glass, which seem to have a feminine significance. On a stone found at Hilton of Cadboll a comb and a glass are set beneath a female figure (a goddess or a queen?) riding her horse ahead of some mounted warriors who all have flowing long hair. Another from Glamis has a fish on it as well as the serpent, hand-glass and comb, indicating a connection with fresh water or the sea. One from Dunnichen has a hand-glass and comb beside other symbols; one from St Vigeans, near Arbroath, has a comb and hand-glass beside a crescent. From Aberlemno comes a stone with an all-male hunting scene on it, and here there is neither comb nor hand-glass, an omission that seems to confirm their feminine connotation. One can guess therefore that the Maiden Stone was raised in honour of a sea or water-goddess. I suggest that a story about a serpent and a fish-maiden, deriving from Pictish times, may have been already in the air, accounting for the serpent, the comb and the glass, but the ballad about the Laidly Worm could have been made by someone in the later Scottish tradition, some imaginative passer-by who was aware of the story, had studied the Maiden Stone and knew about wicked step-mothers.

This answer does not explain the magical significance of the comb and the glass: it merely confirms that they had a magical significance, and that the Ballads were right in making maidens' combs of magical gold. No definite clue is offered, either, by the curious fact that in the tenth century, while Picts must have been still very much in the air, one of the rubrics of the service for the ordination of a Christian bishop has the direction: 'Deinde ministretur ei aqua ad manus et pecten ad caput.' 'Then let there be ministered to him water for the hands and a comb for the head.' Water in a round dish would make a primitive mirror, like Maisry's. What ritual significance from Pictish worship did the comb and the basin of water commemorate? A ceremonial comb was also required at the celebration of a bishop's mass. The comb of St Cuthbert was important enough to be buried with him and is still preserved in Durham Cathedral. Queen Theodolinda's comb (A.D. 590) is kept in the Basilica of St John at

Monza. In A.D. 625 Pope Boniface sent with his blessing a mirror of silver and a comb of ivory to Ethelburga, wife of Edwin, King of Northumbria. These important combs, with or without a hand-glass, could have been taken over from the Pictish climate of belief; they still survive in our mermaid legends; they remain baffling symbols.

One cannot go beyond surmise in accounting for their importance in the Ballads. Often enough they only appear because a girl is asking this kind of question:

> 'Wha will kaim my yellow hair
> Wi the new-made silver kaim,
> (or the tabean brirben kaim)
> And wha will father my young son
> Till Love Gregory comes hame?

Combing hair may have been a ritual of purification before a ceremony, before sacrifice, for instance, before dedicating oneself to die, as the Spartans did at Thermopylae when they combed their long hair before fighting to the death. The long-haired Pictish warriors, like the Homeric Achaeans, may have combed their hair ritually before giving battle. In the ballad 'Child Maurice' (Child, 83) two of the versions make him comb his 'yellow hair' before being killed. Yet the Ballad-makers may have known little more about combs than we do, except that they were perhaps aware of combs having had traditional magic powers.

That the comb and hand-glass were merely toilet instruments in the hands of a water-goddess I do not accept. If they had ministered only to a goddess's vanity the tenth-century bishops would not have included them in ordination ceremonies. Nor would Psellus have been so enraged against them. When he was anathematizing the mysteries of Eleusis he stigmatized the comb as an ultimate obscenity in these rites; he seems to have thought that a comb was a symbol for 'the privities of a woman'. At least he confirms that combs have had important feminine associations.

The mermaid with 'a comb and a glass in her hand' who still lingers in the air today bears witness to the persistence of climates of belief long after their component elements have ceased to be understood. Her survival supports my suggestion that one finds in the Ballads traces of a matriarchal climate inherited, like her comb and her hand-glass, from the Picts, long after the infiltration of patriarchal habits and values. I do not think that I have put the magic-making mothers in a false light by presenting them as matriarchal figures.

The most impressive matriarch of them all is the Wife of Usher's Well. She is the most impressive because she retains some of the attributes of a priestess, which all the others have lost. She exerts her magical powers not to perpetrate domestic tyrannies but to raise her three sons from the dead. In her case family authority is still related to the powers that run the universe, and reaches up to the gods, or the Fates, as it also derives from them. She challenges not rebellious children but Death itself. Elsewhere in the Ballads family authority has receded from the skies and become a closed circuit, related to daily life but not to the cosmos. One belongs to the Family, not to the gods. 'The Wife of Usher's Well' seems a survival from an earlier time before the family ceiling came so far down.

The first verse of her ballad (Child, 79) begins the story with a minimum of description.

> There lived a wife at Usher's Well,
> And a wealthy wife was she;
> She had three stout and stalwart sons
> And sent them to the sea.

Perhaps I should mention that the word 'wife' in North-east Scotland still means simply 'woman'. Any woman can be called a wife, or more endearingly a wifie, whether she is married or not. If the wife of Usher's Well had a husband, or if she were a widow, is not told in the ballad. The father of the family has no part to play in the story and so is left out.

That she lived at Usher's Well may have had some significance, since wells often belong to water-goddesses or spirits. The mention of the Well may be a surviving trace of past priestess functions. It adds only a touch to the religious background of the Wife, and for the ballad is relatively unimportant, although tradition includes it.

The three sons have now left home and the next stanza, instead of short-cutting the story by saying: 'After a week she heard that her sons had sailed', follows Ballad convention in taking the listeners right through the suspense of that week:

They hadna been a week from her,
A week but barely ane,
When word came to the carline wife
That her three sons were gane.

From this point more suspense and tension is built up:

They hadna been a week from her,
A week but barely three,
When word came to the carline wife
That her sons she'd never see.

Her three sons are drowned. She wastes no time in lamentation. A woman whose magic can perturb the sea, she announces at once that she means to draw her dead sons from the Otherworld by the passion of her maternal will.

'I wish the wind may never cease,
Nor fashes in the flood,
Till my three sons come hame to me
In earthly flesh and blood.'

The ballad makes no comment on this announcement; there is no hint of surprise or doubt. What follows comes inevitably.

It fell about the Martinmas,
When nights are long and mirk,
The carline wife's three sons came hame,
And their hats were o the birk.

It neither grew in syke nor ditch
Nor yet in ony sheugh;
But at the gates o Paradise
That birk grew fair eneugh.

The homely detail about the birch-bark hats is all that is needed to convey the Otherworldly nature of the three apparitions, for birch was one of the sacred trees in pre-Christian lore. But the Wife of Usher's Well ignores the hats and stirs up a brisk coming and going in the house: she is not going to relax her will-power now.

> 'Blow up the fire, my maidens,
> Bring water from the well;
> For a' my house shall feast this night
> Since my three sons are well.'
>
> And she has made to them a bed,
> She's made it large and wide,
> And she's taen her mantle her about,
> Sat down at the bed-side.

There is tenderness in that verse. It is a tender as well as a grim figure that sits cloaked beside the bed, willing her sons to stay where they are, since she is going to conquer Death if she can.

Up to this point, the Wife dominates the ballad. She is not described at all; what she says and does is given, but not what she looks like. She is a concentrated force, an embodiment of passionate motherhood rather than a recognizable neighbour. But the 'feel' of her is strongly conveyed; with great economy of means and language listeners are made aware of her forcefulness. One is told that she is a 'wealthy' wife, the simplest way of making clear that she is a woman of power. She has her messengers; word comes to her promptly about her sons—promptly for that time and place. The declaration of her intentions is couched in simple but intense language, made more impressive by spontaneous alliteration:

> 'I wish the wind may never cease
> Nor fashes in the flood,
> Till my three sons come hame to me
> In earthly flesh and blood.'

This is a ceremonial utterance, not a hysterical cry. Such is her power that no one is surprised when her sons do come home, all three of them. She commands her household with accustomed vigour. She tucks her grown children into their bed and sits watchful beside it. And just here, where her powers are most concentrated, she fades out of the ballad altogether. The rest of the story concerns her sons.

I think that she fades out of the ballad because at this point the failure of her bold challenge to Death begins.

Up then crew the red, red cock
And up and crew the gray;
The eldest to the youngest said,
' 'Tis time we were away.'

The cock he hadna crawd but once
And clappd his wings at a',
When the youngest to the eldest said,
'Brother, we must awa'.'

The Wife's passionate force has risen to the sky and has been beaten back. The ballad conveys that rising passion to the listeners and now conveys its failure. No comment is made on the Wife's failure, no surprise is expressed; the situation is accepted in another ceremonially alliterative stanza, uttered by the youngest son:

'The cock doth craw, the day doth daw,
The channerin worm doth chide;
Gin we be mist out o our place,
A sair pain we maun bide.'

The long-drawn vowels 'sair pain' give a sense of inevitable doom. They also suggest Purgatory, yet it is a limbo felt but not described, just as the Wife herself is felt as a passionate force but not described. Despite the birch-bark hats from the gates of Paradise, despite the hint of Purgatory, this is not a Christian ballad. The Wife of Usher's Well belongs to the old heroic world that defies the gods to the limit of human effort and defies them in vain.

One comes now to an interesting difference between Child's two versions of this ballad. In the *A* version the next stanza, the last one, brings the ballad down again to the level of daily life, in the usual manner.

'Fare ye well, my mother dear,
Fareweel to barn and byre,
And fare ye weel, the bonny lass
That kindles my mother's fire.'

But the *B* version, before falling to a close, interpolates a stanza of compassionate anxiety for the mother. One brother says:

> 'Lie still, lie still a little wee while,
> Lie still but if we may;
> For gin my mother miss us away
> She'll gae mad or it be day.'

This sentiment seems out of place in a matriarchal Ballad. When fathers and brothers begin to represent family authority in the Ballads with all-too-ready swords, there is an occasional hint that some woman may 'go brain', go out of her mind, because of the killings, but that occurs only in later Ballads. The early tragic Ballads do not at all interest themselves in the men or women who happen to be left alive at the end of the story. One remembers the ballad of Lord Donald: what does the mother there feel about her son's death? We do not know. Does she die heart-broken or does the Wife of Usher's Well die heart-broken, as she might do in a Yugoslav epic? We are not told. Once the action is completed, or once the wave of passion is spent, as in the Wife of Usher's Well, there is no interest in personalities. Indeed, the women in these ballads have no features, not even the Wife of Usher's Well. She is not a recognizable 'individual'. She is not looked at, she is not described for the eye of an onlooker, she is not 'seen' as a visibly separate human being. None of the matriarchs is 'seen' in this way. These ballads are composed for the ear, not for the eye. The protagonists in them are 'felt' as embodied forces, pulling this way or that, intersecting points in a network of linked relationships, driven by passion to their destiny. By comparison with the invisible but strongly felt network that links them and the Fate that controls them their personalities do not matter. It is in this sense that these ballads are profoundly pagan.

Yet they cannot be called impersonal. They present rather a different kind of awareness of people, unlike our awareness which is much conditioned by the eye and so marks, I think, a more developed state of consciousness. The difference between our awareness and theirs perhaps resembles the difference between daylight photography and infra-red photography, or between a map of the sky as seen by an ordinary telescope and that seen by radio astronomers. The Ballad-makers knew nothing about the invisible and inaudible radiations in the cosmos that we now begin to discover, but they were aware, because they felt their force, of radiations received and transmitted between people. In short, they felt that people 'belonged' and that what they belonged to, Fate or the Family, was an arbitrary Power, stronger than they were.

I am therefore inclined to think that this compassionate stanza introduced before the close of 'The Wife of Usher's Well' is an interpolation from a more self-conscious age, one more concerned with personalities, so that Child's *B* version is later than his *A*.

The closing verses provided by the two renderings, *A* and *B*, are of further interest. The first one, already quoted, makes a gentle farewell to daily life. The second version performs the same function although it is entirely different:

> O it's they've taen up their mother's mantel
> An they've hangd it on the pin:
> 'O lang may ye hing, my mother's mantel,
> Or ye hap us again.'

(In this *B* version the mother has 'happed' her sons in her mantle.)

Either stanza lets the feeling in the ballad sink to a quiet, domestic close. Clearly the raising or lowering of tension in this ballad matters more than the particular form in which the flow of feeling is embodied, just as the force of passionate feeling in the story matters more than the particular person in whom it is embodied. The singer apparently keeps in mind the direction the flow of feeling should take; provided he makes it rise or fall in the appropriate places, he is free to improvise. The main outline of the story is given him; that is traditional, not to be changed, and what he improvises must not contradict it. One might say that he is given a geographically determined landscape, with its configuration of heights and valleys. Yet as he guides the flow of feeling, he can invent at will various features on the way, though he cannot change the lie of the land, and in the last verse he must bring the listeners down to the level. Once on the level, the ballad stops, like a river that has reached the sea. If this is not art, I do not know what is.

I shall now leave the magic-using matriarchs and consider the Ballads in which Family Authority is enforced by other means.

10

Family Authority: Violence, Murder, and True Love

FAMILY authority, as reflected in early Scottish Ballads, is a law to itself, a closed system which cuts off outsiders ruthlessly. To kill someone outside the family is no murder: to kill an outsider for the sake of the family is a virtue. But to kill someone inside the family, without authorization by the family code of honour, is a fearful crime, unless it is a matriarch who does the killing. This contrast between human sensibilities inside and outside the family is strikingly brought out in a curious little ballad, 'Babylon, or The Bonnie Banks o Fordie' (Child, 14), which resembles a good many Scandinavian Ballads. It is shorter than any of the Scandinavian versions, omitting the domestic details and dialogues which they provide, as well as their many references to church services, but its subject-matter is the same: the unwitting slaying, by some member of the family, of sons or sisters, unrecognized because of long absence, and the unbearable sense of guilt that overwhelms the killer when the family relationship is discovered.

'Babylon' follows the earlier Ballad pattern of two-line instead of four-line stanzas, with refrains sandwiched between:

> There were three ladies lived in a bower,
> *Eh vow bonnie*
> And they went out to pull a flower
> *On the bonnie banks o Fordie.*

An Aberdeenshire variant (Greig, VIII) has a slightly different refrain:

> Will ye be a rank robber's wife,
> *Aiken ay so bonnie, O,*
> Or will ye die by my pen-knife?
> *On the bonnie banks o Airdrie, O.*

These refrains, as one can hear, lilt along light-heartedly although this is a murderous ballad. The three sisters—merely picking flowers, not on their way to mass like their Scandinavian counterparts—meet an outlaw, a 'banisht man', who seizes them one by one and asks the above question. The first sister refuses him, and so he kills her with his pen-knife. The ballad puts it like this:

> He's killed this may and he's laid her by,
> For to bear the red rose company.

A pretty sentiment, a touch of aestheticism—a conscious repetition, one would swear, of the flower-picking motif in the first verse. The second sister gets the same treatment; she, too, refuses and is killed in her turn 'to bear the red rose company'. The third sister refuses the outlaw with more spirit, telling him that she has a banished brother in the wood who will kill him should he kill her. He asks her brother's name.

> 'My brother's name is Baby Lon.'
> 'O sister, sister, what have I done?'

Remorse and guilt overwhelm him at once.

> He's taken out his wee pen-knife
> And he's twyned himself o his ain sweet life.

Two murders and a suicide in eighteen couplets: the story could not be more compressed. It reaches its climax in a terse, business-like manner; all feeling is squeezed out of it except the spirited retort of the youngest sister and the passionate sense of guilt that invades the killer. The family bond is apparently so strong that for a man who has unwittingly killed two of his sisters nothing remains but to commit suicide on the spot. The cold-blooded detachment with which the murder of the girls is related must be deliberate, a dramatic contrast to the horror-stricken guilt that follows.

The compression, the detachment, the conscious artistry, all point to a long-lived ballad that has been worked over and then worn down, as it were, to the nub. But all the more saliently does the nub stand out: the overwhelming force of family authority. This is taken for granted, and must have provided a never-failing thrill of fear. 'Babylon', in fact, is a thriller, of the kind that half-grown girls, say, would appreciate, the lack of humanitarian feeling in the murder couplets being unlikely to trouble them. From my own recollection of singing games, I am prepared to believe that this compressed version with its lilting refrains served as a singing game for young people. A line has gone a-missing, too, so that the rhyme sequence is somewhat dislocated, and the loss of a line or two is compatible with adolescent performances.

Yet the lack of humanitarian feeling does not happen by chance, nor is it entirely accounted for by the sense of dramatic contrast. One cannot avoid the conclusion that family solidarity extends no feeling of brotherhood towards human beings outside the family, that respect for the lives of one's kin is a code of etiquette rather than a moral code. The situation in this ballad is formalized, but what it formalizes, the difference between killing an outsider and killing one's sister, reflects a genuine awe before family authority and a genuine lack of concern for human life beyond the family network.

Half-grown girls playing this ballad as a game would be just the members of a family to feel the full weight of family authority, which, in the Ballads following on the matriarchal group, is generally wielded by fathers, husbands and brothers at the expense of wives, daughters, and sisters—daughters and sisters in especial being centrifugal elements in a patriarchal family, liable to elope with any suitor they fancy. The usual Ballad procedure, if a girl elopes, is for the father, backed by a posse of anonymous brothers—the girl's 'seven bold brothers'—to mount horse and away after the errant couple, with the express intention of killing the man and bringing the girl back. This convention gives rise to much sword-play and provides a theme for many Ballads. The girl's lover is always the hero and performs doughty feats. In one of these fighting Ballads, 'Earl Brand' (Child, 7), also called 'The Douglas Tragedy' (Greig, IV), the father's importance is stressed by the heroine herself, Lady Margaret Douglas:

> Sometimes she gaed, sometimes she stood,
> But never dropt a tear
> Until she saw her brethren all slain
> And her father who loved her so dear.

'Hold thy hand, sweet William,' she says,
'Thy blows are wondrous sore;
Sweethearts I may have many a one,
But a father I'll never have more.'

O she's taken her napkin frae her pocket,
Was made o the holland fine,
And ay as she dichted her father's bloody wounds
They sprang as red as the wine.

As Child remarks, in his introduction to 'The Bent sae Brown' (71), 'the killing of a certain number of brothers is not regarded as a very serious matter by the heroine', and the contrast here between the lady's tearless unconcern for her slain brothers and the grief she feels for her father is striking. It is also psychologically sound. Passion for her sweetheart may have, for a while, wiped out all concern for her family—the greatest danger to family authority lay precisely here, in the power of passionate 'true love', which could sweep a sister and daughter beyond family feelings—but when she sees her father bleeding a revulsion sets in, since a girl is usually drawn to her father, and natural grief overcomes her. As a result, when her sweetheart dies of his wounds, she also dies, we are told, of grief.

Yet on these punitive expeditions the posse of brothers represented the executive arm of the Family much oftener than did the father himself. In 'Willie o Douglas Dale' (Child, 101) the heroine says:

'But an my father get word of this,
He'll never drink again;
An gin my mother get word of this,
In her ain bowr she'll go brain;
An gin my bold brothers get word o this,
I fear, Willy, you'll be slain.'

The father comes first in this family catalogue, but it is the brothers who are lethal. Throughout the Ballad world, brothers loom large as a menace to their sisters. In a society where men are brought up to wear and use edged weapons, brothers may well be dangerous, but even so, lethal brothers are more frequent in the Ballads than one expects: they have a sinister aura. A clue to this peculiar characteristic is provided in 'The Cruel Brother' (Child,

11), an early ballad in couplets with light-hearted refrains between the lines, as in 'Babylon', and, like 'Babylon', giving the impression of a singing and dancing game.

> There was three ladies playd at the ba,
> *With a hey ho and a lillie gay.*
> There cam a knight and played oer them a,
> *As the primrose spreads so sweetly.*

The youngest of the three daughters, as usual, is the chosen one; she becomes the knight's bride, stipulating only that he must get the consent of her kin.

> 'Ye may ga ask my father, the king,
> Sae maun ye ask my mither, the queen.
>
> 'Sae maun ye ask my sister Anne:
> And dinna forget my brither John.'

He asked them all, except her brother John, whom he forgot.

> Her mother dear led her thro the closs,
> And her brother John set her on her horse.
>
> She leand her oer the saddle-bow
> To give him a kiss ere she did go.
>
> He has taen a knife, baith lang and sharp,
> And stabbd that bonny bride to the heart.

Or, as another version says:

> She louted down to gie a kiss,
> *With a hey and a lilly gay.*
> He stuck his penknife in her hass.[1]
> *And the rose it smells so sweetly.*

The only motive for brother John's cruelty, as the ballad conveys, is that his consent was not asked to the wedding. In the introduction to this Ballad, Child says (I, p. 142): 'Dr Prior remarks that the offence given by not asking a brother's assent to his sister's marriage, was in Ballad times regarded as unpardonable.' The same motive is found in Scandinavian Ballads. Why should it be so especially a brother's concern whom his sister marries? Again the answer comes down from matriarchal times, when a man's heir was not his own son, but his sister's son. (The

[1] Hass (cf. German *Hals*) is a Scottish term for the windpipe

term 'sister's son' recurs in various Ballads and carries with it a sense of special intimacy, signifying an uncommonly close relationship.) In a matriarchy it was therefore a matter of deep personal concern to a brother what man his sister chose as a father for his heir, and his consent to her marriage might well have been obligatory. Long after the custom had died out the cloud of feeling surrounding it seems to have persisted 'in the air'. In the Ballad world, where feeling is predominant, it survives as a sense that a brother is important when a sister thinks of marrying, that a sister's son is somehow very important to a man, and that these feelings, vague and unaccountable, become dangerous if ignored.

Yet the brother has committed here a crime against the Family, and so, in the usual Family Testament made by the dying victim, his legacy is

'The gallows-tree to hang him on.'

It may be worth noting that there is no Scottish Ballad entitled 'The Cruel Father'. There is a Cruel Mother (Child, 20) and a Cruel Sister (Scott's *Minstrelsy*, II, 143) but the Father escapes calumny altogether. In Continental Ballads he plays a more dominant role, striking off heads and burning down cloisters, but in Scottish Ballads he is more usually only a figure in the family pattern; violent action is reserved for brothers or husbands.

Another complication in the brother-sister relationship is incest between them, a canker, as it were, in the heart of the family. There are two kinds of incest Ballad in Scotland: the earlier styles in couplets with refrains, which are fragments of a brooding cloud of incest themes that stretched from Iceland to Finland, containing various elements which get broken up into separate Ballads in Scotland: the later style in four-line stanzas, dealing with incest in a more matter-of-fact way, but all ending, like the first series, in death, by suicide, murder, or in childbirth. The earlier Ballads are the more haunting, and their refrains, far from being light-hearted, are muted and sorrowful.

It is talked the world all over
The brume blooms bonnie and says it is fair
That the King's dochter gaes wi child to her brither,
And we'll never gang down to the brume onie mair.

('Sheath and Knife', Child, 16)

The best of them, as I think, is the Ballad recently discovered among papers in Panmure House, Angus, by Mrs Helena Mcnnie Shire, a hitherto unknown version of 'Leesome Brand' (Child, 15, Greig, IX), written down by the middle of the seventeenth century. It contains most of the general Scandinavian elements combined in one version, instead of being broken up into two or three Ballads, and its refrains are remarkable.

> Ther was a sister and a brother
> *the sun gois to under the wood*
> who most intirelie loved othir
> *god give we had nevir beine sib.*

These sorrowful refrains reach a deep level of personal feeling not found in Scottish Ballads except in the later self-conscious romantic lyrics. Refrains of the light-hearted flowery kind suggest high-spirited movement and singing-games; they are a framework which keep horrid murders at a playful distance; but the muted refrains of the incest Ballads bring the tragedies of the narrative closer home instead of distancing them, the guilt of incest being too terrible to be played with. The refrains in the incest Ballads survive, I think, as a habit, after the style of the singing games, yet the mournful tone which they set as an emotional framework precludes high-spirited movement: they may be a pointer to the fact that refrains are on the way out, as personal emotion is on the way in. The refrains in Mrs Shire's ballad are those of a poet communing with himself in profound sympathy with the doomed characters in his story, rather than the expression of a collective mood.

Yet this ballad with the new kind of refrains, being in essence no new Ballad, has many old Ballad conventions: commonplace phrases like a steed 'both wight and able', on which the heroine is to flee from her father's court: stereotyped questions from her lover when she begins to groan in labour:

> 'Is ther water into your shoes
> Or comes the wind into your gloves?'

and the conventional romantic ending:

the on was layid in Marie Kirk
othir in Marie Queire
out throch the on ther greu a birke
and out throch hir a breir.

It is likely, therefore, that the lady's reference to another brother, whom she did not love, also reflects a stereotyped convention. She urges flight because, she says, the rumour of her condition

'wil go from on to uthir
until it come to Jhon my brother.

'and Jhon my brothir is most il
he wil hus both burne on a hil.'

Brother John, the Cruel Brother, is 'in the air', part of a climate of belief, and comes naturally to the Balladist's mind.

A chronicle Ballad composed in the seventeenth century, at a somewhat later date than the writing down of the Panmure House ballad, brings out this prejudice against brothers very clearly; it brings out also the actual brutality of Family Authority. By the eighteenth century, especially in France (to judge from Marivaux), there was a belief that only people of position and rank in Society had to contend with Family obstacles to romance: peasants, it was argued, could couple freely, in a kind of pastoral idyll. The kind of thing that really happened in the North-East of Scotland can be gathered from this ballad, which is set in Aberdeenshire and has been—maybe still is—popular there. Greig's version is called 'Tifty's Annie', although Child gives it the name of Annie's sweetheart, 'Andrew Lammie' (Child, 233; Greig, LXXVII). I am using Greig's version. Annie, or Agnes Smith, died in 1673 and was buried in Fyvie churchyard. Tifty was her father who, according to custom, was referred to by the name of his holding, the Mill of Tifty, instead of by his own name, Smith.

Tifty's Annie was a beautiful girl. She fell in love with Andrew Lammie, a trumpeter in the retinue of Lord Fyvie, and he fell in love with her. But her father's ambition for her would not allow a menial trumpeter as a son-in-law.

He'll not have it said that she should wed
The trumpeter of Fyvie.

Andrew Lammie used to blow his trumpet from 'the high house-top of Fyvie' so that Annie could hear it at Tifty; whenever this happened

> Her father locked the door at nicht,
> Laid up the keys fu canny;
> An when he heard the trumpet sound,
> Said 'Your coo is lowing, Annie'.

Mockery of this kind was not all she had to suffer:

> Her father struck her wondrous sore,
> As also did her mother,
> Her sisters also did her scorn
> But woe be to her brother.
>
> Her brother struck her wondrous sore
> Wi cruel strokes an many;
> He broke her back at the ha' door
> For liking Andrew Lammie.

And so she died. But the countryside made a ballad about her and she was not forgotten. The ballad itself is garrulous, sentimental and in some versions tricked out with much eighteenth-century artifice, yet through it all shines an image of constant true love, ill requited by a cruel family and a most cruel brother. Chronicle Ballads, as I have already indicated, stick to the truth of feeling rather than fact; we can accept the countryside's belief that Annie was hounded to death by her family without necessarily allowing the chief blame to her brother; yet we must also accept that the cruelty of brothers was taken for granted by the countryside, which had a strong Ballad tradition. Current Ballads not only reflected the feelings of country people; they were also influential, since their stories stayed 'in the air' for generations.

The tyranny of Family Authority, radiating downwards like all authority in the long history of oral poetry, could survive because, like all authority, it evoked in its recipients a sense of 'belonging' to a secure and powerful group; or, more accurately, it helped to satisfy a basic human need to 'belong' to a secure and powerful group. The Family was, in a way, immortal: it continued to exist although individual members died. Yet it appears in the Ballads without any divine sanctions; it has become a closed system, well below the heights where the gods dwell. Now the world of archaic feeling, being power-conscious rather than self-conscious, had accepted for thousands of years the burden of hierarchical authority which claimed to reach up to the gods, just because that claim gave simple men the assurance of 'belonging' to the supreme powers that ran the universe. The common people in 'Gilgamesh', looking to the King as their shepherd, felt that the King, being the son of a goddess, linked them to the cosmos. Mediaeval peasants had much the same feeling about their King; he still had divine backing although he was not the son of a goddess. A Bushman in Africa satisfies the same need to 'belong' to the universe when he declares, as Laurens van der Post informs us, that Sirius is his grandmother. To be linked to the universe, even by remote control, through an allegiance to Kings and priests or through a Family pedigree deriving from a star or a god, goes far to keep mankind from feeling insignificant in face of the stellar cosmos. The human need to 'belong' to the universe in which one lives can thus provide an upward movement to balance the downward radiation of authority in the underworld of feeling. But with the growth of self-consciousness, reciprocity may fail, the simple equation may no longer work, and should authority appear to reach no longer to cosmic heights, human feelings will then rise against it and try to establish a new authority reaching up higher than the old. Family Authority in the Ballads suffered in this way; its vicissitudes can, I think, be traced.

To begin with, the anonymous block of 'the Family' breaks up into separate components. In the Testament Ballads this process is already at work; the dying victim is asked: what will you leave to your Father, your Mother, your Sister, your Brother? But in later Ballads the pattern is more elaborated; the Ballad love of cumulative repetition gains new opportunities. In an Aberdeenshire version of 'Lady Maisry' (Child, 65), where the heroine is called Janet, the Family is brought in one by one:

In came her sister,
Stepping on the floor;
Says, 'it's telling me, my sister Janet,
That you're become a whore.'

. . . . .

In came her brother,
Stepping on the floor,
Says, 'it's telling me, my sister Janet,
That you're become a whore.'

. . . . .

In came her mother,
Stepping on the floor,
'They are telling me, my daughter,
That you're become a whore.'

. . . . .

In came her father,
Stepping on the floor;
Says, 'they tell me, my daughter Janet,
That you are become a whore.'

These are almost stage directions. The Family block has become a procession. In early Ballads there is no nonsense about putting in such explanatory presentations, and the dialogue is hurled from line to line without self-conscious directions, as, for instance, in 'Hind Horn'. This introduction of the Family, one by one, is a conscious dramatic production, bordering on mime, with the Ballad-singer as compère. The listeners have become more of an audience separated from the Ballad. The whole setting of the performance shows an increase in self-consciousness. It has no need, and no room, for refrains to express a collective mood of listener-participants. The style of it reminds one of the mumming plays in which each character in turn announces himself, with: In comes I. . . . Not that the Ballad-singer here is copying the mumming plays, although he may have known them: his stock of characters is only becoming more multiple, more diverse, and he naturally brings them in separately, in repetitive sequence, to heighten dramatic tension as much as possible. The increase in self-consciousness and the break-up of the Family into separate figures accompany each other.

The next development is the breaking-up of the Family into separate figures at variance with each other. Instead of a solid, aggressive block of seven anonymous brothers, 'Clerk Saunders' (Child, 69) brings in seven separate men differing about what to do with the sleeping lovers in their sister's bower.

Out and speaks the first of them,
'A wat they hay been lovers dear';
Out and speaks the next of them,
'They hay been in love this many a year'.

Out and speaks the third of them,
'It were great sin thir twa to twain';
Out and speaks the fourth of them,
'It were sin to kill a sleeping man'.

Out and speaks the fifth of them,
'A wat they'll neer be twained by me';
Out and speaks the sixt of them,
'We'll tak our leave an gae our way'.

Out an speaks the seventh of them,
'Altho' there were no a man but me,
. . . . .
I bear the brand'll gar him die.'

The variance between them is possible only because a new self-consciousness is in the air: killing is no longer automatic; the Family code of honour can be questioned. So the collective grip of the Family is loosened and conflict arises among its members. This seems a clear sign of its waning power.

The chief danger to Family Authority, the tendency for a sister and daughter to be swept beyond its orbit because of passionate love for some sweetheart outside the Family circle, provides a natural nucleus for situations that further undermine the Family prestige. In Clerk Saunders the girl dissociates herself from the family when her father, 'stout steping on the floor' as seems to be a custom in Northern Ballads, offers to comfort her.

'Comfort well your seven sons,
For comforted will I never bee.'

Concern is shown for her feelings, in a way that was never thought of in early Ballads; her reactions are noted and set out with sympathy.

'Ther'll neer a shirt go on my back,
There'll neer a kame go in my hair,
There'll never coal nor candle-light
Shine in my bower nae mair.'

The implication is not far away that a girl's true-love is worth more than her whole family, father and all.

And presently one finds Ballads that bring this implication more and more into the open. In the 'Janet' version of 'Lady Maisry', after Janet has been burned alive by her family, her lover, arriving just too late to save her, demands to know who has burned her.

> 'O here are we,' her brother said,
> 'This bonfire who set on;
> And we have been so bold,' he said,
> 'Her body for to burn.'

The lover retorts:

> 'O I'll cause burn for you, Janet,
> Your father and your mother;
> And I'll cause die for you, Janet,
> Your sister and your brother.'

Yet, for all its concern about the heroine, after her death, poetic justice of this kind does not much encourage listeners to feel that escape from the Family is possible this side of the grave. That encouragement, however, is explicitly offered in a ballad called 'The Maid Freed from the Gallows' (Child, 95).

A girl—not a Lady Maisry or Lady Margaret, simply a girl, Everygirl as it were—is going to be hanged for losing a golden ball, or a golden key, or, in some versions, for no given reason. She pleads with her father, her mother, her brother, her sister, to bring silver or gold to set her free and is spurned by all of them, one after another in repetitive sequence:

> 'Ye's get nane of my gowd,
> Nor of my well-won fee,
> For I would gie five hundred poun
> To see ye hangit hie.'

The Family is a solid block here; although its members have separate voices they all use the same words. But then the girl's lover appears, like a god from the machine:

'Ye's get a' my gowd
And a' my well-won fee,
To save ye fra the headin-hill
And frae the gallows-tree.'

The Family is cast-off once and for all, while the lovers go away together. Here True Love is shown in concrete terms as finally stronger than the Family block.

This somewhat drastic ballad survived into the nineteenth century as a girls' singing game in Angus, noted by Child. The form in which the girls played it is indicated in version *F*, and it is a form which must have been mimed, from the dramatic beginning:

'Stop, stop,
I think I see my father coming,'

to the triumphant ending:

'I am come to set you free
From this green gallows-tree'.

I wish we had known it in our school.

The higher authority which here over-tops Family Authority is Romantic True Love, yet it could not have remained anything but a wistful aspiration had it not been accompanied by a progressive growth in self-consciousness and the emergence of an interest in the personal feelings of individual people: indeed, the aspiration itself arises out of an awareness of individual difference between one human being and another. Early Ballads are not interested in romantic love; the people in them, token characters, are linked to each other by forces of power and status, family kinship, for instance, or the power of other group loyalties, or of Fate; passionate love is merely one of these forces, accepted as being an arbitrary and perhaps regrettable doom. There is no suggestion that True Love is immortal and eternal, allied to the run of the universe and therefore omnipotent. This suggestion makes but a belated appearance in the Ballads long after it has been familiar elsewhere, but once it does appear it keeps on recurring, fuming up to Ballad skies for many years before it comes down to earth and shows 'The Maid Freed from the Gallows' in plain terms.

The form it takes is that of symbol—the symbol of plants growing on true lovers' graves and twining together as they grow, to intimate that True Love is stronger than Death. This touching symbolism is found, as Child points out (vol. I, pp. 96-98) not only in Scottish and English Ballads but in Ballads and romances all over Europe, and not in Europe only; it extends in space as far as Afghanistan and Kurdistan, in time as far back as Greek mythology. The more it is investigated, the more widespread it will probably appear, for it formalizes an ancient aspiration of naturally aspiring human beings.

Like that of the symbolism in children's games, its significance is immediately felt, no explanation being needed. In the ballad about Lady Margaret Douglas, who grieved so much for her father as well as her sweetheart, it provides the conventional ending:

> Lord William was buried in St Mary's kirk,
> Lady Margaret in Mary's quire;
> Out o the lady's grave grew a bonny red rose
> And out o the Knight's a brier.
>
> And they twa met, and they twa plat,
> And fain they wad be near;
> And a' the warld might ken right weel
> They were twa lovers dear.

But, instead of finishing here as usual, the Balladist adds another verse:

> But bye and rade the Black Douglas,
> And wow but he was rough,
> For he pulled up the bonny brier
> And flang't in St Mary's Loch.

No explanation is needed here to convey to listeners, who knew what the symbolism meant as well as the Black Douglas did, that this was a spiteful attempt to wreak Family revenge beyond the grave.

I do not see how the brutal kind of Family Authority could well survive Ballads like 'The Maid Freed from the Gallows'. By the nineteenth century the Family had indeed made a come-back through trying to over-top romantic true love, a quasi-divine status being accorded to the Head of the Family, the Victorian

Father, among the other Great Men of that era. Yet the upsurge of individual self-consciousness could not be checked, and individual romanticism was already too much 'in the air' to be dispersed. Family Authority in its ancient, tyrannical form was inevitably doomed.

THE REFORMATION AND AFTER

11

The Ballads and Calvinism

i

To suggest that the nature of the Ballads as well as circumstances in Scotland made it difficult for them to explore the new self-awareness except through instances of romantic love, is to tread, however diffidently, on doubtful ground. That they did begin to explore romantic love, showing a greater sensibility, an increased awareness of private feelings, is evident. One remembers the later versions of Young Beichan, where the private feelings of the hero and heroine are probed, with delicate sympathy, in new stanzas interpolated among the old. But how can one be certain that this was the only way the Ballads could reflect that upsurge of individual self-assertion which made the Scottish seventeenth century so turbulent? Why should the style and tradition of Ballad-making prevent Ballads from celebrating the clash of religious beliefs like Calvinism, Presbyterianism, or Episcopalianism? It is not really enough to say that in fact, despite the old tradition of fighting Ballads, the few that were made about the religious wars in Scotland (cf. 'The Battle of Philiphaugh', Child, 202; 'Loudon Hill or Drumclog', Child, 205; 'Bothwell Bridge', Child, 206) would not have stirred Sir Philip Sidney's spirit or anyone else's. There was no lack of passion in the air to inspire good new Ballads, one might think, and perhaps the failure was the fault only of the would-be Ballad-makers? I shall try to show why I think the nature of Ballads themselves prevented Calvinism from being embodied in good Ballads, and why no way was open for the new consciousness to survive in Ballads except the way of romantic love.

From their beginning Ballads were stories sung to tunes. A singable story-tune, which may be also a dance tune, has a marked rhythm and is not too long or complicated to be easily memorized and repeated. The shape of the tune governs the shape of the story, and also the shape of the dance, if there is a dance. Story and dance alike break up into convenient lengths; each fresh repetition of the tune moves the action along a little farther. (I am making these deductions from my own experience of schoolday singing games.)

Early Ballads are sung in rhyming couplets with a refrain after each line, making a stanza that corresponds to the length of the tune. The couplets tell the story, the refrains, I think, express the collective mood of the participants. Tune and stanza begin and come to an end together. The whole Ballad follows this example of shapeliness; the verses rise to a climax and fall to an end of the story. The rhythmical shape, with its rising and falling tensions, is felt by all participants, whether singers or listeners, and the resolution of tensions in the last stanza, as in my experience of singing games, should give general satisfaction.

These story-tunes, extending usually over four lines of song, can be repeated over and over again, depending on the length of the story, but the stories, although they vary in length, tend to be on the short side. The division into stanza-tunes, the need to leap, as it were, from one stepping-stone to another, seems naturally to throw the story into dramatic form, by way of dialogue tossed from one character in the story to another, in a series of leaps apparently followed with ease by the participants; yet where time is needed for listeners' feelings to travel through a situation or where a lapse of time itself is to be journeyed through, the story 'lingers' by using iteration to embody this process. In general, the flow of feeling mounts from verse to verse and is usually allowed to die away at the end of the Ballad instead of being cut short at its climax.

A structure of this kind cannot permit of a too complex or extended theme, like those developed in epics. (Even an epic like the *Iliad*, moreover, could not extend over the whole ten years of the siege of Troy.) Oral tradition sets natural limits to the length of the stories it can tell, and in the Ballad tradition, early or late, the limits are drawn much closer than in epic. There is little room for narrative and less, or none at all, for explanatory comment. The early stories are stories of action, moving through situations and episodes to a climax. And the protagonists in the story, like the story itself, keep on answering the question: what next? They do not pause to ask: why?

By calling characters in a Ballad story 'token characters' I may have obscured their nature. Hindsight makes one aware that whole areas of personality in which we are now interested are left out of consideration in Ballads, and so one feels that the early Ballad heroes and heroines are not presented as rounded, full personalities in our contemporary sense of the words; yet I do not mean to suggest that as 'token characters' they are puppets; nor could they have seemed to be puppets to the people for whom and by whom the Ballads were made. I mean only that their feelings, which are strong and passionate, are of no interest to the Ballad-makers except in so far as they lead to action. Once the action is closed, personal feelings sink into oblivion.

In 'Gil Brenton' the bridegroom jumps out of his bride-bed crying:

'I am the most unhappy man
That ever was in christened lan.

'I woo'd a maiden meek an mild,
An' I've marryed a woman great wi' child.'

This personal statement, or confession, the cry of a hurt child running to his mother, is needed in the story to drive the matriarch into action; that is why it is put in and that is the only reason for its occurrence. As for the matriarch, she expresses her feelings by deeds. 'She gard the door flee aff the ban' ' and 'she gard the door lye i the fleer', but we are not told if she said anything while she battered down that door, nor are we asked to dwell on her feelings. Even the unhappy bride who tells her story at some length does not dwell on her feelings, except to lay the blame for everything on Fate, on the 'Kevil', the lot that was cast and fell on her so that she had to go to the greenwood for flowers, as a domestic duty.

'We cast the kevils us amang,
To see which shoud to the greenwood gang.

'Ohone, alas! for I was youngest,
An ay my weird it was the hardest.

'The kevil it on me did fa,
Which was the cause of a' my wae.'

That is all she says about her unhappiness. If she said more, it would hold up the story, and the story is all. She has, almost inadvertently, answered the question: why? But the question was not directly asked and she answers it only to shrug it off.

The protagonists in an early Ballad, forceful or not, are shaped by the art of the story-teller into functions of the action. Their feelings drive the story on to its climax, and in so far as personal feelings explode in action they are important, but outside the limits of the story they are of no interest. Even the forceful characters, like the 'auld queen' in 'Gil Brenton', or the Wife of Usher's Well, do not stop to consider the purpose or nature of their feelings before going into action. If they had been asked: do you accept responsibility for your actions? they might have said: yes, of course, but the question would have surprised them exceedingly: they might have found difficulty in understanding it. The current of strong feeling in early Ballads naturally carries people along in an 'of course' mood, with no pause for reflection. The headlong rush of these Ballad actions enchants us in our self-conscious modern days and gives us a sense of wild freedom, but it was taken for granted when the Ballads were first made. People in the early Ballad world were not self-conscious. Any reflections they indulged in came after the deed, not before it, and were usually remorseful, not analytic.

This lack of self-consciousness is what I was thinking of when I called them 'token' characters. I should rather have said: stylized figures. Should one infer from stylized figures shaped by art that they resemble living contemporaries? Hardly. In prehistoric cave-drawings men are represented by pin-headed diagrams, but we cannot assume that they were depicted by pin-headed men. On the Warrior Vase from Mycenae the warriors marching round the vase have heads in profile; each of them has a beard and a wide open eye and a salient nose; yet one and all they look like meek anonymous pets being hounded into battle by the formidable goddess at the end of their file. None the less, one cannot suppose that Mycenean warriors, anonymous or not, were at all meek pets. What one can legitimately infer, however, is that the prehistoric artist was interested in the men he drew only in so far as they were functions of the action he was portraying; they were merely structures sustaining the necessary limbs, arms for throwing and legs for leaping. What he was profoundly interested in, the animals to be attacked, he depicted in careful and accurate detail. Similarly the designer of the Warrior Vase was interested in the equipment of his warriors, since that is carefully drawn with distinguishing variations between one group of marchers and another, whereas the men themselves are only stereotypes in a pattern because he was not interested in them as persons. Applying the same criterion of interest to the work of the early Ballad-makers, one can infer that they were not interested in human personalities as such; they were interested in the surge of feeling that made the story rather than in the people who embodied the feelings. As I suggested in discussing 'The Wife of Usher's Well', they were aware of people as forces, driving or being driven; perhaps they were more keenly aware than we are of the unseen and unheard radiations that vibrate from one person to another. But the 'feel' of people was of interest to them only as it contributed to the story. What they were interested in was action, and that they described tersely and well. In 'Lady Isabel and the Elf-Knight' (Child, 4) version *A*, for instance:

> She stroak'd him sae fast, the nearer he did creep,
> Wi a sma charm she lulld him asleep.
>
> Wi his ain sword-belt sae fast as she ban him,
> Wi his ain dag-durk sae sair as she dang him.

Everything in an early Ballad is subordinated to the needs of the action, not only the characters but their surroundings and their 'properties'. Swords are not mentioned except as they go 'through and through' some enemy's body; horses and ships are merely transport; rivers are for fording or drowning in, and woods for amorous encounters, hiding in, or fleeing through. People, properties and scenery are taken for granted as elements in daily life; they are at hand as and when needed; one does not trouble to stop and look at them, far less describe them. This kind of experience resembles what we have in dreams.

Such unthinking movement comes, like dreams, straight out of the underworld of feeling, with little immediate help from consciousness. The story-material is felt, not seen, and where a Ballad lingers in elaboration or iteration, detail is supplied for the sake of the feeling it evokes, not for its own sake. Consider the ships that come bringing the bride in 'Gil Brenton':

> There was twall an twall wi beer an wine,
> An twall an twall wi muskadine:
>
> An twall an twall wi bouted flour,
> An twall an twall wi the paramour:
>
> An twall an twall wi baken bread,
> An twall an twall wi the goud sae red.

This is not, and does not pretend to be, a catalogue of real ships; the improbable cargoes are multiplied to convey a feeling of plenteous richness; the ships are as stylized as the protagonists in the ballad. 'Twall an twall' is a number of conventional significance, like the number twelve in the Epic of Gilgamesh; we can recognize it as the original of the later 'four and twenty' that recur in so many Ballads, but it is an emotionally significant and traditional number rather than an actual sum.

Yet these stylized figures, shaped by art, with their stylized belongings, are given personal names. They are not meant to be non-persons. They are very much alive. One cannot assume that they are realistic contemporary portraits; but can one perhaps infer that they represent contemporary types? No art is accepted and popular if it is too remote in general style from the age it appears in, and the Ballads were accepted and popular. The vitality of oral tradition depends on the extent to which each generation accepts and transmits it, transforming it a little in the process, and the process could not continue if the art were altogether alien. The background of life in the early Ballads, when they were first made, must have then been familiar and credible, the properties being actual objects in common use, the stories articles of common acceptance. Journeys on horse-back or shipboard, knife-play and sword-play, porters at castle-gates, pageboys and armed retainers must have been commonplaces in the daily round before they became commonplaces in the Ballad tradition; domestic and supernatural magic must have been 'in the air'. Once cast into verse-form, these familiar components of daily life, recurring again and again in all stories, become set pieces, like the formulaic pieces in Homer, ready to the hand of the Balladist for building into his story-structure, preserved by style and tradition as well as convenience, and, in time, although by then corresponding to no contemporary reality, taken for granted once more, as well-known and well-loved legacies traditionally 'in the air'. I think one can assume that the characters in the stories were also 'in the air'. Lady Isabel and the Elf-Knight, Hind Horn and Young Beichan, the King and the King's son or daughter, the Lady Margarets and Lord Williams, the Queen of Elfland and the Cruel Brother, the bad stepmother, belonged to some prevailing climate of belief. Kings and princesses, noblemen and noblewomen, still loomed large in that climate of belief, as if they were bigger than ordinary people, so that what happened to them was of more than ordinary interest; although they were sylized into conventional figures, their habits, their passions, their fates could not have seemed incredible to the people who made the Ballads. In time the Kings faded out altogether, the nobles not quite, and the shepherd's daughter, the kitchen-boy, the local laird began to take their places, all recognizable figures, even if partly shaped by wishful thinking; yet I think the earlier traditional characters were also felt to be real enough for the imagination to take hold of.

Alive and active as these early Ballad characters are, they are projected by the 'felt' imagination, if one may call it that, not by the 'seen'. Try to look at them and they become, at most, figures in the flat, like those in early mediaeval paintings. Visual description is rare in early Ballads, and when it occurs is stereotyped. All the people have yellow hair; a woman may have a grass-green sleeve, a maiden a golden comb; armour is bright, water is wan. Horses, so much in demand, get more discriminating description than their riders, but even that is generalized: a horse is berry-brown, dun, dapple-grey or milk-white; that is all. Even the gestures people make, although described, can be stereotyped too. A man always looks 'over his left shoulder' when he is spying for trouble; a woman suggesting a bribe always offers to 'heap' the gold 'with her hand'; a sword is always 'stroked through a straw' before being plunged into someone's body; one always laughs when reading the first lines of a letter, which is always a 'broad letter', but sheds tears over its conclusion. Epithets, phrases and whole stanzas become stereotyped, formular and expected. All this is part of the oral stylization in Ballads.

Does this stylization ultimately remove Ballad characters and stories to a legendary distance, far from reality? I think not. In Chronicle Ballads, the Border Riding Ballads, for instance, which I have omitted so far because they do not belong to North-East Scotland, the actions are stories about real people and real happenings, and yet traditional stereotyped phrases recur, time and again, among the particularized local details, just as traditional iteration is used to take listeners through a local journey:

> As they came out at the Wallpath-heid,
> The Crichtons bad them light and lead.
>
> And when they came to the Biddess-burn
> The Crichtons bad them stand and turn.
>
> And when they came to the Biddess-strand
> The Crichtons they were hard at hand.
>
> (Child, 184: 'The Lads of Wamphray'.)

The Ballad style of iteration does not make this journey less 'real' to the listeners who may, indeed, remember it all the more clearly because of the stylization.

The Ballad style sets a little distance between story and listeners, but this is no more than the distance required by any art. The Ballad stories could not have seemed remote to those who participated in singing or listening to them. People were not detached onlookers when early Ballads were performed; if they were not joining in the refrains they were listening, and they were all sharing the feeling shaped in the Ballad. One cannot be detached in feeling from a group emotion, if one is a member of the group and can feel at all; one is bound to be stirred either to sympathy or hostility. Yet one can look on at a spectacle and be detached from it and from other onlookers, so that onlooking may eventually become critical scrutiny. It seems that the detachment of individual persons from being merged in group feelings is associated with a new, focused attentiveness in the use of the eyes as well as a habit of onlooking. People not only take less for granted and become more introspective; they also develop new powers of observation, an eye of the mind. Seeing begins to predominate over feeling as self-awareness strengthens. One begins to say: 'I see', to prove that one understands something. In every way self-detachment, on-looking, comes more into play.

This process is already at work in the Border Riding Ballads, which deal with 'real' people, mostly of the sixteenth century. The eye is more in evidence here than in the older legendary Ballads. The characters consciously look at each other, sometimes with sardonic humour, and keep a cool, scrutinizing eye on their enemies. The earliest Ballads of the 'felt' imagination have no humour; for that, one needs a certain detachment, a seeing eye. But in 'Jock o the Side', (Child, 187) a Riding Ballad, a rough humour is part of the general atmosphere. Jock has been snatched by his comrades from a dungeon in the New Castle and hoisted sideways on a horse with his leg-irons still upon him:

> Sae out at the gates they a' are gane,
> The prisoner's set on horseback hie;
> And now wi speed they've tane the gate,
> While ilk ane jokes fu wantonlie.
>
> 'O Jock, sae winsomely 's ye ride,
> Wi baith your feet upo ae side,
> Sae weel's ye're harnessed and sae trig,
> In troth ye sit like any bride.'

The Riders' 'properties' are more exactly described than in legendary Ballads: 'Flanders files' for dealing with iron doors, 'Spanish iron' for the prisoner's legs and feet, 'branks and brecham' on the horses. Sardonic comment is not lacking in telling a story:

> Then they're comd on to Hutton Hall,
> They rade that proper place about;
> But the laird he was the wiser man,
> For he had left nae gear without.
>
> ('Dick o the Cow', Child, 185)

When Dick o the Cow rides out after the marauders who have stolen his three cows and three coverlets from his wife's bed, one learns more about his preparations than about any legendary Knight's:

Dickie has tane leave at lord and master,
And I wat a merrie fool was he;
He has bought a bridle and a pair of new spurs
And has packed them up in his breek-thigh.

Local customs are seen with observant eyes:

It was then the use of Puddingburn hoose,
And the hoose of Mangerton, all haile,
Them that came na at the first ca',
Got nae mair till the neist meall.

Together with alert eyesight in the Riding Ballads there is one instance of a capacity to comprehend abstract terms, quite unknown to the 'felt' imagination. Dickie says to his enemy, Johnie Armstrong:

There is a preacher in owr chapell
And a the lee-lang day teaches he;
When day is gane and night is come,
There's never a word I mark but three.

The first and second's Faith and Conscience,
The third is, Johnie, take heed of thee;
But what faith and conscience had thow, traitor,
When thou took my three kye frae me?

And yet, among the visual awareness and conscious comment in this Ballad, Dickie 'looked oer his left shoulder' to see his enemy, exactly like any character in a legendary Ballad, and was none the less 'real' for that.

The raiding described in these Border Ballads must have faded away after 1603, when the Crowns of Scotland and England were united and hostilities between the two kingdoms could no longer be winked at, so we can infer that well before the beginning of the seventeenth century an alert self-consciousness in the Borders already balanced the underworld of feeling. The independence of these Border raiders is witnessed to by an official description of the Liddesdale Armstrongs, the strongest sept among them, as being 'enemies of the King of England, and traitors, fugitives and felons of the King of Scotland'. James V of Scotland, trying to clear out what he regarded as a nest of robbers, hanged Johnie Armstrong in 1530, after having lured him, it is said, to visit his Court. The ballad recounting Johnie's fate, sometimes called 'Johnny Armstrong's Last Good Night', (Child, 169), contains these two verses:

> 'To seik het water beneth cauld yce,
> Surely it is a great folie;
> I haif asked grace at a graceless face,
> But there is nane for my men and me.
>
> 'But had I kend, as I came frae hame,
> How thou unkynd wadst bene to me,
> I wad haf kept the border-syde,
> In spite of all thy force and thee.'

The use of a metaphor, as here, in describing one's own action, is too clear-sighted an achievement, as well as too self-critical, to occur in any legendary Ballad. In such a Ballad one might well have found the third line, with its epigrammatic terseness:

> I haif asked grace at a graceless face,

but not the metaphorical detachment Johnie Armstrong is made to show in the first two lines of that stanza. The second stanza, moreover, is not merely an expression of immediate remorse for an unthinking act; it moves out into the 'might have been', looking back with a considering eye at a possible line of conduct, the spontaneous alliteration giving it a bitter intensity. Johnie Armstrong is communing with himself. Consider the difference in self-awareness between this verse and the petulant last stanza of an earlier ballad, 'Child Maurice' (Child, 83):

> 'Away, away, ye ill woman,
> And an ill death mait ye dee.
> Gin I had kend he'd bin your son,
> He'd neer bin slain by mee.'

Johnie Armstrong's self-communing is of the kind that we find in later Ballads of the seventeenth century:

> 'But had I wist, before I kiss'd,
> That love had been sae ill to win,
> I'd locked my heart in a case o gowd,
> And pin'd it wi' a siller pin.'
>
> (Child, 204)

In these Riding Ballads, then, before the seventeenth century had begun, individual self-awareness and the traditional imagination were successfully interfused. Local group loyalty was still strong; people were confident that they shared the same feelings; the abstract preachings of the new religion (faith and conscience) could still be used ironically by Dick o the Cow; and an observant eye was turned on oneself as well as on other people.

Could not this newly observant eye have been turned on the politico-religious fanaticism that was already convulsing Scotland in the second half of the sixteenth century and became acute during the seventeenth? Chronicle Ballads might seem the proper medium to convey the feelings of country Scots among these turmoils, yet if any such were made there is no record of them. The Border Ballads ignore the troubles entirely; they sing only of local raids and loyalties and pay no attention to religious factions. One is hardly surprised to find that the Borders resisted the new sects and remained Roman Catholic long after Central Scotland had succumbed to Calvinism, as if the Borderers lived within a bell of high atmospheric pressure of their own. The cool balance which they show between the old awareness of tradition and the new-focused eye of consciousness was not to be found among the Reformers farther north or in the still mediaeval regions of the North-East. The Fire of Frendraught, for instance, which belongs in time to the seventeenth century, has none of the humour or detachment found in the Riding Ballads: it is an older style of Chronicle Ballad with a less controlled head of emotion in it. The ambience of the Riding Ballads is a crystalline clarity, such as one recognizes in another ballad of action, 'Sir Patrick Spens', where there is the same fusion of traditional commonplaces and alert eyesight. The commonplaces, the braid letter read first with a laugh and then with a tear in the eye, the voyage lingered out:

> They hadna sailed a league, a league,
> A league but barely three
> When the lift grew dark and the wind blew loud
> And gurly grew the sea,

the unquestioning acceptance of danger and doom, are all traditional; the sharp eye of the mariner who says:

'I saw the new moon late yestreen
Wi the auld moon in her arm,'

the metaphorical detachment of the cry:

'The saut sea's in at our coat-neck
And out at our left arm'

belong to a newer awareness which resembles that in the Riding Ballads. What was to prevent this excellently balanced technique from producing good Ballads about the religious troubles?

This is really a specious question, since it implies that a Ballad-maker has only to use the new technique and make a Ballad, regardless of his audience. The audience for oral poetry is as important as the singer: it is not passive. Yet between the Borders and the North, from around the Forth to around the Tay, that Ballad audience was being thrown into confusion by the new religion, which in its zeal for extirpating Popery was trying to suppress the whole underworld of imagination out of which Ballads arise.

This sounds like, but is not, an over-statement. It is true that Popery, as such, enters very little into the Scottish Ballad background, if we take as a criterion the infrequency with which it is mentioned. A few references of this kind:

When bells were rung and mass was sung
And a' men bound for bed,

or a passing allusion to Our Lady, is about all the Catholicism one meets in Scottish Ballads: there are very few priests, and only one or two of the Ballads which were based on stories from the Apocrypha and composed in England were current in Scotland. Yet Thomas the Rhymer mistook the Queen of Elfland at first for the Queen of Heaven: they were Queens side by side somewhere in the back of his mind. It is possible, and I incline to this opinion, that Catholicism was little mentioned in Scottish Ballads because it consorted comfortably with the traditional background and so was taken for granted. For very many years the Catholic Church had made compromises with pre-Christian pagan elements and adopted them into its rituals and worship: there was a Mother-figure in its pantheon; there was still magic haunting St Mary's

Well; christening was still a magic rite. The old paganism and Christian magic belonged together in the underworld of feeling.

Christian magic did not lie so deep as the old paganism, none the less. The Ballads' deeper strata of feeling contain a pagan awareness of incomprehensible powers in the universe, whose operations are accepted without much question and without a sense of personal guilt. If the 'kevil' falls upon you and you must obey it, that is simply that; you have no bad conscience about it and you try to endure the consequences. You belong to the Universe, and you must 'dree your weird' with courage.

This sense of 'belonging', in some way, to the Universe and to powerful human groups like a family or a tribe, is a characteristic of any old-time community. From the Ballads one can legitimately infer that the Scots, especially in rural districts, felt this sense of community. They 'belonged' also to the places they happened to live in; one finds direct expression of strong local attachment.

> 'Happy the craw
> That biggs i the Trotten shaw
> An drinks o the Water o Dye,
> For nae mair shall I.'

When one adds to this sense of belonging together a common and widely ranging background of traditional legends and songs which avoid the passing of moral judgments although they give shape to violent, unthinking action resulting from vehement passions, one has the impression of a relatively unsophisticated people unused, like the Ballads themselves, to the practice of systematic conceptual thinking, a passionate and highly imaginative people accustomed to live mainly in the underworld of feeling. People of this kind are, I am convinced, peculiarly vulnerable to the attack of systematized power-structures, especially under the guise of religion, and Calvinism directed just such an attack upon them.

ii

It seems easy to see why the first impact of Calvinism on these unsophisticated people should be strong, although not so easy to see why it should ultimately shatter the old sense of community. Destiny or Fate simply appears again as Predestination—an abstract term, certainly, but abstractions impress people unused to them. The Calvinist creed emphasizes the helplessness of the individual, who has no say in the arrangements made for his eternal future. The Confession of Faith drawn up by the Reformers in 1560 describes how 'some are elected to everlasting salvation and others ordained as vessels of wrath without reference to their merits or vices'. The individual has no choice whether he shall be saved or damned, this being solely determined by 'the incomprehensible mercy of God', which is not unlike the arbitrary operations of luck or Fate. The Calvinist creed, that is to say, chimed in with some of the deeper resonances in the imagination of Ballad audiences. The preachers, moreover, proclaimed the doctrine dramatically, staging performances in the pulpit which excited the congregations and reminded them that they were participants in a cosmic drama. The congregations were also incited to violent, unthinking action such as rises easily from the underworld of feeling.

The fierce, intolerant vehemence of these early Scottish Reformers is a phenomenon worth noting. It is difficult to see them except in a red glare of fanaticism. Many elements in them must have contributed to this. At the very heart of their fanaticism lay the quaking uncertainty which every Calvinist was bound at some time to feel about his ultimate election by God, an election defined by his creed as incomprehensible. The more the preachers thundered about the terrors of the Day of Judgment the more their own human doubts and weaknesses could make them quail inwardly. Yet Reforming Calvinists elsewhere must have had the same experience, but outside Geneva they did not compensate themselves by insisting upon the extreme authority, the theocratic absolutism, so fervently demanded by these first Scottish ministers, with a vehemence as narrow and concentrated as the war-passion of ancient Norsemen. That berserk passion seems to have been part of their make-up.

Again, the Pictish traces of matriarchy perceptible in the Scottish Ballads and still lingering in the air may help to explain the venom with which Knox persecuted Mary of Guise and Mary, Queen of Scots, and why he blew a blast of his trumpet against the monstrous regiment of women. Militant cults, regarding women as unfit to be soldiers, usually class them as inferior to men, 'infirm vessels' as Knox called them, but not all militant Reformers have told a queen to her face, as Knox did, that he was 'appointed by God to rebuke the sins and vices of all', while even Calvin regarded with misgiving the untimely blast of Knox's trumpet, as Cromwell later was to regard with misgiving the pretensions of the Scottish preachers.

In fact, the exercise of power was of central importance to them. A Father seemed more powerful to them than a Son, and so what they set up for worship was a projection of Jehovah from the Old Testament, even more jealous and vengeful than the original, dealing out terrible wrath and punishment. As is usual in systems motived by a desire for power, there was no room for love, compassion, or generosity in theirs. When they used the word 'love' it was as a weapon to chastise others; they could not understand love except as an instrument of power. Knox in a letter told Mary of Guise that her religion was poison and whoever drank it drank damnation and death, and informed her that he was warning her 'out of love', on the principle, I suppose, of 'this hurts me more than it hurts you'. It was from the more bitter Old Testament prophets that the Reformers drew their inspiration and their invective. Indeed, one cannot understand how they came to call themselves Christians, especially when one remembers that the Covenanters later went into battle with the slogan: 'Christ and No Quarter'.

In their fanaticism for power, derived, as they claimed, directly from God, they soared above realities, either political or psychological. To some extent they were kept in check by the lairds and nobles in Parliament, which passed an Act, proposed by the Kirk, to make a third attendance at Mass a capital crime, yet refused to do the same for a third adultery. This recalcitrance of Parliament gave great offence to the ministers of the Kirk, who were determined to exert full authority to make congregations godly by legal compulsion as well as by rhetoric. The congregations, moreover, were instructed, in the Book of Discipline presented to Parliament in 1561 but unratified, that after choosing their ministers they must reverence them, 'obeying the commands which they speak from God's mouth and Book, even as they would obey God Himself'. This is the absolute all-or-nothing passion for power that rises from the archaic world of feeling, which the preachers embodied as well as worshipped, conveying a reverence for it to their congregations.

In their political and psychological ignorance, however, the Scottish Reformers achieved unintended effects. The administrative system they drew up looked fool-proof to them, but could not be carried out because the Church land-revenues on which it depended were largely diverted into the pockets of the Protestant nobles, who were following the example of Henry VIII in England. In 1596, more than thirty years after the Kirk was legally established, above four hundred parishes, Dr Hay Fleming reckoned, not counting Argyll and the Isles, still had no ministers. In these parishes Ballads could still survive and did survive, among other superstitions and idolatries which the populace did not yet understand to be criminal works of the Devil. But where the ministers did penetrate, a resistance movement began among the Lowland Scots, which, like all resistance movements, ultimately went underground.

It arose naturally from the provisions in a section of the Book of Discipline relating to the reciprocal duties of a minister and his congregation. This section laid down the principle that congregations were to be corrected by their Ministers, the Elders of the Kirk Session, and one another, but that Ministers were also to be corrected by their colleagues and their Elders. The Elders in turn were to be corrected by their Ministers, their congregations and their fellow Elders. As Edwin Muir says in his *John Knox*, p. 225:

> A church such as this, held together by universal and reciprocal fault-finding, could not but encourage the self-opinionative and the censorious at the expense of the sensitive and the charitable... it substituted for the particular tyranny of the priest a universal and inescapable public tyranny.

It may lie in the nature of power-systems that they cannot flourish without spies and informers as well as drastic penalties. The Calvinist Kirk, anyhow, here enjoined its adherents to become spies and informers, keeping watchful eyes upon each other to make sure that the Devil was not at work in apparently godly bosoms. There was also a private probably unacknowledged motive for this scrutiny: the desire to assure oneself that other candidates for ultimate sainthood were no better than oneself. Paradoxically, therefore, the individual Calvinist who had no say in deciding his eternal fate, helplessly at the mercy of his God, was encouraged to exercise a scrutinizing, censorious eye that necessarily detached him from his brethren and strengthened his individualism. The scrutinizing eye gained in importance until in time it became a symbol for God—a large, watchful eye scrutinizing humanity from heaven, engraved, framed and hung up in bedrooms with the caption: 'Thou God Seest Me'.

Along this narrow way the Lowland Scots advanced into self-conscious individualism, finally saying to themselves: 'Let ilka herring hang by its ain tail.' Their road led into a theocratic, not a contemporary, scientific world, but they did advance. And as they read the Bible and exercised their imaginations upon it, the Word of God became rather the Words of God, since there were many varying voices in it, and each self-conscious individual could find his own interpretation of these. The godly became practised casuists, and later split up into warring splinter sects.

At this stage, I think, among those who felt oppressed by the scrutiny of social and ecclesiastical inquisitions, the natural human reflection crept in: 'what the eye doesn't see, the heart needn't grieve over'. The resistance went underground; that is to say, many people began to acquire the habit of professing one thing openly while furtively following another. Neither adultery nor Catholic idolatry, Knox's chief targets, was ever stamped out. Drunkenness increased greatly; fornication, as the Kirk called it, went on much as usual; and among these guilty indulgences Ballads also survived. But the old sense of unthinking community survived only precariously, more strongly in the wild North-East than elsewhere and in parts of the Borders, where Calvinism did not make such a strong impression as in the central Lowlands. There the dead hand of conforming 'godliness' lay heavy, especially on Sundays.

A common front against the Devil cannot cement a community. A war against the Devil is an ideological war in which partisans wear no recognizable uniform. Any neighbour, even a member of one's own family, may be an enemy agent. The Devil, also, unlike pagan demons, spreads a sense of personal guilt wherever he goes: one feels immediately guilty if one yields to his temptations. A general atmosphere of potential guilt, anxiety, fear and worry over one's qualifications for saint-hood makes not a community but a mistrustful congregation of introspective individuals who feel a constant need to justify themselves. The Calvinist religion claims 'justification by faith', yet in practice the impression it gives is that of 'faith by justification', a continuous argumentative ordeal that wears out the nervous system. Understandably, the more all possible sources of temptation are banned, the easier it becomes to feel armoured in self-righteousness. So prohibitions in Scotland, as in other Puritan countries, were not lacking. Resistance naturally followed.

To appreciate the strength of the resistance one must appreciate the relentless pressure exercised upon congregations by their Elders and Ministers. This may be gauged from the length of time its influence has lasted. For hundreds of years pious Scots have been gloomily obsessed by Death and Judgment Day, and, like other people who find relief in jesting about their oppressors, have fabricated countless jokes about funerals and ministers. As long-lasting have been the more subtle effects of the split in the Scottish personality between open profession and furtive indulgence. A self-conscious split of this kind falsifies, by putting on the defensive, what lies on both sides of it: the open profession can become sanctimonious, the furtive indulgence can grow coarse with bravado. The resulting dualism in Scottish culture has been noted by many critics. The split helped to alter the pattern of daily living in many ways which it would be tedious to enumerate, from Saturday-night drunkenness to Sabbath observance. It also affected the layout of Edinburgh. When I was young there was not a public-house or public bar in the whole length of Princes Street, which was openly respectable. Round the corner, however, two narrow furtive streets immediately behind and parallel to Princes Street consisted of practically nothing but public-houses.

This distortion of the Scottish spirit was bound to affect the standing of the Scottish Ballads. They were devalued, true, in good company, including Shakespeare, since all prose and poetry that was not sacred could be nothing but profane, while plays for the theatre were felt to be especially wicked, inviting people to act and believe in bogus lying fictions, at the peril of their souls. But most prose and poetry had the protection of being already in print, which the Ballads did not have. It is possible that they might have been pushed out sooner among the hedges and ditches where they mostly found refuge in the late nineteenth century, as the property of travelling tinkers and gypsies, had they not been rescued by a surge of interest in Scottish Ballad and folk-song that spread in the eighteenth century in Edinburgh from Allan Ramsay's book-shop, reinforced by Percy's *Reliques* in 1765. They were then widely collected and taken down, mostly from the singing of old women who had learned them as girls from the singing of other old women. Part of their devaluation in the seventeenth century may have consisted in their being relegated to 'women and bairns', as being unworthy of potential Kirk Elders. In any case, women have always tended to conserve a tradition of song and story, as they conserve the ramifications of kinship networks, and did I not know that ploughmen in the Mearns were still singing Ballads in 1906, I should have assumed that only women kept them going after the Reformation.

A traditional background, a whole climate of belief, is not at once dissipated by hostile storms; it tends to linger in pockets of the countryside, so that changes in the status and themes of Ballads took more time than this summary account might imply. The language in which they were sung, however, current Scots or 'Doric' as it came to be called by classicists, began to be devalued as soon as the Bible and the metrical Psalms and Paraphrases were reverentially accepted. These sacred works were presented in English, not in Scots, and English was thus exalted into a 'Sunday-best' medium, leaving the Scots vernacular for the homely discourse of every day. This looks like a deadly blow at the self-confidence of a community, yet, for a time, the vernacular, as it were, merely joined the resistance and re-inforced it, as well as being saved from pretentious rhetoric. (The Calvinists liked bigger rather than smaller abstract words; they always used a Scottish legal term for truth; 'the verity'.) Terse and racy Scots vernacular lived on for centuries, especially in rural districts. Some time after the Union of Parliaments in 1707 the vernacular began to be thought vulgar in the towns, which were trying to become very English, so that when Ballads came to be collected and written down, well-meaning gentlemen could not resist trying to 'improve' them. But until about 1760 the vernacular was safe, even among the upper classes.

The habit of making and singing rhymed verses, deeply implanted in the Scots by the Ballad tradition, also continued and probably to this day adds to the stream of libellous, witty and bawdy Scots verses, locally composed, that was running strongly in my youth beneath the ice of respectability. The Scottish Reformers could not help knowing that everyone sang Ballads; they felt it needful to provide metrical, rhymed verses for their congregations to sing. The metrical versions of the Psalms and Paraphrases are a curious tribute to the strength of the Ballad tradition.

There can be no doubt that the Ballads belonged to the resistance, not to the godly. The early Ministers denounced them, as they denounced theatrical plays, for lying and superstitious fictions. In the underworld of feeling, whatever could not be controlled, funnelled into a blast of godly zeal, was then labelled profane and devilish, including all the arts, except sacred prose, poetry and music. But what the Calvinists banned as profane were basic human needs, such as the need for love and the need for play. Like other arts, Ballads spring from a play of imagination in the underworld of feeling, the pleasurable discharge of energy into satisfying shapes a little removed from actual living so that there is a gamesome freedom in the exercise. This is a very ancient habit of mankind. The Ballad tradition was therefore both older and more deeply founded than the Calvinism which tried to repress it.

Yet the Ballad tradition, as I have emphasized, depended on shared communal feelings. What it played with were emotions and stories acceptable to all listeners, things taken for granted, made familiar both by daily custom and by inheritance. It was neither analytic nor critical to begin with, and could not absorb experiences wholly novel. For this reason alone it could not give expression to Calvinist attitudes and proscriptions until these had seeped into daily life and become sanctioned by custom. Even then it had to contend with the fear of social and ecclesiastical disapproval, since the word 'story' had become a synonym for a lie. Once the Calvinist Kirk really got a grip on its congregations, the making of Ballad stories about public events became a risk people were disinclined to take.

Members of the resistance then tried to save the face of favourite Ballads by inserting godly verses, as was done in 'Young Beichan':

> He viewd the fashions of that land,
> Their way of worship viewd he,
> But into onie of their stocks
> He wadna sae much as bow a knee.

Yet one must note that not all members of the resistance were timid and conformist. There exists a delightful fragment of verse which is anything but timid:

> Eh, sic a parish,
> Eh, sic a parish,
> Eh, sic a parish is Little Kinkell.
> They've hangit the minister,
> Drooned the precentor,
> Dung doon the steeple
> An' drucken the bell.

Beyond their conscious knowledge, however, waves of new self-consciousness were surging in on the Scots from outside Scotland altogether, and although hampered by their religion, they could not avoid being affected, as has been already noted in the chapter about Family Authority. Romantic True Love, a force the Calvinists never understood, was very much in the air, and the new, scrutinizing eye, which could not turn outwards without ecclesiastical risk, could and did turn inwards to trace the vicissitudes, the personal sorrows and exaltation, of love-affairs. Calvinism ignored the Queen of Love, as it ignored all Queens, since it concentrated on Death rather than Birth, but it could not destroy her. The Ballads composed after the Reformation became more and more romantic.

12

Post-Reformation Ballads

THE habit of resistance developed by the Borderers during centuries of fighting against the larger kingdom of England now kept Calvinism also at bay for a time. As is shown in their Riding Ballads, they had advanced farther along the road to individual self-consciousness than their Lowland countrymen elsewhere, and had achieved it in a more wholesome manner than those who were later to take the narrow path provided by the Kirk. A very early example among the Ballads of self-conscious introspection is found therefore in the Borders; it is called the 'Lament of the Border Widow'. Tradition ascribes it to the wife of Piers Cockburn of Henderland, who was hanged above his own door by James V in 1529. Here are two of the verses:

> I took his body on my back,
> And whiles I gaed, and whiles I sat;
> I digg'd a grave and laid him in,
> And happed him wi the sod sae green.
>
> But think na ye my heart was sair
> When I laid the mools on his yellow hair?
> And think na ye my heart was wae
> When I turned aboot, awa to gae?

The fine feeling in this Lament is deeply personal, anticipating the personal sorrow in seventeenth-century Ballads yet to come. But it is still a Ballad of movement, without any metaphorical imagery.

The North-East of Scotland, in its way, was also a Border country, for Highlanders neighboured Lowlanders there. Yet self-awareness was slower in developing along these marches and personal feeling took a longer time to become articulate. The issues for which men fought and resisted encroachment were less clear-cut than on the Southern Border, and perhaps less consciously observed; too often Lowland Scots were merely brawling with each other, as in the time when Frendraught Tower went up in a blaze. The Highlanders, also, in those days were despised in the North for bare-bottomed savages, not taken seriously as political enemies. In 1592 the North was still concerning itself more with action than with reflection, as can be seen in the difference between the expression of feeling there and in Edinburgh concerning the same event, the Earl of Murray's murder by Huntly, which both North and South turned into Ballads (Child, 181, *A* and *B*).

The Northern version, composed at a farther remove from the scene of the murder, makes Murray's wife a sister of Huntly's, although being the Regent Murray's daughter she had brought the Murray title to her husband.

'Open the gates
and let him come in;
He is my brother Huntly,
He'll do him nae harm.'

The gates they were opent,
they let him come in,
But fause traitor Huntly,
He did him great harm.

He's ben and ben
and ben to his bed,
And wi a sharp rapier
he stabbed him dead.

. . . . .

Huntly lap on his horse,
rade to the King;
'Ye're welcome hame, Huntly,
and whare hae ye bin?'

'Whare hae ye been
and how hae ye sped?'
'I've killed the Earl o Murray,
dead in his bed.'

'Foul fa you, Huntly,
and why did you so?
You might have taen the Earl o Murray
and saved his life too.'

'Her bread it's to bake,
her yill is to brew,
My sister's a widow,
and sair do I rue.

'Her corn grows ripe,
her meadows grow green,
But in bonny Dinnibristle
I daurna be seen.'

The words, the metre and the feeling are clipped down almost in Norse style. The Ballad may well have been made by a fighting man on campaign, for the Northern Highlanders, led by the Macintoshes, took the murder as an excuse to attack Huntly's possessions and violent brawling broke out. Auchindown, a castle belonging to Huntly's uncle, was burned by Willie Macintosh; another clipped-down ballad was made about this exploit, in five short verses, of which these are the first three:

'Turn, Willie Macintosh,
Turn, I bid you,
Gin ye burn Auchindown
Huntly will head you.'

'Head me or hang me,
That canna fley me,
I'll burn Auchindown
Ere the life lea me.'

Coming down Deeside
In a clear morning
Auchindown was in flame
Ere the cock-crawing.

The terseness of these ballads does not imply a lack of passionate feeling behind the actions they describe; it means only that the feeling expresses itself in direct action rather than in reflection and is not lingered over. A very different atmosphere is provided by the Edinburgh version. This is a vehicle for the incantatory heightening of feeling, built up by repetition from verse to verse, with a passion of loving regret for the lost young nobleman. In the Northern version there is no personal regret for Murray; the regret indicated by Huntly, the 'wicked brother', is for his sister's grief.

The Edinburgh populace were nearer to the murder, which happened on the opposite bank of the Forth, at Donibristle. The bodies of the Earl and his friend the Sheriff of Murray were brought in their coffins to the Church of Leith and defiantly kept there for months unburied while the people clamoured more and more loudly for the punishment of Huntly. James VI was frightened enough to flee to Glasgow, where he stayed until Huntly 'did enter himself in ward', as he was charged to do. Huntly was let go 'upon caution', being sheltered under the King's commission, and was not punished. Agnes Mure Mackenzie, in the second volume of her *Scottish Pageant*, page 50, says of the Edinburgh Ballad that it 'was once on a time a street song in Edinburgh; it nearly dirled a sovereign off his throne'.

The Edinburgh populace, noted at that time for turbulence, were passionately against all Establishments and were given to breaking open the Tolbooth, the town jail, and setting prisoners free. On one such recorded occasion, in 1561, a certain James Gillon was to be hanged by the magistrates and the Kirk for playing the part of Robin Hood on a summer's day, but after vain appeals for mercy to the magistrates and to Knox in person, the Edinburgh populace, on the day appointed for the hanging, locked the Provost and Bailies in the Town Lawyer's office, then 'dang doun the gibbet', broke the Tolbooth door, with 'foirhammers', let out all the prisoners as well as Gillon, and had a running fight with authorities sent to control them, even exchanging shots as well as throwing stones, until the Constable of the Castle had to come down and arbitrate between the parties. Once it was settled that no one was to be arrested, the crowd released the trapped magistrates and went home. This traditionally formidable mob was devoted to Murray, a well-made, handsome young man, and the Ballad is in essence a Lament.

Of some general interest are the first two lines, setting a tone of reproach as well as sorrow:

> Ye Highlands and ye Lawlands,
> O whaur hae ye been?
> They hae slain the Earl o Murray
> And layd him on the green.

At that time no one in the Northern marches would have

coupled Highlands and Lowlands together as a whole; the conjunction is a surprising find even in this Southern Ballad. I incline to think that these lines came into the song nearer the time of printing it (1763) when public opinion about Highlanders was beginning to change. If they do belong to the year 1592, that is worth noting.

The Ballad is full of feeling, deliberately heightened by the recurrence of the words 'the bonny Earl o Murray' in the third line of each stanza, a device that reinforces the yearning and the tension, verse by verse, like a repeated sob:

> He was a braw gallant
> And he rid at the ring,
> And the bonny Earl o Murray,
> He micht ha been a King.
>
> He was a braw gallant
> And he play'd at the ba',
> And the bonny Earl o Murray,
> Was the flower amang them a'.
>
> He was a braw gallant
> And he play'd at the glove,
> And the bonny Earl o Murray,
> He was the Queen's love.

The romantic insinuation, baseless but dear to the populace, that James's Queen, now three years married, had cast a loving eye on Murray must have added an extra sting to the ballad. It may not have nearly 'dirled' James off his throne, but it certainly helped to frighten him away from Edinburgh.

Besides being romantic, the Murray ballad in its present form is a fine work of art. It is shapely and singable, nearly as popular now as it was in 1592. The last verse, in traditional style, brings one down to everyday level:

> O lang will his lady
> Look frae the Castle Doune,
> Eer she see the Earl o Murray
> Come sounding through the toon.

The three long -oo sounds in the last line, as pronounced by Scots, beautifully suggest the echoing of Murray's trumpets.

Even if it were altered in the course of time, before printing, this ballad must have been strongly emotional when it was made. The Edinburgh populace in 1592 were apparently more inclined to dwell on their emotions in song, and more capable of articulating them, than the Northerners. They were also equally unaffected by Calvinism, of which there is no trace in either version of the Murray song. How is this possible, thirty years after the Confession of Faith and the Book of Discipline? The legal Establishment of the Calvinist Kirk may to some extent account for the Edinburgh mob's indifference to it. Well-to-do burgesses and merchants supported it from the beginning, while the populace stayed suspicious of any established authority. But since 1560 the Scots had had other matters to preoccupy them, for Lowland Scotland was in continuous turmoil, fomented, like much turmoil in Scotland, by political intrigue hiding behind religious motives. What became a hell's-brew of violent civil war between the King's party and the Queen's party boiled up, between, that is to say, the influence of England and the influence of France. There were Protestants on both sides; whole families and parishes were split. The Kirk, in any case, was in difficulty for lack of revenues. Once James VI came of age, it concentrated on disciplining him rather than on administering the country. For the Murray rioting Andrew Melville, Knox's successor, rebuked him roundly, making it clear that the Kingdom of Christ as represented by Melville should rule King, Kirk and Kingdom. None the less, the Edinburgh populace were not yet persuaded to join the Elect. Later in the same year, 1592, they provided another non-Calvinist ballad, based this time on a Court scandal.

That favourite practice of Scottish mobs, the rescuing of prisoners from jail and execution, was also a favourite Ballad theme. When it became known, then, that one of the Queen's ladies, a Dane like her mistress, had rescued her sweetheart, young Wemyss of Logie, from imprisonment in the King's palace, under the very nose of the King, this combination of jail-breaking and romance could hardly help turning into a Ballad (the Laird o Logie', Child, 182).

The heroine's foreign name puzzled the chroniclers of the day, for she appears in historical records as Margaret Twynstoun, Margaret Twinslace, Margaret Vinstar and Margaret Weiksterne. The records agree that, being lady-in-waiting in the bedchamber where the King and Queen lay sleeping, she went to the prisoner's guard and told them that Their Majesties wished to interview him. The guard naturally accepted her as a trustworthy messenger and escorted Young Logie to the door of the royal bedroom. Here she bade them wait, smuggled Young Logie past the sleeping royalties and let him out of a 'backside' window by a rope, while the guard waited outside till morning. This exploit, as a State paper says, 'ministered great occasion of laughter'. None of the Ballad versions is aware of what really happened; they all invent details made up from conventional Ballad material.

In each of the four complete versions almost every stanza has for end-rhyme the syllable -ee, or -ie, a monotonous fashion which perhaps came in about this time, although one cannot be sure of that, since these were printed in the eighteenth century. Three of them, anyhow, have an almost identical last stanza with the same -ee endings and one of these was nearly contemporary with the scandal, since it knows the name of the Captain of the King's Guard, Sir John Carmichael.

There is no strong group feeling behind the Logie ballad, and it falls rather into the jog-trot style of Chronicle Ballads. The *A* version, which names Carmichael, sees him looming large; that Carmichael gets into trouble over the escapade interests the Ballad-maker more than the escapade itself. In this version 'May Margaret' is supposed to have begged for Logie's life on her knees to the King and to have got a refusal. Then she steals the King's 'redding-kaim' and the Queen's 'wedding-knife' and sends these tokens to Carmichael as evidence that Logie is to be set free. Like the sweetheart in 'Young Beichan' she bestows gifts:

> She sent him a purse o the red gowd,
> Another o the white monie;
> She sent him a pistol for each hand
> And bade him shoot when he gat free.

The King hears the shot as he lies in bed, and guesses that it is Young Logie's. He summons Carmichael at once and threatens to hang him instead of Logie. Carmichael hurries to May Margaret's bower, asking to speak with Young Logie.

> May Margaret turnd her round about,
> I wot a loud laugh laughed she:
> 'The egg is chippd, the bird is flown,
> Ye'll see nae mair o Young Logie.'
>
> The tane is shippd at the pier o Leith,
> The tother at the Queen's Ferrie,
> And she's gotten a father to her bairn,
> The wanton laird o Young Logie.

Margaret is supposed to be pregnant, because that is how the man in the street sees her love-affair. This version is clearly the work of some member of the populace well outside Court circles, someone, moreover, who has a lively awareness of Carmichael, probably because of a hostile encounter with the King's Guard. And Margaret's exploit is under-played, through ignorance.

A later generation, perhaps not much later, found this story vaguely inadequate and changed it to suit their own notions of romance, bringing in the Queen as a protagonist. In 'The Bonny Earl o Murray' the populace could not resist trying to involve the Queen, but here they make her the chief character. In all the remaining three versions, one of them a printed stall-copy, it is the Queen's mother-wit and kindness that shape the ballad; she is the high source of mercy. The Kirk's obliteration of queens from the Calvinist world seems now to have provoked a counter-reaction in the underworld of feeling.

Version *B* changes the name of young Logie to Ochiltrie, who was a partner with Logie in the young Earl of Bothwell's plan to force himself into the presence of his cousin, the King. But the change of name does not really matter. What matters is that the Queen is given all the credit of the prisoner's rescue. May Margaret tears her yellow hair and threatens suicide; Carmichael is simply left out; it is the Queen who acts. After begging in vain for Ochiltrie's life, the Queen steals the prison-keys and herself sets the young man free, all for the love she bears to her distracted lady-in-waiting. She it is who presents the purses of gold and silver and the two pistols. The King, hearing the shots and the triumphant shout of Ochiltrie as he rides off, behaves as a King is expected to behave:

'Call to me a my gaolours,
Call them by thirtie and by thrie;
Whairfoir the morn, at twelve a clock,
It's hangit schall they ilk ane be.'

'O didna ye send your keyis to us?
Ye sent thaim be thirtie and be thrie,
And wi thaim sent a strait command
To set at lairge young Ochiltrie.'

'Ah, na, Fie, na' quoth the queen,
'Fie, my dear luve, this maunna be.
And iff ye're gawn to hang them a,
Indeed ye maun begin wi me.'

The tane was schippit at the pier o Leith,
The ither at the Queen's ferrie,
And now the lady has gotten her luve,
The winsom laird of Ochiltrie.

There are no metaphors here about chipped eggs and flown birds; this is a more unsophisticated voice. It is, in any case, the voice of high romance. A lady here may be deep in love without being pregnant, and an authentic queen sheds loving-kindness around her. The introduction of that archetypal figure, the queen, gives more resonance to the ballad and improves it—not to mention the touch of sly humour she imparts.

There is still no trace of Calvinism in this ballad. But eight years later, in 1600, another public scandal gave rise to a ballad (Child, 194) well indoctrinated with a variety of Calvinism. The Laird of Wariston, an estate about a mile from Edinburgh, was murdered at the instigation of his wife. They were both young—the girl being only twenty-one, some say nineteen—and had been married against their inclinations, with the result that they had quarrelled continuously. The Laird had been brutal, 'biting of her in the arm and striking her divers times', until in rage and despair she sent her nurse to beg a former servant of her father's to come and murder him. The nurse and the serving-man were both on the young wife's side; the serving-man arranged that he should flee and take all the blame on himself if the crime came to light.

Wariston was murdered on a Tuesday. On Thursday his wife and the nurse were tried and condemned. Early on Saturday morning the girl was beheaded, because she was of good family, not strangled and burned like the nurse. Four years later the serving-man was caught and broken on the wheel.

A Calvinist minister who visited her in jail found the girl hysterical and recalcitrant before the trial. Once she had been condemned, he 'wrought' with her till after midnight on Friday, when she said that she felt in her heart 'a free remission of all her sins'. Next morning she was still 'full of the grace of God' and went to the scaffold as 'a constant saint of God'. A Memorial of her conversion, printed from manuscript in 1827, refers to her repeatedly as 'this dear saint of God'.

The *A* version of the Ballad was taken down by Sir Walter Scott from his mother's 'recitation'. I give it from stanza 4.

He spak a word in jest;
Her answer wasna good;
He threw a plate at her face,
Made it a' gush out o blood.

She wasna frae her chamber
A step but barely three
When up and at her richt hand
There stood Man's Enemy.

. . . . .

The Foul Thief knotted the tether,
She lifted his heid on hie,
The nourice drew the knot
That gard Lord Waristoun die.

Man's Enemy, the Foul Thief, the Devil in person, tempts people to sin so that they have the chance of repenting before they die and perhaps earning as a reward the dismissal of that even blacker bogey, Eternal Damnation. This is the subtle Calvinist doctrine that comforted Lady Wariston. It is not understood by the Ballad-maker, who sees her not as a potential Saint but as an Awful Warning. In the ballad the Devil comes between the distraught girl and her husband, between her and listeners to her story, between her and all human feeling except moral reprobation. This seems to be Calvinism as it appears to the man in the street. There is a lapse of only eight years between Young Logie's rescue and Lady Wariston's execution, but the difference between the ambience of the two ballads can hardly be measured; they belong to different worlds.

Here are the last two stanzas, banal and didactic, with monotonous -ee endings:

> 'Now, a' ye gentle maids,
> Tak warning now by me,
> And never marry ane
> But wha pleases your ee.
>
> 'For he married me for love,
> But I married him for fee,
> And sae brak out the feud
> That gard my dearie die.'

In this ballad listeners cannot identify themselves with the protagonist; they are invited instead to stand aside and disapprove. How long it took after the event to steep the ballad so thoroughly in such sour moralizing one can only conjecture. The cramping effect of Calvinism, which confines within its own pattern the flow of human sympathy, is shown in the clipped-down metre, resulting here from repressed rather than inarticulate feeling.

The North-Eastern variation of the Wariston ballad has got away from clipped-down terseness; it is looser, more garrulous and more humane than the Southern version. The Devil has vanished from it, but there is a self-conscious agony of repentance in the girl's heart. The story has been changed; the reason for her 'gude lord's' murder is that he has wrongly accused her of making another man the father of her baby. She pays the nurse well for the murder; the serving-man is left out. The nurse is hard of heart, but in prison the 'bonny lady' falls into a swoon. One by one her brother, her mother and her father come in, offering to 'borrow' her. Family sympathy in the North is apparently stronger than in another Southern version where Lady Wariston's father, on being told what his daughter has done,

Cries, 'Gar mak a barrel o pikes,
And row her down some lea.'

She refuses to be borrowed, saying only:

'I that is worthy o the death,
It is but right that I should die.'

Then the King himself 'steps in the fleer' like any Ballad head of a Northern family, and tells her that he will pardon her because she is so young. She begs to be taken instead to the heading-hill, by night, and executed there secretly. Her plea is granted.

They've taen her oot at nine at night,
Loot not the sun upon her shine,
And had her to yon heading-hill,
And headed her baith neat and fine.

Her own family and the King call her 'bonny Jean' throughout; she is never beyond the reach of their sympathy. The only disapproval in the ballad is what she feels for herself, and, in the last stanza, disapproval of Wariston, uttered by the King:

'But Wariston was sair to blame
For slighting o his lady so;
He had the wyte o his ain death
And bonny lady's overthrow.'

The scrutinizing eye is beginning to function, for the King passes judgment here on Wariston although none of the others does, but feelings of common humanity can still rise unhampered. The sense of community is strong enough not to exclude a wrongdoer from human sympathy. Clearly Calvinism has not yet 'taken' in the North-East, although self-consciousness is beginning to glimmer.

The extreme secrecy of the execution is curious. The ballad lays emphasis on the girl's going to the scaffold of her own accord, and then sends her there at night, with no one to see, as nearly as possible blotting the execution out of mind and sight. It is fair to deduce that the people of the countryside were uncomfortable about, and did not want to feel responsible for, the girl's beheading. The execution had to happen, since it was the climax of the story, but they were unwilling to imagine it, to 'see' it.

In shrinking like this from condemning the girl these Northerners may seem to be merely following the tradition of early Ballads, where deeds of violence happen as a matter of course and incur no moral reprobation, even if penance has to be done or head-money paid. These early Ballads were made before self-consciousness began to detach action from feeling. A passion of feeling then inevitably brought instant action, so that a murderer was held to be a victim of Fate rather than a criminal. Yet in the Wariston ballad there is already a dawning of self-awareness, in the girl herself and in the King, who, as a superior, represents the community in his utterances. He passes judgment on Wariston in the last stanza, and in the last stanza but one he says:

> 'I've travelld east, I've travelld west,
> And sailed far beyond the sea,
> But I never saw a woman's face
> I was sae sorry to see dee.'

This is really the verdict of the community itself, although the responsibility for it has been shuffled on to the King's shoulders. One cannot therefore put this ballad on the same footing as earlier, unself-conscious songs. Why, then, were the Northerners so unwilling to condemn the girl?

I suggest that they were unwilling because they were in the first throes of becoming self-conscious. The advance of a personality into full self-consciousness leads through difficult country. As I have ventured to say in a previous chapter, unself-conscious people lack experience in applying systematic moral concepts, acting as they do on impulses from the fluid, unstable underworld of feeling; they have also little or no sense of personal guilt, since they feel driven by forces beyond themselves and do not look inside themselves for motives. Consequently, when some degree of self-awareness comes upon them they are easily bewildered, being unused to it, and may flinch from accepting personal responsibility for their actions. Blame, if blame is in the air, can be attached to someone else, or to external circumstances, not to oneself, and scapegoats are easy to find. I think that one can almost pin-point the dawning of self-awareness in passionate, unsophisticated people by the vehemence with which they push blame away from themselves and refuse personal responsibility.

In the Northern Wariston ballad the community clearly feels unable to cope with moral responsibility; it leaves moral judgment to its superior, the King.

The question now arises: is this where sentimentality begins to creep in? Sentimentality, if we take it to be the outpouring of vicarious emotion on some inappropriate or imaginary object, that is to say, the expression of bogus feeling, is not found in the unselfconscious early Ballads, although they are so fluid that they change from generation to generation and from singer to singer. No extraneous, bogus feeling comes into them unless interpolated by a later age. I think this immunity is largely due to the fact that the singer himself is not self-conscious as he sings, nor is self-consciousness in the air. The singer lets the story carry its own weight and tell itself; he can trust listeners to feel the fitting responses; he does not intrude. When singer and listeners become self-conscious the danger of sentimental intrusion begins, and it is the onset of self-consciousness itself that makes sentimentality possible. Feeling and direct action are then no longer inseparable. Action may be deferred, feeling may be repressed and unrealized. The self-aware personality, becoming more of an onlooker at his social group and at himself, may generate an excess of displaced feeling which will then, often enough, seek another outlet, under cover, evading recognition by the self and giving rise to sentimentality. And the evasion of personal responsibility, if persisted in, also leads to sentimentality. The evasion of responsibility and the evasion of facing one's real feelings are closely akin in their origins. Let us look again at the King's statement in the second last verse of the Northern Wariston ballad:

> 'But I never saw a woman's face
> I was sae sorry to see dee.'

Is this sentiment to be described as sentimentality in embryo? It could be.

There is a danger, then, of Ballads becoming sentimental once they grow self-conscious. Intrusions of sentimental piety are to be found in 'The Fire of Frendraught', and sentimental romantic stuff pads out 'Tifty's Annie', which are both seventeenth-century Ballads; one cannot be certain, however, that this sentimentality worked its way into them during the seventeenth century.

Even early Ballads of action did not escape the revising work of later sentimentalists. A clear example both of sentimentality and evasion of blame, for instance, can be found interpolated into a sixteenth-century ballad, 'Captain Car or Edom o Gordon' (Child, 178), whose deeds go back to the dreadful 'killing times' in the fifteen-seventies. In the *D* version, recorded in 1755, stanzas 19 to 23 are repudiated by Child: he calls them 'deplorable interpolations', and if we look at them we can well see why. I shall begin quoting the ballad at stanza 17, as given by Child.

Edom o Gordon is burning down a castle in which are a lady and her 'babies three'. Her lord is absent and she has refused to surrender.

Stanza 17 has had an emotional 'O' inserted at the beginning of it. The usual form of this carry-over line is: Out then bespake, or: Up then bespake.

17. O then bespake her dochter dear,
She was baith jimp and sma;
'O row me in a pair o shiets
And tow me owre the wa.'

18. They rowd her in a pair of shiets
And towd her owre the wa,
But on the point of Edom's speir
She gat a deadly fa.

19. O bonny, bonny was hir mouth
And chirry were her cheiks,
And clear, clear was hir yellow hair
Whereon the reid bluid dreips!

20. Then wi his speir he turnd hir owr;
O gin her face was wan!
He said, 'You are the first that eer
I wist alive again.'

21. He turned hir owr and owr again;
O gin her skin was whyte!
He said, 'I might ha spard thy life
To been some mans delyte.

22. 'Busk and boon, my merry men all,
For ill dooms I do guess;
I cannae luik on that bonny face
As it lyes on the grass.'

23. 'Them luiks to freits, my master deir,
Then freits will follow them;
Let it neir be said brave Edom o Gordon
Was daunted with a dame.'

Stanza 19 is a comment from outside the story suddenly thrust into the ballad, a comment as from an onlooker, describing the dead girl, a comment with an emotional 'O' at the beginning of it and an ejaculation mark at the end. The ejaculation mark, added by the printer, does not belong to oral poetry at all, but it shows that the printer or an editor appreciated the rhetorical stanza, finding it right and proper, and suggests, therefore, a climate of opinion in which rhetorical comment is acceptable. Yet in a traditional sixteenth-century Ballad rhetorical comment from outside the story has no place. In such a Ballad, description comes from inside the story, as part of narrative or dialogue advancing the action; no one stops the action to look at it from outside, as is done here, and however grim the description no comment is made. Here is a verse in the traditional style:

Out then spake the lady Margaret,
As she stood on the stair;
'The fire is at my gowd garters,
And the lowe is at my hair.'

Or stanza 18, in this rendering:

They rowd her in a pair o shiets
And towd hir owre the wa,
But on the point of Edom's speir
She gat a deadly fa.

No comment on these happenings is expected or made in a Ballad that has not been tampered with. The singer chants:

'She gat a deadly fa'

and leaves it at that. There can be no doubt that stanza 19 begins an interpolation much later in time than the original version of the ballad.

The emotional 'O', again, is used in traditional Ballads before the utterance of some strong feeling, but the utterance is made by a protagonist inside the story, not by an outsider:

> 'O is your bairn to laird or loon
> Or is it to your father's groom?'
>
> 'O row me in a pair o shiets
> And tow me owre the wa.'

These are natural expressions of strong feeling made in their proper place in the course of the story. But here we have another kind of emotional 'O':

> O, bonny, bonny was her mouth,
>
> O gin her face was wan!
>
> O gin her skin was whyte!

These are rhetorical appeals made by an onlooker to intensify the emotion he insists on indulging, inflating its importance and holding up the story to do so.

But the interpolated emotion here is not merely intrusive, it is also ambiguous; it is not what it seems. It pretends to be grief for a fair young dead girl, yet it lingers over details of her murder in a way one cannot help suspecting. There is a suggestion of gloating over the red blood that 'dreips' and Edom o Gordon turns the dead girl 'Owr and owr again'. Some emotional need, forbidden direct expression, is here being satisfied vicariously, under cover. The feeling in these stanzas is entirely sentimental.

The next stanza, with its:

> 'I cannae luik on that bonny face
> As it lyes on the grass',

calls to mind the King's remark in the Wariston ballad:

> 'But I never saw a woman's face
> I was sae sorry to see dee.'

Edom o Gordon, being himself the murderer, is here made to carry evasion of responsibility a step farther than the King does.

His uncomfortable awareness of possible blame is at once counteracted by the dry response of a proper man of action, untroubled by self-consciousness, his subordinate:

> 'Them luiks to freits, my master deir,
> Then freits will follow them;
> Let it neir be said brave Edom o Gordon
> Was daunted with a dame.'

The word 'daunted' is appropriate, for new-growing self-awareness does have a daunting effect; that is one reason why people have recourse to sentimentality.

In itself sentimentality seems to be a technique of evasiveness that cannot be used until some degree of self-consciousness has developed; it is a result, though not an inevitable result, of increased self-awareness. Naturally, it is influenced by currents in prevailing climates of opinion; some ages are more generally sentimental than others, and the objects or attitudes sentimentalized vary from generation to generation. It was a sentimentally inclined age anyhow, that took the trouble to interpolate these five stanzas into 'Edom o Gordon'. I suspect the eighteenth century, which in Scotland was an age of growing sentimentality as well as of reason: quite different things went on in the back of Lowland Scots' minds from the rational policies consciously prevailing in the front of them.

One of these almost unconscious processes was the shift in public opinion from despising the Highlanders to enveloping them in sentimental glamour. Until the eighteenth century, contempt for Highlanders was well rooted in Lowland Scotland. About 1560, only 32 years before the Murray ballad, the following lines were written down in the Bannatyne MS.,[1] entitled: 'How the first Helandman of God was maid of Ane horse turd in argylle as is said.'

> Sanct petir said to god in a sport word
> Can ȝe no^t mak a helandman of this horss tourd
> God turnd owre þe horss turd w^t his pykit staff
> And vp start a helandman blak as ony draff
> Quod god to þe helandman Quhair wilt thow now
> I will doun in þe Lowland lord and thair steill a kow

[1] Bannatyne MS., ff. 162b-163a

And thow steill A cow cairle thair thay will hang the
Quattrack lord of that ffor anis mon I die.

This popular rhyme may havc bccn current for some time before it was written, for ridicule and contempt were poured upon Highlanders as far back as the fifteenth century when the poet Dunbar consigned Erse-speakers to be 'smoorit' in the deepest pit of hell where they belonged. And as late as 1948 a children's rhyme,[1] recorded by Norah and William Montgomerie, still preserved in Aberdeen an old fleer at the Highlandmen:

'Hielanman, Hielanman,
Far wis ye born?'

'Up in the Hielans
Among the green corn.'

'Fat gat ye there
But green kail and leeks?'

Laugh at a Hielanman
Wintin his breeks.

The breeklessness of Highlandmen has long been, and still is, a matter of interest to trouser-conscious societies. Besides being breekless cow-thieves they spoke an unintelligible language once called by Lowland Scots Erse or Irish. In 1720, the Society for the Propagation of Christian Knowledge, which sent Presbyterian missionaries to the Highlands, refused a Minister's plea that people who knew no English might learn their catechism in Irish. School-children were punished for speaking Gaelic among themselves. In the name of Christian enlightenment Gaelic songs were forbidden, fiddles were broken across the Minister's knee and Highland dancing was put down. Right into the nineteenth century this superior attitude to Highland culture was consciously maintained by many Lowland Scots, who added the cant of economic progress to the cant of spiritual progress, claiming that Highlanders were unprofitable tenants, fit only to be cleared out and sent to the colonies.

How has it happened, then, that the public image Scotland now presents to the world is composed of elements from Highland

[1] *Sandy Candy*, p. 117, The Hogarth Press

culture? Among the tartans, whiskies, bag-pipes and Highland dances the Lowland Scots contribute nothing to it unless, perhaps, Robert Burns: yet even Burns may exist in someone's imagination as a ploughman in a kilt, considering that Staffordshire made a pottery figure of him in 1850 clad in a kilt beside his Highland Mary. An extraordinary shift must have taken place in the back of the Lowlanders' minds.

Some evidence of the shift can be found in Ballads. In 'The Baron of Brackley' (Child, 203), an old ballad in couplet form, perhaps of the sixteenth century, the Highlanders are still despised as 'widifus wi belted plaids'. A widifu is a gallows-bird: the widy, or wuddie, refers to the withy with which victims were then hanged on a gallows. The belted plaids are an accurate description of their dress; the separate kilt was invented later as a regimental garb. Both earlier and later Ballads than this see the Highlanders not merely as lawless robbers but as fighting savages to be put down in the cause of civilization. A big battle fought between Highlanders and Lowlanders in 1411, the Battle of Harlaw, not far from Aberdeen, in which more than nine hundred Celts were killed and five hundred Lowlanders, including nearly all the gentry of Buchan, 'was felt', says a Scottish historian, Burton, in 1883, 'as a more memorable deliverance even than that of Bannockburn'. It was celebrated in a Ballad mentioned in the *Complaynt of Scotland*, 1549, and was still celebrated in a much-revised more modern version in 1858, which must have been worked over for four hundred years; in the course of time the ancient ballad disappeared and successive versions glorified families who played no part in the original encounter, but they still preserved the old feeling of enmity to Highlanders with some ridicule of bag-pipes added.

The reputation of Highlanders as fighting men began to improve a little in the seventeenth century, especially after they won the battle of Killiecrankie. A Covenanting ballad, 'Bonny John Seton' (Child, 198), with the solemn cadence of a metrical psalm, gives them grudging praise:

The Highland men, they're clever men
At handling sword and shield,
But yet they are too naked men
To stay in battle field.

The Highland men are clever men
At handling sword or gun,
But yet they are too naked men
To bear the cannon's rung.

But not until the eighteenth century, after the Jacobite risings of the 'Fifteen and the 'Forty-five, did sentimental glamour begin to surround the Highlanders. Because of these risings, especially the 'Forty-five, the Government in London cruelly oppressed the Highland clans as a matter of official policy. Before that, while Lowlanders themselves were the despisers and oppressors, there had been no need for them to feel sentimental about Highlanders, since the despising was done with a good conscience; but after the Union of Parliaments in 1707 many Lowland Scots strongly resented the London Government for its new taxes, its legal breaches of the Treaty of Union, and its apparently unfair discrimination against Scottish industries, so that in the back of their minds, beyond reason, beyond surface loyalties, beyond the conscious policies they thought to follow, they felt uneasy, were stirred by the gallantry of the Risings, and began to be sentimental about them. This ambivalence in the Lowland Scottish make-up was sensed by Walter Scott, who embodied it in the character of Bailie Nicol Jarvie, canny merchant in Glasgow and kinsman of the Highland freebooter, Rob Roy. The personal appearance of Prince Charlie and various great Highland chiefs in Edinburgh during the 'Forty-five deepened the impression in the background of people's minds, where the Ballad tradition still lingered, and symptoms of romanticizing sentimentality began to find expression in songs and Ballads. The following song comes from Royalist Aberdeen:

'My love was born in Aberdeen,
The bonniest lad that e'er was seen;
But now he's made our hearts fu' sad
He's ta'en the field wi' his white cockade.'

The third verse shows a complete swing-over from previous ridicule of Highland dress:

'O leeze[1] me on the philabeg,
The hairy hough and garter'd leg!'

[1] Leeze me on = My delight is. (Lief is me.)

The lady goes on to aver:

'I'll sell my rock, I'll sell my reel,
My rippling-kame and spinning-wheel,
To buy mysel a tartan plaid
A braid sword, durk, and white cockade.'

The men in Aberdeen might still be singing 'The Battle of Harlaw', but the women were already shifting their allegiance. This shift appears in Ballads, as might be expected, in romantic form. Instead of Chronicle Ballads describing the kidnapping of unwilling Lowland heiresses by wicked Highlanders,[1] which did in fact happen as late as 1750, we find romantic Ballads celebrating true love-affairs between a Lowland maiden and a Highland chieftain. The Highlander disguises himself at first as a poor man and then turns out to be the lord of wide domains; the old image of the Highlander as a poverty-stricken cateran is thus replaced by a new image of grandeur. In 'Glasgow Peggie' (Child, 228), version *B*, which begins with the firm statement:

The Lowland lads think they are fine
But the Hieland lads are brisk and gaucy,

bonnie Peggy has first to spend a night on the open moors:

Gude green hay was Peggy's bed,
And brakens were her blankets bonnie,
Wi' his tartan plaid aneath her head;
An she's lain doun wi her Hieland laddie.

But her lover, once he has made sure of her, announces:

'I am Donald, the Lord of Skye,
And why sud na Peggy be calld a lady?

'See ye no a' yon castles and towrs?
The sun sheens owre them a sae bonnie;
I am Donald, the Lord of Skye,
I think I'll mak ye as blythe as onie.'

Bonnie Lizie Baillie (Child, 227) provides a variation on the theme; her wooer, Duncan Grahame, says:

[1] 'Bonny Baby Livingston' (Child, 222); 'Eppie Morrie' (Child, 223); 'Rob Roy' (Child, 225)

'My bonny Lizie Bailie,
I'll row thee in my pladie,
If thou will go along with me
And be my Highland lady.'

She has misgivings:

'If I would go along with thee
I think I were not wise;
For I cannot milk cow nor ewe
Nor yet can I speak Erse.'

Yet she goes with him because she loves him:

'Should not I fancie Duncan Grahame
When Duncan fancies me?'

Here the Highlander is loved forthrightly as a man, not as a glamorous chieftain. But the glamorous chieftain has the longer life in Ballad memory. The ballad of Lizie Lindsay (Child, 226), once very popular in the North-East, begins with the Highlander pretending to be a poor man who can promise his lady only curds and green whey, so that she is convinced she has to 'gang wi a bare-houghed puir laddie'; he even, following Ballad precedents, persuades his shepherd's wife to pretend to be his mother when they arrive at her hut; then, after this disguise, puts on splendour like Hind Horn:

He led her up to a hie mountain
And bade her look out, far and wide;
'I'm lord o thae isles and thae mountains,
And ye're now my beautiful bride.'

A satisfactory outcome, later condensed into a short ballad, or song, still widely known in Scotland.

'Will ye gang to the Hielands, Leezie Lindsay,
Will ye gang to the Hielands wi me?
Will ye gang to the Hielands, Leezie Lindsay,
My bride and my darling to be?'

'Tae gang to the Hielands wi you, sir,
I dinna ken how that may be,
For I kenna the land that ye live in,
Nor ken I the lad I gang wi.'

'Leezie, lassie, 'tis little that ye ken,
If so be you dinna ken me,
For my name is Lord Ronald Macdonald,
A chieftain o high degree.'

She's kilted her coats o green satin,
She's kilted them up to the knee,
And she's aff wi Lord Ronald Macdonald,
His bride and his darling to be.

This song, with its delightful tune, is perhaps all that is left in general memory from among these image-making Ballads. Yet the glamorous effect of the forgotten Ballads remains.

So the Lowland Scots themselves projected the public image of Scotland which now seems to exclude them, although when they began projecting it they were only satisfying a vague need. One must remember that sentimentality is a technique of evasion; what it evades is the conscious recognition of some human need which none the less makes itself felt as a source of uneasiness, a sense, perhaps, of something lacking to the full enjoyment of the human condition, something, certainly, which might cause social discomfort if brought into the open. What the Lowland Scots shrank from bringing into the open was disloyalty to the Treaty of Union: what they felt uneasy about was their sense of being no longer an independent people, separate and different from the English. Under Calvinist guidance they had been attaching their values to shrewd, logical reasoning, keeping a wary eye on each other while saving their own souls, and in the cause of self-interest many of them had now a conscious desire to become as like the English as possible. They were, indeed, not startlingly unlike the English, in their own eyes, yet the English seemed to regard them as inferior Englishmen, and, as they thought, high-handedly oppressed them. They needed a new sense of nationhood. What they had previously taken for granted had now to be given shape. Hitherto their monarch had been a King of Scots, but now he had to become a King of Scotland, the whole of Scotland. Highland dress, Highland music, Highland temperament were all sufficiently unlike the English to make part of a nucleus for the crystallizing of this new separateness, this new nationhood, and although many Lowland Scots were not Celts, being, in the

Lothians for instance, of the same stock as Northumbrians, they were in a condition of emotional shock because of the Union that made them susceptible to the glamour of the Celts. The attitude to the Highlands began to change. By the seventeen-nineties bag-piping contests were held in Edinburgh. Bag-pipes were already popular and had been strongly influencing the style of fiddling in Lowland country districts. Whisky needed no recommendation. Tartans became a commercial asset: it is said that clan tartans were mostly invented by a Lowland woollen-draper. Slowly the new public image was formed, and it was largely a Highland image. When the small principalities of Germany felt the need for a unifying myth, they invented the *Volks-seele*, the Folk-soul, but Calvinist Scots had had no truck with folk-souls and did not yet sentimentalize their peasantry. Instead, they now idealized the Highlanders, who represented an ancient and persisting heroic legend, the 'chieftains of high degree'. At the same time, because this idealization was sentimental, they evaded doing anything about official persecution of Highlanders, or about the eviction of Highland crofters from their holdings, as late as the nineteenth century,when thousands of them either starved or were packed off abroad by the ship-load.

The argument has since been advanced that Lowland Scotland, excluding the Lothians, was originally Celtic, since its people were Picts if not Scots, so that the Celtic public image means only the revivifying of a very old pattern. It is true that Fife was long regarded from the Lothians as a separate kingdom inhabited by queer folk; a Lothian man crossing the Forth would speak of going 'out of Scotland into Fife', and popular Lothian maxims, such as: 'It tak's a lang spoon to sup wi a Fifer', and 'F-L-Y spells Fife' show the same wariness of wily aliens as do English rhymes about the Welsh. Fife may have preserved a Strathclyde culture, or even a Pictish culture, between its two estuaries for a long time. It is also true that from Angus and the Mearns as far North as beyond Aberdeen the local speech still pronounces 'what' as 'fat', and 'wha' as 'fa', and 'whaur' as 'faur', in what seems to be Celtic fashion. Yet this possible Celtic heritage, with its legends, superstitions and enduring interest in far-flung kinship networks, had already assimilated itself to Lowland tradition well before Ballads began to circulate; it was neither recognized nor acknowledged by the fifteenth century. I think one should not lay any emphasis upon it. These Ballads which I have called the 'image-making' Ballads provide as good a clue as any to the way in which the Celtic public image was shaped during the eighteenth century. Ballads have a knack—shared by written literature—of picking up whatever is 'in the air'. How it comes to be in the air I do not pretend to explain, although I believe that it has to do with the invisible radiations which people daily receive from others and give out in turn, vibrations which make what are called 'climates of opinion', or 'climates of belief', about which we still know too little. On this hypothesis, at any rate, when one says that something is 'in the air', the expression means more than one usually supposes it to mean.

There was less sentimentality in the air of Scotland during the seventeenth century, to judge from its Ballads, than during the eighteenth. People were travelling through the Debateable Land of increasing self-awareness, which almost inevitably brings self-pity, but I do not think that self-pity is necessarily sentimental. Consider this song, which must have existed by the late seventeenth century, since stanzas from it were incorporated into a ballad about the break-up of a Douglas marriage in 1681:

'O waly, waly up the bank,
And waly, waly down the brae,
And waly, waly yon burn-side
Where I and my love wont to gae.

'I leaned my back unto an aik,
I thought it was a trusty tree;
But first it bowd and syne it brak,
Sae my true-love did lightly me.

'O waly, waly, but love be bonny
A little time, while it is new;
But when 'tis auld it waxeth cauld
And fades away like morning dew.

. . . . .

'When we came in by Glasgow town
We were a comely sight to see;
My love was clad in the black velvet,
And I mysell in cramasie.

'But had I wist before I kiss'd
That love had been sae ill to win,
I'd lockd my heart in a case o gowd
And pin'd it wi' a siller pin.'

There is sentiment here, but no sentimentality; the singer is taking a straight look at her predicament and evading none of it, nor is she 'showing off' her feelings as people do in a sentimental age. She has detached herself from her grief sufficiently to see her past happiness as past, and she has no hope of renewing it. The last verse makes that clear:

'And O, if my young babe was born
And set upon the nurse's knee,
And I mysell were dead and gane,
For a maid again I'll never be.'

In another version the last line reads:

'And the green grass growing over me.'

The scrutinizing eye of self-awareness, turned here upon interior experience, brings out visual imagery in the form of metaphors and it is of interest to note that the stanzas borrowed by the Douglas ballad (Child, 204) except for the introductory lament, are precisely those with the pictorial imagery; in version *J*: 'I leaned my back against an aik', in version *F*: 'But gin I had wist or I had kisst', and in all versions but one a riddling stanza that occurs only in the *Orpheus Caledonius* rendering of the song (1725):

'When cockle-shells turn siller bells
And mussles grows on evry tree,
When frost and snaw shall warm us a',
Then shall my love prove true to me.'

The slight variations in the lines that have been borrowed, as, for instance: 'But gin I had wist or I had kisst', instead of: 'But had I wist before I kissd', suggest that they have been heard rather than read; the Ballad-makers have retained the sense and rhythm, but not the exact wording, in the usual style of oral transmission. Yet only the metaphorical stanzas stuck in their memories, and these they must have borrowed because they admired the metaphors as an exciting novelty. Metaphors were indeed novel to the Ballad tradition, although familiar enough in other kinds of poetry, in the court poetry of mediaeval Scotland as well as elsewhere. Until now, until about the late sixteenth and the seventeenth centuries, emotional situations were not summed up in pictorial imagery in Ballads. One cannot make a visual image unless one first has a standpoint from which to see it, and that standpoint can be provided only by detached self-awareness, a new element in Ballads, as I have tried to show.

The harbingers of self-aware metaphors in Ballads were symbols, like the flower symbols in the dancing refrains of 'The Cruel Brother', which, as I have surmised, expressed the mood of the participants, probably girls playing a singing and dancing game. 'And a lilly gay, As the primrose spreads so sweetly', or another variant, 'And the rose it smells so sweetly'—these refrains do not form an integral part of the Ballad story but are merely added to it, laid alongside, as it were, suggesting an implicit not an explicit connection. Like the 'cold, cold frosty morning' in our singing game at school, the added symbol is understood without explanation; its meaning is felt but not formulated; the lily, the primrose or the rose are not consciously looked at, not even with a side-glance; they simply suggest girlish youth and gaiety. Any sweet-smelling flower would have served the purpose equally well. In a mournful incest ballad ('Sheath and Knife') the flower-refrain comes nearer to metaphor; the broom, like rye, is associated with love-making, and the refrains:

> The brume blooms bonnie and says it is fair.
> And we'll never gang doun to the brume onie mair.

provide more than an atmosphere; they suggest a taboo on love-making, made more explicit by a variation:

> And we daurna gae doun to the brume nae mair.

Here no other flower but the broom would have served the purpose. Still more explicit, more nearly verging on metaphor, are the symbol-stanzas about the twining plants on true lovers' graves; these are also added to Ballads as extras, not integrated into the story. With the coming of self-awareness the visual image is at last fully seen and becomes part of the story, as here:

'I leaned my back unto an aik,
I thought it was a trusty tree,
But first it bowd and syne it brak,
Sae my true love did lightly me.'

What happens in the underworld of feeling when it sends up a Ballad without visual imagery should not perhaps be called imagination in the strict sense of the word: to use a term like 'dramatic invention' would be more accurate. The action in early Ballads is dramatic, with tension mounting to a crisis, a confrontation, a challenge and usually a death or two. Being entirely within the drama itself, an early Ballad cannot get outside an action to mirror it in an image. The kind of world represented is one that lives wholly by doing, by exercising a power inherent in all living creatures, but especially in man, who either subdues other forces to his own uses or is subdued by them. In such a world the only alternatives are victory or defeat: there is no third way out of this dilemma, which seems final to the primitive mind although when seen by more consciously developed people appears to be a false dilemma. One might say that the world of early Ballads knows the Active Voice of grammar and the Passive Voice, but is not yet aware of the Middle Voice. There is no space for reflection, for self-awareness. Consequently there is no awareness of the external world as existing separately by right of itself. A matriarch picking a bush of woodbine for magical purposes would not pause to admire it, or to wonder at the difference between its mode of growth and other plants; she would see it merely as an embodiment of the power to bind, something she could use against her pregnant daughter-in-law, because she is stronger than the woodbine and can break it off and carry it home. Everything belongs to man if he can but subdue it. He does see the external world, since he is not blind, but he is not detached from it as an onlooker; he is too busy conquering it, using it, or defending himself from it to see it except as an instrument, a possible enhancer or diminisher of his own power. This world of action, of tensions, of pressure from above and below, of overwhelming passions, defiant challenges and desperate fighting, seems a more primitive world than that in which Ballads are first known to have appeared, but it is the world they sing about.

The early Ballads are shaped for drama alone, for on-goings that make stories of action, for carryings-on that often end in tragedy. There is no room for visual imagery in that world, although each Ballad embodies a pattern of feeling which might in time become the source of an image.

The growth of self-awareness and of an awareness that the external world has a separate existence of its own are one and the same process in Ballads. Animals and birds are closer at first to human life than plants or flowers; when men go out with hounds to 'ding the dun deer doun' a white hind can be a woman, and Johnie Cock can say, on being surprised asleep by arrow-flights from foresters:

> 'There's not a wolf in a' the wood
> Woud ha done the like to me;
> She'd ha dipped her foot in coll water
> And strinkled above my ee,
> And if I would not have waked for that,
> She'd ha gane and let me be.'

As time goes on, animals lose their ambiguous humanity, until in the Border Riding Ballads horses and cows have become simply horses and cows. Presently flowers, nuts and berries separate themselves from the greenwood, as if newly observed. It may be relevant to note here that in the upsurge of consciousness called the Renaissance animal motifs were common at first in decorative work and were later replaced by twining plants and foliage, just as in Ballads flowers come in later than animals to hover, in refrains, on the verge of human awareness, as symbols of young gaiety. Still later, plant symbols begin to occupy whole stanzas instead of merely being hinted at in refrains, and presently occasional similes appear—blood is 'as red as the wine'—and full metaphors, as in 'Johnie Armstrong's Last Goodnight', and 'Sir Patrick Spens'. The achievement of metaphor seems to me to mark a high-water level of Ballad-making, a level at which Scottish Ballads did not—perhaps could not—stay.

At this time, in the late seventeenth century, the scrutinizing eye was fresh and often penetrating in its interior observation. Even in the Douglas ballad ('Jamie Douglas'), a usual type of jog-trot Chronicle Ballad except for its lovely borrowed verses, which describes in banal style the troubles of the Marchioness of Douglas after her husband has falsely accused her of adultery and repudiated her, there are flashes of insight which one does not find earlier in any Ballad version of relations between men and women. The Marchioness suddenly sees that there ought to be a symmetrical balance between the sexes:

> 'O what need I care for Jamie Douglas
> More than he needs to care for me?'

And again:

> 'Thou thocht that I was just like thyself,
> And took everyone that I did see.'

This perception is echoed in another ballad, a broadside supposed to have been printed towards the end of the seventeenth or the beginning of the eighteenth century, which also incorporates stanzas from 'Waly, waly', such as this one:

> 'Martinmas wind, when wilt thou blow
> And blow the green leafs off the tree,
> O gentle Death, when wilt thou come,
> For of my life I am wearie.'

Yet, in the very middle of so much despair, we find again the hint that love should have reciprocal obligations:

> Should I be bound that may go free?
> Should I love them that loves not me?
> I'le rather travel into Spain,
> Where I'le get love for love again.'

'Love for love again' actually becomes the central motif in a little ballad found only in the North-east of Scotland, where it was very popular. In Greig's version ('The False Lover Won Back', LXIX) the phrase is enlarged into a stanza that functions as a refrain:

> 'It's love for love that I do want,
> An love for love again:
> It's hard when I like you sae weel
> An ye nae me again.'

In this simple and endearing ballad the lady kilts up her 'gay clothin'' and follows her faithless lover, who is riding away, until, at the third town they come to, he buys her a wedding ring and her refrain changes:

> 'It's love for love that I do want,
> An love for love again,
> An there's neen but you for me, bonnie love,
> An there's neen but me for you.
>
> 'There's comfort for the comfortless
> An honey for the bee;
> An there's neen for me but you, bonnie love,
> There's neen for you but me.'

Reciprocity in love is clearly in the air of the late seventeenth century, a new look at relationships between men and women. In general, one would expect the growth of self-awareness to provide a new look not only at oneself but also at other people, men and women, and at the external world of animals, vegetation, natural forces, stars and suns. But to ask Ballads to do this is asking them to rival the Royal Society. They were first made by people who felt the impact of power and enjoyed few or none of its privileges, people who were sustained by a sense of vicariously belonging to powerful groups but had to spend their lives in continuous toil; consequently early Ballads express only patterns of action, which become traditional, familiar, well-loved and resistant to change, formed into dramatic stories in a style that cannot lend itself to non-dramatic subjects. When Ballads get as far as expressing dramatic self-revelations they cannot penetrate farther within their own tradition: they would have to become lyrics or stage plays, not Ballads. Indeed, 'Waly waly' is as much of a lyric as a Ballad. People in a Ballad must be in motion, journeying, shall we say, or fighting. In 'Waly, waly' the singer, perhaps unconsciously, keeps herself and her lover moving as much as she can:

> 'Waly waly yon burnside
> Where I and my love wont to gae.'
>
> . . . . .
>
> 'When we came in by Glasgow town—'

All her metaphors move; the oak bows and breaks, love fades like dew, she might have locked her heart in a golden case and pinned it with a silver pin, she wants to be blown from the tree of life like a leaf in a Martinmas wind. In every stanza there is action of some kind, and so one can call her Lament a Ballad, but the exploration of interior feeling is more suited to a lyric. And the expression of that in metaphor seems to have been too difficult for Ballad audiences, since metaphors are almost entirely dropped from subsequent Ballads, which confine themselves to singing dramatic stories in traditional fashion.

Yet, even had their style permitted, Ballads were not free to develop far-reaching self-awareness without hindrance. One must not forget that influences 'in the air' have always determined the kind, even the existence, of Ballads. In the re-making of Scotland after the Treaty of Union, for instance, Ballads helped to form the popular image of the glamorous Highland chief, and so were subject to the growing sentimentality of the age. It seems, moreover, impossible for any institution which becomes part of a public image to escape being sentimentalized, since a public image itself is a by-product of self-consciousness and offers too easy a focus for displaced and homeless feelings. The Kirk of Scotland which naturally became part of the new public image differentiating Scotland from England was inevitably sentimentalized, and, as inevitably, affected the tone of Ballads. The Ballad of the Queen's Maries, or Mary Hamilton, which is still well known in its shortened version and which was given its present shape in the eighteenth century, acquired in the North-East this bit of pious cant as a final stanza:

> 'O what care I for a nameless grave,
> If I've hope for eternity?
> For it was for the blood of the dyin lamb,
> That's granted through grace unto me.'[1]

Nor did Ballads escape unharmed from the attention bestowed on them by literate townspeople, who were beginning to take an interest in them and trying to correct their vulgar vernacular. The traditional commonplace stanza for reading a 'braid letter' which is used in Sir Patrick Spens, for instance:

[1] Greig, *Last Leaves*, LII, version *B*

The first word that Sir Patrick read
Sae loud, loud laughed he;
The neist word that Sir Patrick read,
The tear blinded his ee.

was transformed, in the interests of 'poetical propriety', into this:

The first line that my lord lookd on
Struck him with strong surprise;
The second, more alarming still,
Made tears fall from his eyes.

The influence of the printed word, too, was spreading widely, even into rural districts, with the circulation of chapbooks, broadsides, weekly and monthly magazines and news-sheets. Unlettered people, especially when they are given authoritative scriptures and feel reverence for the printed word of God, extend that reverence to all print that comes their way; they begin to think that the printed version of a song must be correct and that the fluid rendering of an orally transmitted song is somehow full of incorrect deviations, a misconception which for some time was shared by most of their literate fellow-countrymen in Scotland. Print disseminates information but in this way also hardens it: what is down 'in black and white' seems more rigidly true than what comes by word of mouth. Print also has to be paid for, in cash; it belongs immediately to the new world which is set on money-making, not on subsistence farming, and so helps to shift people's minds away from older values. The country people, it is true, went on singing Ballads in the old style, yet they could not but feel the new currents setting against them. Whatever the reason, a dimension vanishes from Ballads in the eighteenth century. No longer, that is to say, do they reach up to the sky, either with a sense of overbearing powers or of triumphant human hopes; they leave such matters to the Kirk and become domestic dramas. Moreover, romantic Ballads in which the hero weeps as readily as the heroine and as easily dies for love, are now scorned by a new generation in the towns, where industry and finance, following their own patterns of increasing power, are bringing back the old Norse feeling that men of power do not allow emotions to govern them. Consequently the hint of a symmetrical balance between the sexes, perceptible in the late seventeenth century, disappears altogether; the masters of industry now claim, with a vehemence sometimes amounting in the nineteenth century to hysteria, that women should be their obedient subjects, not their equal partners.

Another sign of the times is the shortening of Ballads into songs. The ballad of Lizie Lindsay becomes a song, and so does the Queen's Maries. The Jacobite Risings, proper subjects, one might think, for Ballads, raise a crop of songs but no Ballads. And Robert Burns devotes his genius to songs. There had always been songs in Scotland, but there were as many Ballads as songs; now songs come into the forefront and are multiplied. Some of them have a cosy domestic humour, which also appears in Northern Ballads. One feels that both song and Ballad are ready to cross the invisible line leading into the world of entertainment, which postulates a public rather than an intimate audience and presently insists on being paid for in cash, either in print or personal performance.

I think that increasing self-consciousness tends to prefer short-cuts rather than long journeys through stories, and that the shortening of Ballads and the prevalence of briefer songs owes much to this. Perhaps also there was an increased awareness of clock-time, of time too precious to waste. Even in the rural districts of North-East Scotland the re-making of Scotland was going on at a fast pace throughout the eighteenth century. The 'seven ill years' at the end of the seventeenth century had killed off hundreds of starving country people, and the first priority in the minds of the intelligent men known as the 'Improvers' was the improvement of agriculture. Great energy was bent towards achieving this. Importing new ideas from Holland, such as the use of turnips for winter feeding, was only a part of the process. Men were now busier fighting Nature than fighting each other; a different kind of 'action' was in the air; a different devotion to acquiring power, and the money which meant power. If many a waste patch of broom was uprooted and many a strip of greenwood felled, would that not have some effect on the Ballad tradition also? Let us consider the Ballads still being produced and sung in the North-East of Scotland after the Treaty of Union.

13
From Ballads to Corn-kisters

THE habit of Ballad-singing in the North-east of Scotland lasted until the twentieth century. Gavin Greig, born in 1856, a native of Aberdeenshire and a schoolmaster there until he died in 1914, collected more than seven hundred Ballads, tunes and all, which were alive and circulating in the countryside he knew. As a memorial to him, about a seventh of these were published in 1925, in a volume called *Last Leaves of Aberdeen Ballads and Airs*, and the editor, Alexander Keith, says in his introduction to it that Ballad-singing in Aberdeenshire 'is only now dying out'. In the neighbouring county of the Mearns, Kincardineshire, Ballads were being sung by ploughmen in 1906, as I know from personal experience. Today, in the sixties, the School of Scottish Studies in Edinburgh is still recording Ballad-singers here and there, including that great Ballad-singer from the city of Aberdeen, Jeannie Robertson, who renders her songs in high traditional style, having learned them from her mother, a travelling tinker. This part of Scotland has put up what seems to be a stout resistance to any influences which might have undermined Ballads, from the eighteenth century onwards.

According to John Allan, the people of North-east Scotland began to come out of the Middle Ages only about 1713; before that, they had resisted in turn Calvinism, Cromwell and the Treaty of Union; clearly they were a conservative, stubborn people. Yet they did not go on singing Ballads into the twentieth century only out of sheer stubborn conservatism, out of duty to the past or defiance of the future. Ballads must have been a satisfying, enjoyable element in their way of life. They were lucky, perhaps exceptionally lucky, in having that way of life improved but not basically changed when they emerged from the Middle Ages to help in re-making the agriculture of Scotland. They had been, and they remained, rural farming people; their farming merely became more intelligent, better organized and more productive than it had been before; the new ways did not unsettle them and drive them into cities but stirred them up and gave them new confidence. Continuity in their lives seemed assured, and Ballads were a part of it.

Yet living Ballads change with the generations who sing them, and the Ballads current in the North-East naturally changed with the times. They were bound to gain in self-consciousness, and perhaps to lose something through being affected by the new sentimentalities of their age. Whatever the changes, the people who sang them went on feeling, suffering, loving, and in their Ballads rehearsed, exercised and contemplated these activities with apparent satisfaction.

Why, then, did I suggest that Ballads lost a dimension somewhere about the eighteenth century? Possibly an answer could be found to this question by comparing newer and older versions of the same Ballad, or by looking at a typical Ballad or two from the eighteenth century. Among hundreds of random Ballads, with a range as varied as that of human nature, selection is difficult,but, as it happens, in 'The Kitchie-Boy' (Child, 252) there exists a good example of an old Ballad made over again in the North-East.

'The Kitchie-Boy' is 'Hind Horn' re-told in eighteenth-century terms. The course of the story is much the same. A lady of high rank falls in love with a young man of lower standing, gives him a ring as a love-token when he goes overseas, meets him on his return, when he comes back disguised, recognizes first the ring then her lover as he drops his disguise, and marries him. Yet the elements of the story have all been reduced in strength. The lady is no queen or princess, merely an earl's daughter. The young man is her father's menial kitchen-boy. The golden ring she gives him has no magic in it. He does not come back in the nick of time to keep her from marrying another: indeed, her father seems anxious just to get her married off. The current of emotion that carries the ballad along brings a sense of triumph for the hero, yet it is a shallower current and a lesser triumph. This hero is not winning a kingdom from rival adventurers, or being borne into harbour at the last dramatic moment by a magical Fate. His adventures while overseas are reduced to flirtations with other ladies who try in vain to seduce his affections, in London and in Spain. The emphasis in the story is on love-affairs: there are no less than eight stanzas of dialogue between the ill-matched pair before the lady sends the kitchen-boy off to sea. When this ballad was made it marked, I should think, a new Ballad interest in personal romantic relationships, but nowadays it could be called 'novelettish'.

What it has lost is magic and high adventure. One little touch of the old Ballad magic is left, the ship that the lady fits up for her love:

> The topmasts war o the red goud,
> the sails of tafetie.

What it has gained, besides being interested in the lovers as 'Hind Horn' is not, is an entirely new element of irony.

The first stanza betrays the influence of the scrutinizing censorious eye, which seems to have reached the North-East at last:

> There was a lady fair
> An een a lady of birth an fame,
> She eyed her father's kitchen-boy,
> The greater was her shame.

After this perfunctory tribute to conventional social morality the next stanza at once enters with understanding into the lady's difficulties:

> She could never her love reveal,
> Nor to him talk,
> But in the forest wide an brade
> Where they were wont to walk.

The seductive greenwood, one notices, has lost both its magic and its danger: it has become merely a trysting-place.

> It fell once upon a day
> Her father gaed frae hame.
> And she sent for the kitchen-boy
> To her own room.
>
> 'Canna ye fancy me, Willie?
> Canna ye fancy me?
> By a' the lords I ever saw
> There is nane I loo but ye.'

We are now well into the novelette. She sends him off to sea in grand style with her 'gay goud ring' on his finger, for no apparent motive except that the original story postulates a return by sea. But here the element of irony comes in, a self-conscious achievement not possible for the earlier ballad, 'Hind Horn'. She has fitted up the 'bonny ship' in order to outwit her father: the young man is to come back in his rich ship looking like a rich squire from overseas. An eighteenth-century rendering of 'Young Beichan' also makes the lady slily outwit her father; it appears that outwitting one's father was then a popular theme.

Two years later the hero duly returns in his magnificent ship and the deluded father says:

'Gae busk ye, my dochter,
Gae busk ye unco fine,
And I'll gae down to yon shore-side
To invite the squar to dine.
I wad gie a' my rents
To hae ye married to him.'

As the ballad comments in the last stanza:

Little did the old man ken
It was his ain kitchen-boy.

The twist of irony in the story leads to satisfied laughter at the ending of it. But is this still the story that once formed the core of the *Odyssey* and reverberated down the ages till it produced 'Hind Horn'? It has lost the sense of over-riding Fate, the power of magic, the adventurous glory of taking a kingdom as well as a wife. Instead of Fate there is a woman's guile; instead of magic there is plausible, realistic intrigue; instead of glory there is a comfortable marriage. The added detail, moreover, makes the ballad much longer than 'Hind Horn'. Yet the derivation from 'Hind Horn' is clearly shown when the lady recognizes the ring:

'O gat ye that ring on the sea sailing?
Or gat ye it on the land?
O gat ye it on the shore lying
On a drowned man's hand?'

'I got na it on the sea sailing,
I got na it on the land,
But I got it on the shore lying
On a drowned man's hand.'

This extra ironic screw on the tension, frightening the lady at first into believing her Willie drowned, does not obscure the likeness to 'Hind Horn'.

Many of the Northern Ballads, especially those collected in the early nineteenth century by Peter Buchan, of which this is one, are long, often garrulously long. Perhaps the piling on of detail was a conscious attempt to make up for the vaguely sensed loss of magic? Or was it the natural consequence of a more observant and scrutinizing eye? Or, if the singer were a peripatetic beggar, did he feel he had to entertain his hosts for as long as possible? That such 'gangrel bodies' did travel from farm to farm with a store of Ballads is known; there was one James Rankin who supplied many Ballads to Buchan. But Ballads also descended in families, usually from grandmother to granddaughter, and if they were sung by old women with failing powers might they not have become looser in structure? Yet 'The Kitchie-Boy', which comes from an Old Lady left anonymous, is terse enough in its single stanzas:

'O latna this be kent, lady,
O latna this be,
For gin your father get word of this
I vou he'd gar me die.'

Whatever may be lost here, it is not the power of terse statement. I incline to think that the addition of so much detail was meant to carry conviction to listeners who, like Burns's Mauchline belles, might be also readers of 'novells' which were comparatively lavish in the provision of detail. This presupposes a slight feeling of uncertainty separating the singer from his listeners: the Ballad-singer no longer enjoys a monopoly either of tales or of his listeners' attention. Let us consider another ballad, to see if this impression is borne out, and if the loss of a dimension can also be felt in it.

'Lady Isabel' (Child, 261) is a ghost story, in which a dead mother appears and counsels her daughter. It can be contrasted with an older ballad, 'The Wife of Usher's Well', in which the ghosts of three dead sons come home at their mother's command.

Like 'Hind Horn', 'The Wife of Usher's Well' is told straightforwardly in continuous narrative and dialogue. The story flows along in simple, familiar phrases, except for two ceremonial utterances, one by the Wife—her challenge to Death—which rings out in language heightened by alliteration:

> 'I wish the wind may never cease
> Nor fashes in the flood,
> Till my three sons come hame to me
> In earthly flesh and blood.'

and one by her youngest son, also made formally ceremonious by alliteration:

> 'The cock doth craw, the day doth daw,
> The channerin worm doth chide,
> Gin we be mist out o our place,
> A sair pain we maun bide.'

These ceremonial stanzas are not in any way 'staged' by the singer; they are neither foreshadowed nor emphasized nor repeated. They swell out in the story at the appropriate places in the narrative, which then relapses into ordinary language again. One gets the impression that the singer is not consciously thinking about the listeners: he is quite absorbed in the ballad story and takes his listeners for granted. Without straining or effort he has his listeners' entire attention and need not bother about them.

The three ghosts are also taken for granted; they come home as if returning from an ordinary journey and are welcomed in the same way by their mother. Realistic detail is put in, but economically; the fire is to be blown up, water fetched, and a feast prepared. Meanwhile the Wife makes up a large bed for the three of them. The only hint that they come from the Otherworld is that they wear hats 'of the birk' which once grew at the gates of Paradise, and even that hint is ignored by the mother. There is no attempt to make one's flesh creep; it is all very matter-of-fact. This makes the younger son's utterance more effective when it comes, but the ballad sinks again to a quiet domestic level in its close. As it is a ballad with four-line stanzas and no refrains, the listeners have only to listen; one feels that when the song ends singer and listeners come out of a trance together.

For all the quietude of the ballad, in that trance singer and listeners have been transported into a larger air. The Wife is a hieratic figure with magical powers that can compel the sea to give up its dead. Her challenge to Death is the ultimate challenge a human being can make. The matter-of-fact treatment of the ghosts makes them eerier than self-conscious shuddering could do. That extraordinary happenings can be taken for granted increases the strangeness of the mystery surrounding human life. Singer and listeners have been taken out of their ordinary, daytime selves to stand for a moment on the brink of what may be an infinite void, the void of the Unknown, where human personalities may be of no account. As I said in Chapter 9, this ballad is profoundly pagan in its atmosphere, despite the reference to Paradise and the hint of Limbo.

In the first two stanzas of 'Lady Isabel' we are at once aware of a difference in tone, a different relationship between singer and listeners. The singer is almost coaxing his listeners to attend to his story, promising them adventures to come:

> 'Twas early on a May morning,
> Lady Isabel comb'd her hair;
> But little kent she or the morn[1]
> She woud never comb it mair.
>
> 'Twas early on a May morning,
> Lady Isabel rang the keys;
> But little kent she or the morn
> A fey woman she was.

Her step-mother comes 'ben' and accuses her of being her father's whore. In two repetitive stanzas (repetition is a headmark of this ballad) she enjoins the step-mother to mind her own business. One gets an impression that Lady Isabel is a self-reliant personality, taking responsibility for her own actions.

> 'For if I be the same woman
> My ain sell drees the pine.'[2]

[1] or the morn = ere the morrow
[2] pine: perhaps a local pronunciation of 'pain'

And then the step-mother produces surprising evidence:

> 'It may be very well seen, Isabel,
> It may be very well seen;
> He buys to you the damask gowns,
> To me the dowie green.'

Even more surprisingly, Lady Isabel retorts in the same kind of terms:

> 'I hae a love beyond the sea,
> And far ayont the faem;
> For ilka gown my father buys me,
> My ain love sends me ten.'

Can incest be reduced to a matter of squabbling about wardrobes? Yet any trivial possession may be shown up in a lurid light by jealousy, and in the Middle Ages, after all, a gown lasted nearly a lifetime. The really surprising element in this personal exchange is that it comes so near the modern commercial world, where the buying and wearing of fashionable gowns is important. The Wife of Usher's Well, one feels, had her gowns spun, woven and made on her own premises; in any case, they are of no importance in her ballad, which is concerned with timeless issues of life and death. Here in 'Lady Isabel' one comes upon arguments from a merchandizing society, a more organized civilization situated at a definite and later stage in time, with a very different ambience.

The step-mother then proffers a reconciling invitation:

> 'Come ben, come ben now, Lady Isabel,
> And drink the wine wi me;
> I hae twa jewels in ae coffer,
> And ane o them I'll gie.'

Lady Isabel, very courteously, defers accepting it until she has paid a visit to Marykirk:

> When she gaed on to Marykirk
> And into Mary's quire,
> There she saw her ain mother
> Sit in a gowden chair.

The golden chair, once a magical chair, is the only indication that the figure sitting there comes from the Otherworld. Like the Wife of Usher's Well meeting her dead sons, Lady Isabel meets her dead mother as if by appointment. The Otherworld is still taken for granted in this ballad.

But now the wicked deception in the step-mother's proposal is unmasked, and to achieve this is partly why the self-reliant Lady Isabel consults her mother:

> 'O will I leave the lands, mother?
> Or shall I sail the sea?
> Or shall I drink this dowie drink
> That is prepared for me?'
>
> 'Ye winna leave the lands, daughter,
> Nor will you sail the sea,
> But ye will drink this dowie drink
> This woman's prepared for thee.
>
> 'Your bed is made in a better place
> Than ever hers will be,
> And ere ye're cauld into the room
> Ye will be there wi' me.'

The little detail: 'ere ye're cauld into the room' is the kind of realism which the Scottish imagination touches in with fine effect.

Now comes a curious piece of manipulation by the Ballad-singer; the step-mother's invitation stanza is repeated, word for word, like a stage direction, to introduce each phase of the ensuing action. The next phase is Lady Isabel's second courteous deferment of the drinking cermeony, almost in the same words, until she has seen her 'maries' in 'yon garden green'. That they are her 'maries', not her 'maids', suggests an earlier date for the ballad than the eighteenth century, but this may be an older ballad worked over again in the eighteenth century. The use of the step-mother's invitation stanza as a structural device is conscious and deliberate, like the conscious use of miming technique in 'Lady Maisry' (see Chapter 10) where members of the family are brought on the scene in procession, one after the other. Such deliberate staging of a Ballad story is not only self-conscious but makes for excessive repetition of lines and stanzas. I think it cannot be earlier than the eighteenth century.

The third phase, like a third act, leads on to the climax of the ballad. Lady Isabel drinks the poison and tells her step-mother:

> 'My bed is in the heavens high
> Amang the angels fine,
> But yours is in the lowest hell,
> To dree torment and pine.'

I suppose this represents a kind of Christianity. The pagan Wife of Usher's Well desires only life for her dead sons: the Christian mother of Lady Isabel desires death at another woman's hand for her daughter, so that she may enter a Better World. Certainly a prevalent sentimentalism in the eighteenth and nineteenth centuries saw Heaven as an immediate escape from the ills of life, and this ballad has picked that out of the air. There is something touching about the idea of Heaven's providing a comfortable bed, a Himmelbett.

The ballad ends with a commonplace, a closing verse used in various murder Ballads, mostly rather late ones.

> Nae moan was made for Lady Isabel
> In bower where she lay dead,
> But a' was for that ill woman,
> In the fields mad she gaed.

Here it is neither very apposite nor well-turned. In 'Willie and Lady Maisry' (Child, 70), perhaps its first appearance, it comes in better:

> Nae meen was made for this young knight
> In bower where he lay slain,
> But a' was for sweet Maisry bright
> In fields where she ran brain.

This ballad shows a greater distance between singer and listeners than 'The Wife of Usher's Well'. The singer is consciously staging and presenting the story like a compère making things easier for an audience. He is aware but not sure of his audience: he cannot take their attention for granted: he tries to anticipate and control their reactions. He is 'putting the ballad across', and is therefore coming much nearer to the rôle of a public entertainer putting himself across. The intimate relationship between singer and listeners has been to some extent eroded.

'Lady Isabel', compared with the older ballad, has also lost something else which might be called a hieratic dimension, magic and the sense of the unknown void that frustrates human aspirations. The Otherworld of ghosts is still accepted quite simply but it seems to pose no unanswerable questions. Heaven and Hell are taken to be evident facts closing the door on inquiry or doubt, cutting off speculation and wonder. The domestic human world, in itself sufficiently mysterious to demand wonder as well as exploration, is treated in the relatively prosiac way that satisfied the eighteenth century up to its last three decades, which then brought in a revulsion from the penny plain and a growing appetite for tuppenny-coloured Gothic. At this stage, however, the horizon has certainly narrowed. Yet was not the loss of the hieratic dimension bound to follow on the advent and growth of self-consciousness?

In 'The Wife of Usher's Well' some last traces of the hieratic dimension are just perceptible. In Chapter 9 I mentioned that the Wife is not described in visual terms as a neighbour with recognizable features but is felt rather as a force. That is her hieratic quality; she is no ordinary woman; she is all that is left of an ancient priestess beside a sacred well, a priestess with magical powers, though now dwindled into a matriarch without a face. What is essential in hieratic figures is that they have no recognizable faces, coming as they do from the pre-conscious world of ritual, where they originally belong.

In stage plays which, like the Greek tragedies, evolved many years later than tribal ritual dances, there was still a ritual continuity, for the protagonists at first wore masks to hide their faces and heightened themselves beyond normal human stature to make themselves hieratic. When masks and buskins were discarded, players still represented high-ranking noble potentates, kings, queens, princes, princesses, whose faces were disguised behind a conventional make-up and whose height was increased by crowns or head-dresses so that they still loomed larger and more mysterious than ordinary human beings, in the imagination of those who watched their doings. In Ballads the early protagonists also were kings or queens, nobles or noblewomen, figures possibly magical, larger than life, of unceasing interest to the little people who sang about them. All of them, in plays and

Ballads alike, are far-off descendants of hieratic figures in ritual dances like those still danced in New Mexico by the Zuni Indians. When the Zunis dance their yearly ceremonial Shalako, figures representing the gods are not only twelve feet high but wear cylindrical masks to make them appear blank-faced, featureless. These numinous gods wield magical powers and can never be entirely known, so they have no faces; they come out of the Great Unknown and return to it; the tribe hopes only to propitiate them. With the growth of self-consciousness, when people begin to know each other face to face, the Great Unknown begins to shrink and the hieratic figures gradually lessen in majesty and acquire features. Finally, when men and women have emerged as individual personalities from the collective group, when the private, scrutinizing eye begins to function, high representative functionaries on earth also begin to shrink, and the numinous power of magic shrinks with them, being replaced by the conscious knowledge later called Science. In the eighteenth century, the Age of Reason and Science, it is not surprising that the hieratic dimension, with its shrinking traces of ancient magic, should now at last vanish from the Scottish Ballad world. Together with the kings, magic and magical properties begin to disappear. The golden chair in the ballad 'Lady Isabel' is one of the last of these. As for the Otherworld, it is left undisturbed in the keeping of the Kirk, perhaps on the principle of letting sleeping dogs lie, perhaps because the Scots have now had enough of religious wars for the time being.

One other consequence of advancing self-awareness is the release of comedy in Ballads. The primitive mind, not being given to categorizing, does not separate fun from solemn grandeur. In the Shalako dance of the Zuni Indians, the masked, faceless giant gods are accompanied by equally divine animal-like clowns capering around them. But by the time the Greeks staged their tragedies, the comic element was already segregated from the solemn, being attached as a pendant, a satyric comedy, to three tragic productions. Still later, comedy was felt to be entirely incongruous with tragedy—although Shakespeare did not think so—and when Ballads appeared they maintained the distinction between these two modes. Early tragic Ballads have no fun in them, no by-play.

Humorous comedy can hardly be looked for in early Ballads since, like visual metaphor, it needs a conscious standpoint to operate from, but knockabout farce, horse-play and ribaldry belong to the same unself-conscious world as passionate tragedies of action and one would expect ribald Ballads to be more numerous than they are. Perhaps the men who collected and recorded Ballads were too high-minded to approve or listen to, or even encounter, those that were ribald. Early comic Ballads are mostly English, many of them in the Robin Hood cycle. A certain amount of fun is got out of riddles, fantastic challenges or wagers, and a great deal of fun from outwitting respectable authorities by some kind of trickery. One such early tale of trickery is a Scottish ballad, 'The Lochmaben Harper' (Child, 192).

This is a kind of Riding Ballad, for it has to do with horse-stealing from across the Border. A blind Scottish harper outwits King Henry of England by stealing his famous Wanton Brown, which in some versions is a mare and in others a stallion. Not only does he 'get away with it', he demands and obtains compensation for the alleged loss of his own mare, which in fact he has sent home by night to her waiting foal at Lochmaben with the Wanton Brown tied to her tail.

The wily harper succeeds in his ruse because he is an excellent harper. After meeting King Henry at the castle gate and, thanks to the king's good nature, having his mare stabled beside the Wanton Brown, he harps the king and his nobles into a trance:

And ay he harpit, and ay he carpit,
Till a' the lords had fitted the floor;
They thought the music was sae sweet
And they forgot the stable-door.

And ay he harpit, and ay he carpit,
Till a' the nobles were sound asleep;
Then quietly he took off his shoon
And safly down the stair did creep.

There is a touch of magic about this harping which rightly belongs to the early Ballad world. But the trickery is timeless and so is the fun of the mare's early morning arrival at Lochmaben with the Wanton Brown behind her. Like other old Ballads, this one has a refrain expressing the mood of the singer or singers: the mood is entirely nonsensical and daft, for the differing refrains in the various versions are all made up of nonsense syllables, like:

> Fadle didle dodle didle,
> Fadle didle fadle doo.

The tune this ballad was sung to, as reported to Child in 1883 by a man who had heard it, was: 'a very simple but particularly plaintive lilt—more like a rapid chant than an ordinary song—which rings in my ear yet, although I only heard it once, when a lad'. Comic Ballads, one may infer, were sung faster than tragic Ballads, but shared with them the curious traditional resonance of their music, which went on ringing in the ear for a lifetime.

With the shrinking of the hieratic dimension, the authority radiating from hieratic figures also shrinks, so most comic Ballads are devoted to the further sapping and mining of that authority through tales about outwitting those who exercise it, as the blind harper outwits the King of England, or as daughters outwit their fathers in 'Young Beichan' and 'The Kitchie Boy'. The fun of outwitting powerful figures, whether public functionaries or private enemies, seems to be one of the touches of nature that make the whole world kin. The use of magic is the oldest method of outwitting, next to that comes simple disguise; once self-consciousness has begun to grow recourse is had to psychological means of deception such as impersonation, lying and false pretences.

'The Duke of Athole's Nurse' (Child, 212, Greig, LXIII), recorded not long after 1800, uses disguise to outwit a posse of brothers bent on murder. Its double feminine endings give the story a tripping, light-hearted rhythm all through, so that one feels the outcome will not be tragic.

The Duke of Athole's nurse hears her sweetheart's bridles ringing and so she sings in her 'bonnie voice':

> 'O I'm the Duke o Athole's nurse,
> My post is very weel becomin,
> But I wad gie a' my half-year's fee
> For ae sicht o my leman.'

This he obligingly grants her, yet, leaning from his saddle bow to kiss her, tells her that she may have his heart but another has his hand, words which, she says 'hae fairly undone me'. She proposes that they should 'twine' in good friendship: he is to go to the tavern and drink her health and by dawn she will be with him to settle his reckoning. Following her instructions he drinks freely:

> He spared na the wine, altho it was fine,
> The sack nor the sugar candy.

Yet she did not come:

> 'He's teen him up to a shott window,
> A little before the dawin,
> An there he spied her brothers three
> Wi their swords a' weel drawn.'

One version makes it nine brothers, another twelve; three, however, are dangerous enough.

> 'O where shall I rin, or where shall I gang?'

He appeals to the landlady, who dresses him up in 'female claes', including, one feels, a mob-cap, and sets him to work at the baking-board. She rebuffs the armed incomers who ask: where is the 'quarterer' who spent the night drinking? She denies that any quarterer is on the premises; a man came, she says, drank a pint, paid for it and went off. One of the brothers tries to flirt with the baking-maid, but the landlady is equal to that:

> The wife took her foot an' gae him a kick,
> Says, 'Be busy, ye jilt, at yer bakin.'
>
> They socht the house up an they socht the house doon,
> An they spared nae the curtains for the riving
> An ilka ane o them, as they passed by,
> For a kiss of the Knight they were striving.

This is very simple fun, asking for and probably getting only a pleased laugh at the end of the ballad. More elaborate entertainment is to be found in 'The Knight and Shepherd's Daughter' (Child, 110, Greig, XLIII), an old ballad, parts of which were enlarged in Scotland and recast to suit the country people's notions of fun.

The original story, probably Elizabethan (Fletcher put a verse of it into his comedy 'The Pilgrim'), runs like this: a shepherd's daughter is waylaid and ravished by a Knight who then rides away. She follows him to the King's court and accuses him before the King, who promises that he is to marry her if he be a bachelor, and if a married man that he will be hanged. She reviews the courtiers one by one, and picks out Sweet William, who then tries to buy her off with as much as five hundred pounds in gold, which she refuses. He mourns his bad luck, to which she retorts:

> 'You might have let me be.'

Once they are married, she turns out to be a duke's daughter, so that they go off

> 'linked fast
> And joyning hand in hand.'

On this skeleton story the Scots have put much flesh and blood. The lady was only pretending to be a shepherd's daughter, so she must have greatly enjoyed misleading her lover, they inferred, and there seemed no reason why the ballad should be deprived of all the fun that could be got out of verbal exchanges between them. A long stretch of dialogue is invented and stage-managed with repetitions in eighteenth-century style.

The ballad pair in England cross the river Tyne; in Scotland the river becomes the Clyde, the Tay, and finally in a Deeside version the 'water o Dee'. The gentleman rides, and the lady runs on foot, but at the river he offers her a seat on his horse. She retorts that she has learned to swim like an otter, or an eel, and gets across the water before him. In the Deeside version it is the Queen's court she makes for, not the King's, and she sends in a message by the porter, as well as the usual 'guineas three', which would tell any Ballad listener that she is no 'beggar's brat', but a lady born and bred.

> 'Ye will gang to the queen hersell
> And tell her this frae me.
>
> 'There is a lady at your yetts
> Can neither card nor spin;
> But she can sit in a lady's bower
> And lay gold on a seam.'

To 'lay gowd wi her hand' is an old and well-known Ballad

accomplishment for a lady.[1] At Queen's court or King's court, the procedure is the same; when the culprit is identified, a ring and a sword are laid before the lady; if she chooses the ring, the pair are married, if the sword, the man is slain.

'Three times she minted to the brand,
But she took up the ring.'

They gad ón to Mary kirk, and ón to Mary quire,
The nettles they grew by the dyke:
'O an my mither wer here,
So clean as she would them pyke!'

'I wiss I had druken water,' he says,
'Whan I drank the ale,
That ony cerl's daughter
Sud tell me sick a tale.'

'Perhaps I am a cerl's daughter,
Perhaps I am nane;
But whan ye gat me in free forest
Ye sud ha latten me alane.'

These two last stanzas are used like a recurrent stage direction, between every flight of fancy that is now indulged in. They pass a mill, for instance, and the lady reminds herself of the meal dust she and her mother have scraped into their pokes. She refuses silver spoons:

'Tak awa yer siller speens,
Tak awa fra me,
An gae me the gude horn speens,
Its what I'm used tee.'

In another Northern version, after Earl Richard and the beggar's daughter are married and laid in one chamber, the lady says:

'Had far awa your fine claithing
Had them far awa frae me,
And bring to me my fleachy[2] clouts
That I was best used wi.

[1] See 'Fause Foodrage' (Child, 89) verse *A*. 23
[2] fleachy = flea-infested: ch pronounced as in loch

'Had far awa your holland sheets,
Had them far awa frae me,
And bring to me my canvas clouts
That I was best used wi.

'Lay a pock o meal beneath my head,
Another aneath my feet,
A pock o seeds beneath my knees
And soundly will I sleep.'

Here, I think, one can recognize the kind of detail put in by guffawing ploughmen in a bothy. The Ballad has become a spontaneous game, with improvizations that vary from one version to another. But it is held in shape by the stage-managing recurrent stanzas, and brought to a happy ending by the Billy Blin who may be a far-off reminiscence of the fairy magic in the Gawain tales, which this ballad calls to mind:

Up it starts the Billy-Blin
Just at their bed-feet,

and says:

'I think it is a meet marriage
Atween the tane and the tither,
The Earl o Hertford's ae daughter
And the Queen of England's brither.'

Another ballad, 'Lang Johnny More' (Child, 251), seems to me also a product of authentic ploughboy humour. It may be a re-working of an older Ballad, 'Johnie Scot' (Child, 99), which has essentially the same theme, the story of a Scot who goes to London, gets the king's daughter with child, and with help from Scotland rescues both her and himself from her father's wrath. Yet Lang Johnny More has what may be an even older traditional element in it, for Lang Johnny is a giant, and needs only two other giant Scots of the same breed to come to his assistance, although Johnie Scot, a little Scot, needed five hundred armed men to help him. The giants are like Norse folk-lore figures translated into realistic contemporary terms. All of them come from West Aberdeenshire, at the foot of Benachie: they are firmly localized.

Young Johnny was a clever youth,
Fu sturdy, stout and wight,
Just full three yards around the waist
And fourteen feet in height.

A formidable figure, and yet the English get the better of him, in spite of his ten-foot sword:

But the English dogs is cunnin rogues,
An roon him they did creep,
They've gien him drams o laudamy
Till he fell fast asleep.

So he wakes up with

'his jaws an hands in iron bands
An his feet in fetters three.'

In this *impasse* the Ballad-makers are helped by a well-known Ballad commonplace, the 'bonnie boy' who is always ready to take a message:

'O here am I, a bonnie boy,
That'll win baith meat an fee,
And will rin on to your uncle,
At the fit o Benachie.'

Lang Johnny More instructs him, in traditional Ballad style:

'Faur ye fin' the brigs broken
Ye'll bend your bow an swim,
An faur ye fin' the grass growin
Ye'll slack your shoes an rin.'

When he got to Benachie he would not fail to recognize Lang Johnny's uncle, three feet taller than anyone else, and he was to deliver a broad letter and the message that 'the body Jock o Noth' should also come to London.

Auld Johnny More and Jock o Noth are gigantic men:

They were three feet atween each brow
An their shoulders broad yards three.

They run to London in a day, these two, and it does not take them long to terrorize the trembling keeper of the gates, which are locked. There is also a trumpeter, and drums are beating and bells ringing, all because a 'wighty' Scot is to be hanged.

So Jock o Noth acts:

> 'Open the gates,' said Jock o Noth,
> 'Open them at my call.'
> An wi his fit he has dung in
> Three yard-breadths o the wall.
>
> They are doon through fair London
> And doon by the town hall,
> And there they saw young Johnny More
> Stand on the English wall.

They loose the knot and slack the rope and take him from the gallows-tree, and then they demand the lady:

> 'O tak the lady,' the king he says,
> 'Ye're welcome to her for me,
> For I never thocht to see sic men
> Fae the fit o Benachie.'

Jock o Noth, with Aberdeenshire dryness, remarks that if he had known they would wonder so much at him, he would have brought with him 'Sir John o Erskine Park' who is thirty-three feet tall. The lady is delivered up, and a cleric appears to marry her to Lang Johnny More; a 'tocher' is offered with her, which the giants refuse with scorn since they have thirty ploughs and three and an estate at the foot of Benachie. The king has threatened to hang the 'bonnie boy', but the giants threaten in return to attend his burial and reward the king in their own fashion, so the boy is also set free:

> Now auld Johnny More and young Johnny More
> An Jock o Noth, a' three,
> The English lady an little wee boy
> Went a' to Benachie.

In 'Lang Johnny More' it is clear that Ballad tradition, with its commonplace precedents, provides timely help to ploughmen who look like getting stuck in an improbable story. Daft and improbable stories with nonsensical refrains are much appreciated in bothies, but as self-consciousness comes more into play, the ploughmen begin to concoct sardonic individual songs about their employers, the farmers. During the nineteenth century, especially the latter half of it when farming became less prosperous, many of these were composed; they were called Cornkisters, because one sat on the 'corn-kist', the meal chest in the bothy, to sing them to one's friends. Here is an anonymous Cornkister roughly dated about 1850, 'The Barnyards o Delgaty':

As I cam in by Netherdale
At Turra market for to fee,
I fell in wi a farmer chiel
Frae the Barnyards o Dalgety.

(*Refrain*) Linten adie toorin adie,
Linten adie toorin ae,
Linten lourin, lourin, lourin,
Linten lourin lourin lae.

He promised me the ae best pair
I ever set my een upon:
When I gaed hame tae the Barnyards
There was naethin there but skin and bone.

The auld black horse sat on his dowp,[1]
The auld white meer lay on her wime,[2]
And aa that I could hup and crack
They widna rise at yokin time.

Lang Meg Scott she maks ma brose
And her and me we canna gree;
First a mott and syne a knot
And aye the tither jilp o bree.

Jean McPherson maks ma bed,
Ye'll see the marks upon ma shins;
For Jean, the coorse ill-tricket jaud,
Has filled the bed wi prickly whins.

When I gae to the kirk on Sunday
Mony's the bonny lass I see,
Prim, sittin by her daddy's side,
And winkin owre the pews at me.

[1] dowp = bottom [2] wime (wame) = stomach

I can drink and nae be drunk,
I can fecht and nae be slain,
I can court anither's lass
And aye be welcome to my ain.

This is individual transmission, not traditional, except for the last verse which was 'in the air'. Many Corn-kisters were later composed for presentation in music-halls; they were modern semi-professional compositions fitted to well-known traditional tunes, and were usually sung at top speed, as fast as the words could be got out. One of these lively tunes, the Muckin' o' Geordie's Byre, is commemorated in the last two verses of its narrative:

A hunder years hae passed and mair,
Faur Sprottie's was, the hill is bare,
The craft's awa, so ye'll see nae mair
the Muckin' o' Geordie's Byre—

His folk's a' deid and awa lang syne,
So in case his memory we should tine
Jist whistle this tune tae keep ye in mind
o' the Muckin' o' Geordie's Byre.

These so-called Bothy Ballads were published in Glasgow and were recorded in London about 1930: they are still on sale. The tunes are familiar, known to this day, with or without the words; some of them go back for two hundred years. It looks as if the music of Ballads can haunt the air longer even than Ballads themselves. With the arrival of the individual 'I', the Bothy songs now merge with the come-all-ye clowning songs that have accompanied them for some time at no great distance; there are no more of the traditional Ballads, none, at least, that are recorded.

This proviso is necessary, since unprintable bawdy Ballads were still being made in the nineteenth century, the most famous of which, 'The Ball o' Kirriemuir' is still, I believe, going strong. A bowdlerized version has been published, but it is a travesty of the original, a wonderful male wish-dream, which celebrates in loving detail the happenings at a farmyard ball where everyone, man or woman, has been dosed beforehand with an aphrodisiac. During the two world wars of the twentieth century this ballad spread through our armies, gathering new verses as it spread; it looks like lasting as long as we do.

Besides such entertainment in the bothies, up in the farmhouse domestic comedies were much in favour, many based on local happenings, and, whether true or not, full of local names and detail. 'Jean of Bethelnie', or 'Glenlogie' (Child, 238, Greig, LXXXI), goes back to the eighteenth century and tells a familiar story of how a girl eventually marries the man she loves; this girl, however, unlike fashionable heroines about that time, is not oppressed by family authority, but merely makes up her mind to die if she cannot wed young Glenlogie, after seeing him only once, and nearly does so. The family, full of concern for her, gets a letter sent to Glenlogie:

> O ben cam her father's chaplain, a man of great skill,
> He has written a broad letter, and he has penned it well.

Glenlogie, moved by the letter, arrives:

> O pale and wan was she when Glenlogie came in,
> But red rosy grew she or Glenlogie got ben.

After telling this story of 'bonnie Jean o Bethelnie, scarce sixteen years old', the ballad ends with a lyrical appreciation of Bethelnie:

> O Bethelnie, O Bethelnie, it shines where it stands,
> An the heather bells round it shines oer Fyvie's lands.

The new, scrutinizing eye is now looking at scenery as well as at people.

This was a very popular ballad. Another, even more popular, was the story of the Laird of Drum's marriage (Child, 236, Greig, LXXIX) which happened in 1681, when the widower Alexander Irvine of Drum at the age of 62 married a young girl, Margaret Coutts, aged about 16, 'a woman of inferior birth and manners, which step gave great offence to his relations'. The ballad makes her a shepherd's daughter. In the later versions it is stage-managed with repetitions and the help of commonplaces, in eighteenth-century style, to throw into high relief the churlish behaviour of Drum's family and retainers, but it is not merely a Cinderella fairy tale; it has an eighteenth-century moral. A feeling about egalitarian rights has reached not only Robert Burns, whose father, after all, came from the North-East, but the North-East itself:

> When they had eaten an drunken weel,
> An a' were bound for bed, O,
> The laird o Drum an the shepherd's dachter
> In ae bed they were laid, O.

And this is how the shepherd's daughter concludes the ballad:

> 'I tell't ye weel ere we were wed,
> Ye was far too high for me, O,
> But noo I'm wed an in your bed laid
> An I'm just as good as ye, O.
>
> 'When I am deid an you are deid
> An baith in ae grave laid, O,
> They wad need to look wi very clear een
> To ken your mould by mine, O.'

That is the voice of an individual self-conscious personality with clear enough eyes. The exercise of the scrutinizing eye and the shrinking of the hierarchic dimension entail, as is shown here, a shrinking not only of hierarchic princely authority, the authority of rank, but of all authority, including that of the family.

There are so many Ballads, and so many variants of each, that one could go on quoting and quoting. I shall, however, finish with a version of a comic Ballad, dated 1776, which comes as near to being a stage entertainment as a Ballad could. 'Our Goodman' (Child, 274, Greig, XCI) is well known in other European countries, but here is some of it in what may be its original Scottish make-up:

> 1 (Sung) Hame cam our goodman
> And hame cam he,
> And there he saw a saddle-horse
> Where nae horse should be.
>
> 2 (Sung) 'What's this now, goodwife,
> What's this I see?
> How cam this horse here
> Without the leave o me?'

Recitative: 'A horse?' quo she,
'Ay, a horse,' quo he.

3 (Sung) 'Shame fa your cuckold face,
Ill mat you see!
'Tis naething but a brood sow
My minnie sent to me.'

Recitative: 'A brood sow?' quo he.
'Ay, a sow,' quo she.

4 (Sung) 'Far hae I ridden
And farer hae I gane,
But a sadle on a sow's back,
Saw I never nane.'

5 (Sung) Hame cam our goodman
And hame cam he,
He spy'd a pair o jack-boots
Where nae boots should be.

6 (Sung) 'What's this now, goodwife.
What's this I see?
How cam these boots here
Without the leave o me?'

Recitative: 'Boots?' quo she.
'Ay, boots,' quo he.

And so on, as long as invention holds out. This is a pleasant game for two; it is stage-managed, with repetitions, like other eighteenth-century Ballads, but also introduces recitative in ordinary speech. Only a step or two is now needed away from Ballad structure to reach something like a music-hall 'turn'. Here the Ballad as an art-form has been stretched to the limit of its tether. Music-hall songs, with their appreciation of the correspondence between rhythmical tunes and rhymed verses follow as natural consequences; the performers merely enlarge recitative into 'patter' to put themselves across as well as the song.

Ballads faded out of the air much sooner in Aberdeen city than in the rural districts. Middle-class families, it is true, were now interested in them, and even the ministers of the Kirk who had once denounced Ballads collected them eagerly by the late eighteenth century and through the nineteenth, passing them on to their children, who were thus conditioned, in the back of their minds, at an impressionable age, to the Ballad style of romance. (The effect of this conditioning can be seen in Scottish writers of fiction, good or bad, from Walter Scott to John Buchan. Even Rudyard Kipling, although not a Scottish writer, had some share in the Scottish Ballad tradition, inherited from his mother. I feel that when he wrote the comic short story 'The Lang Men o Larut' in 'Life's Handicap' he had 'Lang Johnny More' somewhere in the back of his mind.) Yet the addiction of respectable professional families to Ballads did not make up for the waning interest of most other people in the city. By 1850 a simple, romantic ballad, 'Lord Lovel', (Child, 75, Greig, XXIX) was presented in Aberdeen by a favourite comedian, Sam Cowell, as a comic song. 'Lord Lovel', by the way, is sung by Jeannie Robertson with utter conviction; she does not find it funny that a laggard lover should weep over the corpse of Lady Nancy Bell who has died of love for him. But the audiences who listened to Sam Cowell did.

The appearance of a public who pay to be entertained was bound sooner or later to put an end to Ballads, which are made to be sung for love in an intimate circle familiar with the traditional background from which Ballads spring. That background happens to be rural, the old prevailing background of agriculture and gentry which lasted for hundreds of years, and which is now out of date. It cannot be reconstituted, nor can the Ballads which grew out of it. Yet the human need which shaped the Ballads remains, and, likely enough, will shape another culture to express itself in.

We have now inherited the possibility of more self-awareness, as well as more conscious awareness of the natural world around us, than the Ballad-makers and Ballad-listeners of North-East Scotland. Yet, from childhood on, we still travel the road they trod and whatever grown-upness we achieve includes all our experiences on that road, to which Ballads may still be relevant. The Ballad tradition made a culture for ordinary rural people; they transmitted into the air and received images of life as they felt it to be and whatever meaning they found in it, exercising in this way a basic human gift of imagination which gave them much satisfaction and fun.

The Ballad culture is not like a mass-culture, for that term seems to me an abstraction connoting a mass of humanity which is merely recipient and submits to purposive manipulation by various agencies. Like other abstractions, mass-culture is 'in the air', but the air has always been full of chimeras, some of which are inspiring and some preposterous. Mass-culture, unless its meaning changes radically, remains a preposterous statistical abstraction produced by the categorizing intellect. The kind of culture presented by the cinema or by television, the latter of which especially is closely related to clock-time and the focused eye of consciousness, is also unlike the Ballad culture. Whether mankind will again shape a popular culture that provides as much deep satisfaction as Ballads have done I cannot tell; I can only hope so.

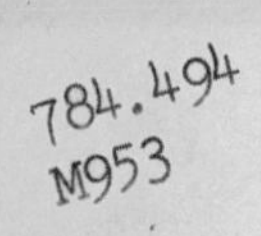
784.494
M953